THE
WRITING GAME

Also by Rosemary Friedman

The Life Situation
The Long Hot Summer
Proofs of Affection
A Loving Mistress
Rose of Jericho
A Second Wife
To Live in Peace
An Eligible Man
Golden Boy
Vintage

Juvenile:

Aristide
Aristide in Paris

as Robert Tibber

No White Coat
Love on my List
We All Fall Down
Patients of a Saint
The Fraternity
The Commonplace Day
The General Practice

as Rosemary Tibber

Practice Makes Perfect

THE
WRITING GAME

ROSEMARY FRIEDMAN

*For Helen & Michael
with best wishes
Rosemary Friedman.*

Oct. 1999.

EMPIRICUS
BOOKS
London, England

First published in Great Britain 1999
by Empiricus Books,
Janus Publishing Company Limited,
Edinburgh House, 19 Nassau Street,
London W1N 7RE

www.januspublishing.co.uk

A CIP catalogue record for this book
is available from the British Library.

ISBN Paperback: 1 902 83501 8
Hardback: 1 902 83500 X

Phototypeset in 11 on 14 Sabon
by Keyboard Services, Luton, Beds

Cover design John Anastasio, Creative Line

Printed and bound in Great Britain by
Athenaeum Press, Gateshead, Tyne & Wear

For Susan, Louise, Charlotte and Emma.

Acknowledgements

Thanks are due to my husband Dennis for his unfailing support during the writing of this work and for his sharp editorial eye. I would also like to thank my agent, Sonia Land, for her faith in the project, Mark Le Fanu (Society of Authors) for his helpful comments, and my publisher Sandy Leung for his enthusiasm and commitment. Thanks also to Wendy Cope for her kind permission to use *Where Do You Get Your Ideas From?*

The publisher and author would also like to thank the Fraser family and the *Radio Times* for their permission to use 'The Modern Muse' for the cover of this book.

Contents

'The Muse ushers the artist into the empty room and points silently at the tightrope.'

Jean Cocteau

author, n. Originator (*of* a condition of things, event etc.) writer of book, treatise, etc.; (loosely –'s writings. Hence – ESS' n.' authoria'IAL a. [ME *autor, -teur* f. L *auctor* (augere *auct-* increase, originate, promote, see -OR); *auth-* appears as scribal var. of *aut-* in Eng. *c.*1550]

Preface

My very first literary agent, the late, redoubtable Joyce Weiner (at first to terrify me and later to become a valued friend) used to say that it's not how you start out that is important, but how you end up. This dictum has been framed and hung in my head for the 30 odd years of my writing life. It has sustained me when I was down and been validated when I was up. Vicissitudes are the hallmark of the seasoned writer. There is no steady progression from first faltering steps to certain success, but rather a series of peaks of exultation and troughs of despair, etched upon the graph of one's chosen profession.

I am often called upon to give lectures on fiction writing. Audiences are surprised to learn that luminaries such as George Bernard Shaw, Scott Fitzgerald, Beatrix Potter, George Orwell, Vladimir Nabokov, Lewis Carroll, Somerset Maugham, Joyce Cary, Frederick Forsyth, Kingsley Amis and Catherine Cookson have in their time had manuscripts turned down by short-sighted publishers. They are equally amazed to hear that Charles Dickens originally called *David Copperfield* 'Old Saying', that

THE WRITING GAME

The Mill on the Floss (George Eliot) was once 'The Tulliver Family', that Aléxandre Dumas's The Three Musketeers started life as 'Athos, Portos, and Aramis', that Jane Austen's 'First Impressions' subsequently became Pride and Prejudice, and that Catch 22, a sobriquet now part of the English language, was submitted by Joseph Heller under the title 'Catch 18'.

In the following chapters I will try to dispel a few of the myths that surround the writing of fiction and in so doing share some of the experiences encountered in an adult life spent largely, but not exclusively, before the typewriter or word processor.

At school, Queen's College, Harley Street, the pioneer institution for the academic education of women (founded under Royal Charter in 1848 by Frederick Denison Maurice), I was lucky enough not only to be taught to appreciate the first rate in everything, but to be instructed in mathematics by Mrs Margaret Truman who had a very clear sense that teaching should be connected with life. Whilst introducing us to the logarithm and revealing, to our surprise, that E equalled mc^2, she regaled her class of adolescent female dreamers with such nuggets of practical advice as how to change an electrical fuse and wire a plug, how to make a fail-safe chocolate cake, and such gems of personal philosophy – germane to those chauvinist between-the-wars days – as that it was necessary to be attractive to get a man but that one must be useful to keep him. Although this work is in no way a confessional, it is my intention, like Margaret Truman, to share some general views, some observations acquired along the way, which seem pertinent to both writing and a writer's life. It is not intended as a vade mecum. If standing back to review the past 30 years helps me to jump better over the final hurdles, it may also provide a few short cuts and eliminate some of the heartache for those lucky enough

Preface

to be starting out. That there is a vast number of aspiring writers, is confirmed by the recent initial response of more than half-a-million applications for a new literary prize for unpublished authors.

Before winding back the clock I would like to lay my cards unequivocally on the table. I do not believe that creative writing can be taught, only encouraged. If someone were to ask me 'how do you write a novel?' I would reply like Alice: 'Begin at the beginning; carry on till you come to the end; then stop.' I offer no advice, illuminate no easy route along the snake-path of the written word. The memoir (how one remembers one's life) which ensues, is both more and less than a conventional autobiography. Deeply personal, yet surrounded by a sense of privacy, it represents a leisurely and self-indulgent stroll through the *arrière-pays* of one author's working life which, for the record, has to date produced 18 novels (translated into several languages), two books for children, a miscellany of short stories, various contributions to anthologies and symposia, a stage play (with a four-month run), three screenplays, a pilot and a six-part series for television, newspaper and magazine articles and sundry book reviews.

Rosemary Friedman

CHAPTER ONE

Setting Out

'Writers come predominantly from the middle class.'
Anthony Storr

The question I am asked most frequently is: have you always wanted to write? It would be romantic but untrue to say that my childhood was spent scribbling away in the solitude of a tree-house weaving fantasies about owls and witches, or dashing off precocious three-act plays to be performed by my peers. The fact of the matter is that until I was in my early 20s, married, and a mother of two, I did not put pen to paper in other than an epistolary capacity.

February, when I was born, is distinguished not only by the fact that it is uniquely affected by the leap year, but it is also the month during which there are more babies born who are likely to develop schizophrenia, as well as the highest number – if the *Encyclopaedia Britannica* is to be believed – predestined for eminence. Despite the fact that at the moment of my birth the stock market plunged, the temperature plummeted and the pipes froze, mine was not a traumatic or deprived childhood demanding any obvious catharsis. I was not amongst the 90 odd well-known writers who were orphaned, did not suffer from the cruelty and neglect which inspired writers as diverse as Kipling and Swift, nor lived through the great historical convulsions which informed the writing of the likes of Günter Grass, Salman Rushdie and Milan Kundera. I was not born into Bohemian poverty like Jean Rhys, was never hungry, was not abused, did not have to battle my way out of a slum, reject my background, endure political oppression or suffer the psychological or geographical exile which provides rich pickings for so many writers of fiction.

While many British novelists seem to be afflicted by a compulsion to appear more proletarian than they are, the novel is inherently a middle-class form 'its narrative voice apt to betray this bias in every turn of phrase',* and many of the finest writers are uncompromisingly middle class.

The seemingly impoverished soil of an unremarkable upbringing in a far from Bohemian house with a monkey-puzzle tree in the front garden and a tennis court in the back, appeared a poor culture medium for literary *angst*. To begin with, there was little literature. Books, yes; current novels culled from Boots's or Mudie's lending libraries on the recommendation of the librarian or on the strength of newspaper reviews – stronger on fiction then than now – which I suspect were often prized more than were the works themselves; Arthur Mee's *Children's Encyclopaedia* kept prohibitively behind the diamond-paned glass of a bookcase in the hall together with the complete works of Byron,

* David Lodge

Setting Out

Tennyson and Shelley (my mother briefly taught elocution) bound in plum-coloured suede; a selection of comics, plus the *Children's Newspaper* delivered weekly but which, as far as I was concerned, remained unopened and unread.

In our house, books, like ideas, sex, and cancer (mentioned only if unavoidable in hushed not-in-front-of-the-children tones) were not subjects for discussion. Such dialogue as there was, around a table which did not recognise children's basic rights to speak (up) for themselves, centred around the quotidian lives of our close network of relatives and the synagogue, in which my father took an active part and to which, from the age of five, I had to walk four miles each Sabbath morning. Family conversation rarely transcended the humdrum, although the *idées reçues* were enlivened at times by passages from Shakespeare or verses from Hiawatha, recollected from my parents' schooldays and trotted out self-consciously at appropriate moments. Nothing to inspire. I did read, perhaps because in those days there was no competition with other kinds of entertainment; my passion for reading encompassed everything I could lay hands on. I indulged it when I was supposed to be doing other things and traditionally, by torchlight, far into the night. From an early age I was addicted, as I still am, to the written word. Even the crude rhyme on the breakfast cereal box 'High o'er the fence leaps Sunny Jim'/'Force is the food that raises him' and the legend on the jars of familiar Cod Liver Oil and Malt (for colds) and Elliman's Embrocation (for aches and pains) were a source of daily delight, although, unlike Proust, I never had to resort to a train timetable for my bedside reading.

Mrs Trollope's advice to her sons was to read and read before they ever considered setting pen to paper themselves. The family

3

adage applied to myself was 'read, read, read and you'll have to wear glasses'. The family was right. And I do: three pairs in constant trajectory. With the years my dependence on the written word has increased. I am an insatiable reader and tend to panic if I have to wait anywhere for a few moments and there is no print to hand. Anything will do: time-expired magazines, telephone directories, advertisements for jobs in which I have no interest and for second-hand cars in which I have even less, restaurant menus, bus schedules, concert programmes including the minuscule note: 'A warning gong will be sounded for five minutes before the end of the interval. First aid facilities are provided by the British Red Cross Society. Steinway pianoforte.' Unfortunately, like that attributed to Colette, I have an *oublieuse mémoire*, a memory that forgets because it selects, and by its selection creates. For this reason, apart from the slogan on the cereal box which has somehow stayed with me, and the William novels of Richmal Crompton, I cannot recall exactly what it was that I read during those years soon to be rudely interrupted by the alarums and excursions of the Second World War. What was there then, in this tranquil, if not idyllic, childhood, to animate my future and life-long affair with the written word?

My upbringing, like that of Kafka, was a fiercely paternalistic regime administered mainly by my 'just' and well-meaning father: 'From your armchair you ruled the world. Your opinion was correct, every other was mad, wild, *meshugge*, not normal.' The twin pillars of duty and blind obedience on which this domination was based – then unremarkable, now utterly incomprehensible to my own four daughters who simply cannot understand why we stood for it, why we never argued our case or answered back – were at least in part responsible for the hundreds of hours spent later in life contemplating the richly encrusted ceiling of my central European psychoanalyst, if not for fostering my creative bent. Perhaps, like Virginia Woolf, my writer's life was driven by the desire to say 'look at me' to loving but critical parents who were to die before I had really proved myself as a writer. The firmly instilled principle that achievement comes from doing what is difficult, self fulfilment from facing responsibilities, and character from triumphing over circumstances rather than changing them when they become awkward, certainly left me with one endowment later to prove of immense value in my professional life: an infinite capacity for taking pains.

Subsequently I found this gift endorsed by Flaubert, whose letters are essential reading for any novelist: 'When one does something, one must do it wholly and well. Those bastard existences where you sell suet all day and write poetry at night are made for mediocre minds and are like those horses that are equally good for saddle and carriage, the worst kind, that can neither jump a ditch nor pull a plough.'

While I do not boast about the quality of my work, I can pride myself upon the gift, promoted by my upbringing, for steady application. Even today, when I am working, I require neither silence nor cups of tea.

If I was not a writer in those early days I was certainly an entertainer, possibly because, like many middle children, I was passed over in terms of parental concern, which fostered my need to attract attention to myself, while at the same time leaving me alone to develop an inner life. I could sit at the piano for hours churning out prose lyrics based upon any suggested topic. Once the penny was in the slot it was hard to stop me. I seemed never to run out of words. This ability, and my fondness for games of imagination in which the doors of the nursery toy cupboard could be turned at will into prison gates or submarine hatch, were the only pointers I can find to later proclivities. I did like *writing*. I still do. I liked making marks upon paper and even now, although I have graduated from pen to typewriter, typewriter to electronic typewriter, and electronic typewriter to computer with word processing program (about which more later), I still find the act itself, and the mystique which surrounds it, both satisfying and exciting. The stationery shop, rather than the fashion boutique, sets my heart pounding. I would much rather browse amongst day-glo textliners and jiffy-bags (selecting, with the attention paid to the purchase of a pair of shoes, exactly the right size and fit), Post-it notes and paperclips, than contemplate any amount of new clothing, although this too has its place. I do not have to wear corsets like Disraeli in order to release the flood gates, neither, as did Tolstoy that consummate infiltrator of the hearts and minds of women, do I smother myself with French perfume, but I cannot compose in any other than my writing clothes – trousers, sweaters, and bare feet which, like Terence Rattigan's silk dressing-gown, seem to trigger the free flow of thought – certainly not in 'going out' garments which are the kiss of death to creativity.

I waste paper. It is one of my indulgences. A few unwanted words render an entire sheet of A4 unusable. Unsullied stacks of rose-pink, yellow, turquoise, or white (according to which draft I am working on) 8Ogm paper are the catalyst for any torrent of words which may be forthcoming.

As far as writing (as in creative writing) was concerned, I did not, as did Kafka and Proust, have to free myself from the expectations of my parents. They did not give me the least encouragement. No one ever said, at any time: 'You should be a writer'. Perhaps it was just as well. In my experience when people in their formative years are told what they should do, they will do anything but that which has been proposed.

My father was a 'mantle manufacturer' (coats not fireplaces), my mother played afternoon bridge whilst having not-in-front-of-the-children conversations with her lady friends who sported slim, shagreen cigarette holders. She made me take off my shoes – because of the white carpet in the drawing-room – when I was exhibited, suitably scrubbed and primped, for a few brief moments after they had taken tea. A crippled manicurist with long red talons, called Miss Noah, came every week to do her nails. Like other middle-class households, we had a cook, a housemaid, and a nanny to look after my older brother, my younger sister and myself. On the nanny's day off, or when we were ill, there was another nanny. My parents lived their lives in the context of their extended families, my aunts and uncles who were in need of constant visiting and who were consulted upon every detail of our lives. Their friends were in business, manu-facturing, considered a cut above retailing. My maternal grand-father, who always smelled of Pears' soap, had a large wholesale warehouse in Houndsditch bearing his name and was shaved daily with an impressive cut-throat razor by a barber, Mr Cokeman, who came to the house. My grandfather was driven round in a Hispano-Suiza and later a Minerva, with a fur rug over his knees, by a sadistic, Hitler-moustached chauffeur named Selston (given to inflicting 'electric burns' upon the arms of small children) who was later to seduce and jilt our nanny. I did not know any writers. I did not know anyone who knew any writers. I had no idea that such prestigious and significant creatures as publishers, agents and editors existed. It was not my world.

THE WRITING GAME

It was not until I moved house, as adult, mother of four, and published author, that I found among the attic memorabilia an English Composition book written when I was 14. I was genuinely astonished to find essays, such as 'Travelling by Train in Wartime', another on Charles Lamb, and a critique of Van Dyck's painting of *Charles I attended by the Marquis of Hamilton*, that I realised that my efforts had been rewarded not only with an 'A+' but in addition with a red-inked complimentary remark. I do recall, sometime later, my facility at composing a story. One subject which was summarily thrown at us was 'the chimneypiece'. Since the one in our classroom was decorated with stucco, grape-bearing vines, I had no difficulty whatever in filling many impromptu pages of my notebook with the delights of Bacchus (was this the precursor of my novel *Vintage* set in the vineyards of Bordeaux?) while those around me chewed their pens. With other more pressing matters on my adolescent mind I was, fortunately, not aware of any competence with words at the time.

For those of my generation, the early years are unambiguously divided into 'before' and 'after' the war. The cataclysmic events of 1939 swiftly put paid to the upstairs world of bridge afternoons and weekly manicures, as it did to the downstairs world of buckets of coal carried up five flights of stairs for my grandfather's shaving water, and the daily whitening of my grandmother's front doorstep (ours was 'cardinaled' red). By 1945 the patterns in the kaleidoscope of lives too young to be actively involved in the least unexpected war in history, were no longer recognisable.

I was on holiday with my grandparents in a Bournemouth hotel (owned by the grandparents, and later the parents, of biographer Ronald Hayman), when the prime minister, Mr

Setting Out

Neville Chamberlain, solemnly announced from the cabinet room of number 10 Downing Street that the German government had refused his request to withdraw its troops from Poland and that 'this country is at war with Germany'. As the national anthem was played and the hotel guests – many still licking their wounds from the catastrophic 1914–1918 débâcle – tearfully reassured each other that it would 'all be over by Christmas', I had no idea what they were making such a fuss about. Like Virginia Woolf I had a curious sense of personal immunity and 'It always seemed impossible one should be hurt.'

I grew accustomed to the ullulations of the air-raid warnings, followed by the optimistic notes of the all-clear, tried on and carried my gas-mask at all times and set off unquestioningly, like others of my age, for a succession of homes and various schools in which jingoistic tunes such as 'Land of Hope and Glory' and 'I Vow to Thee my Country' replaced traditional hymns, and in some of which I was singled out and taunted by both teachers and pupils for my adherence to the Jewish faith with its alien ritual. For the first time I became uncertain whether to be proud or ashamed of being Jewish, and although my harassment could in no way be compared with that of my extended family in Holland (my father's Polish antecedents had long ago sought refuge in England) later to be deported and to disappear for ever, I spent much of my time hiding and in tears.

Many city children, some no more than four or five years old, were summarily separated from their parents, labelled like so many parcels, and put on trains for foster homes in rural areas (evacuation was voluntary but billeting compulsory). I was lucky enough to move out of London together with my family, at first to the seaside, where the bitterest winter in living memory was followed by the finest spring, and later to the depths of the country which was considered 'safe'.

With my father, who was too old for active service, a squadron leader in the Royal Air Force Special Investigation Branch, and our nanny, no longer white-aproned but smartly uniformed, away in the ATS, the seemingly immutable pattern of life changed abruptly. I helped my mother to put up the black-outs, to preserve eggs in buckets of waterglass (from which they often emerged stinking), to make 'fruit' flans (out of carrots and turnips), and to 'dig for victory' in our vegetable patch.

When, after a peripatetic existence, we finally settled, it was in a large and rambling house in the old village of Brackley in Northamptonshire which became home to my elderly grandparents (who eventually died there), as well as to sundry male cousins waiting for call-up papers, whose parents had taken their younger siblings away from a potential war zone to the safety of the United States.

Our extended family was joined by a bewildered, intensely shy, 12-year-old refugee boy, with not one word of English, who escaped to England on the last *Kindertransport*. We had no idea what Max was a refugee from and, consistent with past attitudes, we were never told. In the manner of children we accepted that he had left his family behind in Germany, but euphemisms such as *Kristallnacht*, designations such as Dachau and Theresienstadt, metaphors such as Belsen, had yet to enter the language. My older brother, my younger sister, and I had no notion of the Nazi persecution from which Max had escaped, no idea how this bereaved child must be feeling, no inkling of the unimaginable fact that he would never see a single member of his large and loving family again.

Setting Out

When my father was posted to SIB Headquarters in Knights-bridge, my mother decided that in the deceptive lull which followed the Blitz she would like to be near him, and we returned to a London flat (our old house had been 'requisitioned') in time for the 'little blitz'.

During the war my organizational talents, later to prove indispensable in juggling with family life and a writing career – getting the balance right – stood me in good stead. During the years in Brackley, I queued up for and hoarded scarce chocolate bars (first intimations of my future addiction), was first in line for luxuries such as tins of peaches (some people went so far as to keep theirs in the safe), and sussed out a farm willing to supplement our weekly ration of a single egg. The egg-lady, with her blue, cross-over pinny, was one of the first in the panoply of characters to be unconsciously filed away in the card-index of my mind. She became reincarnated many years later as Mrs Little in my first published novel *No White Coat*. The egg-lady was exceptional in the fact that she was never seen without a brown, pudding-basin hat. Did she ever take it off? What happened when she washed her grey, wispy hair? Did she wear the hat in bed?

The country was a revelation. From my labours in our kitchen garden, I learned to my great surprise that rhubarb, one of the staples of our restricted diet, actually *grew* beneath massive leaves in giant sticks which must be pulled from the ground, and that the walnuts from the majestic tree on our lawn, had to be extricated from soft green carapaces which permanently stained the fingers. Another thing which I discovered was that no matter what the horrors of inner-city life I am essentially a town person. The writer, *qua* observer, needs anonymity. She needs to mingle with the crowd and to merge

11

with it. It is the urban soup of colour, race and creed, the diversities of class, the odours of street life, the intriguing snatches of overheard conversation, rather than, as is generally supposed, the peace and serenity of the countryside, which set the wheels in motion and provide the stimulus for imaginative thought.

My memories of wartime London, illuminated by the glare of the searchlights which criss-crossed the night skies looking for enemy aircraft, are still lucid. Despite the poignant morning newspaper reports of digging for bodies beneath houses which had received 'direct hits', pictures of flames more reminiscent of Dante's *Inferno* than the City of London which they consumed, there was no fear and little terror. Perhaps it was my embryo writer's mind, but as we selfishly waited with bated breath for the 'buzz bombs' or 'doodle bugs' (as the unmanned aircraft or V1s were known) to fall on someone else's house, and grew crick-necked from identifying overhead planes as 'theirs' or 'ours', it felt neither threatening nor alarming but more like an exhilarating game of chance. Wearing an abandoned tin hat and convinced of my immortality, I foolishly refused to go down to the air-raid shelter.

We were bombed out of one flat, fortunately when we were all out, and moved to another. I learned to find my way by torchlight (the bulb covered with a statutory three layers of tissue paper) through the blacked-out streets, and had my first serious romance with an Air Force officer who only nine months later was reported missing and '... believed to have lost his life as the result of air operations'.

The stark telegram from the Air Ministry, facsimiles of which had been delivered daily to households up and down the land, brought home the fact that the past five years had been more than a matter of civilian hardship and deprivation, more than a question of collecting waste-paper and scrap-iron and limiting ourselves to the mandatory five inches of water in the bath. It was my first trenchant intimation of the real implications of war, an experience I was to draw upon 50 years later in *Mein Offizier*, my contribution to Bertelsmann's *Besiegt, befreit...,** a German symposium on the feelings of politicians, philosophers, historians, writers and others (including Manfred Rommel and Klaus von Bismarck) in Europe and the USA at the close of the Second World War.

Devastated by my pilot officer's death, only four short weeks before the war in Europe ended, I did not dance in the streets on VE day. It was perhaps my earliest experience of reserving for myself Montaigne's 'little back shop, all our own, entirely free, wherein to establish our true liberty and principal retreat and solitude'.

On leaving Queen's College, Harley Street, at the age of 18, with Higher School Certificate in English, French, Latin, and German, and no guidance whatsoever as to any future career other than marriage – I was a girl was I not? – I drifted off to London University to request a place to read English. There was none available until the following year, which – since a degree in Eng. Lit. is often thought to be an impediment to writing – was, in view of my future career, perhaps in my best interests.

On the way out of the building I passed the Law Faculty. Half-heartedly I enquired from the dean whether I might perhaps read law. One of the three places available to women was reluctantly given to me, together with the caveat that I would

* Eds Werner Filmer and Dr Heribert Schwan (Hrsg.)

probably get married before the course was finished. Fortunately the dean was right. I never did master the Legislation of Tiberius Gracchus, and the case of The Carbolic Smoke Ball left me cold.

CHAPTER TWO

Writing For Pleasure

———————

'It is a delicious thing to write. To be no longer yourself but to move in an entire universe of your own creating.'

Gustave Flaubert

First novels are not usually first novels. *No White Coat*, published by Hodder & Stoughton and launched in the same year as the first Russian Sputnik (1957), was no exception to this paradox.

My husband, a doctor, was in general practice. The newly formed National Health Service provided no support system, but relied upon the goodwill of the doctor's wife for secretarial and ancillary help. A cavalcade of patients called at the house and attached surgery from morning till night (and very often during the night), and I had little idea that together with their clumsily wrapped specimen bottles and their ailments, they brought to my doorstep sufficient testimony of the 'quiet desperation', which governs the mass of people's lives, to furnish

15

many of my future novels. I did not put the patients into my books. 'Do you put real people into your books?' is a favourite question which was briskly dealt with by Mrs Trollope: 'Of course I draw from life, but I always pulp my acquaintance before serving them up. You would never recognise a pig in a sausage.' Somerset Maugham made no secret of the fact that he not only described people he knew (Miss Thompson, the prostitute in *Rain*), but even filched their names. Simenon got his names from the telephone directory; Jonathan Swift took 'Gulliver' from a tombstone, while Robert Louis Stevenson made use of two names which were engraved on the stained-glass windows of Middle Temple Hall where he happened to be dining: Sir Joseph *Jekyll* and Sir Robert *Hyde*. My own answer to the question is no. And yes. Evelyn Waugh's disclaimer to *Brideshead Revisited* 'I am not I: thou art not he or she: they are not they', or the more usual declaration at the beginning of a many works of fiction: 'The characters in this novel bear no relation to any living person' is more often than not untrue. It is the universal custom to *base* characters upon living persons and the identification of the originals need in no way detract from any writer's artistic integrity. Dickens based most of the important figures in *Bleak House* on prototypes: Harold Skimpole, upon the romantic essayist Leigh Hunt; Boythorn, upon the poet Walter Savage Landor; Bucket, upon a noted London police inspector. Dr Joseph Bell, an Edinburgh surgeon and friend of Sir Arthur Conan Doyle, provided the inspiration for Sherlock Holmes, and Delphine Delamère, a French doctor's wife who had many love affairs and was later to commit suicide, was the model for Emma Bovary. Turgenev could not create a character at all unless as a starting point he used a living person. Writers who deny that they make use of people they either know or have encountered, deceive themselves, and no writer should be ashamed to admit it. A. A. Milne (Christopher Robin), the Rev. Charles Dodgson (Alice in Wonderland), and John le Carré (George Smiley), all based their characters on real people.

My own wartime egg-lady was the model for Mrs Little (*No White Coat*) who, like her begetter, wore a pudding-basin hat which she seemed never to remove. Superimposed upon Mrs Little's physical appearance however, was the distinctive and lugubrious voice mouthing fabricated opinions (I had never heard the egg-lady utter other than to confide the current price of an egg) of a woman who came on the scene many years later, coupled with a fictional personality of her own. Writers who do not make use of people they know, or have met, in order to get a 'fix' on them, rarely create believable characters. 'It is only if you have a definite person in your mind that you can give vitality and authenticity to your own creation.'*

Somerset Maugham confirmed that it is a creation: 'We know very little even of the persons we know most intimately; we do not know them enough to transfer them to the pages of a book and make human beings of them ... The writer does not copy his originals; he takes what he wants from them, a few traits that have caught his attention, a turn of mind that has fired his imagination, and therefrom constructs his character ... no one has the right to take a character in a book and say, "this is meant to be me." All he may say is, I provided the suggestion for this character.'

Readers of course will have it otherwise. A South African reader of mine insisted that she had actually met Kitty Shelton

* Turgenev

17

(the protagonist of *Proofs of Affection*) sitting by the swimming pool in a Cape Town hotel, while an Australian lady from Perth swore that I had used her father as a model for Sydney Shelton in the same novel. Although I had at the time set foot in neither country, I do not argue. The author can have no greater compliment paid to him than to be told his characters are 'real people'. If the core quality of your writing is human, if you succeed in transmitting not only images and events but thoughts, feelings, longings, if your words, like Kafka's ice-axe, break 'the sea frozen inside us', it is inevitable that you hit chords.

After I had had two of my four daughters I began to write short stories. According to Cyril Connolly 'there is no more sombre enemy of art than the pram in the hall' and it is perhaps significant that of the four great women novelists – Jane Austen, Charlotte Brontë, Emily Brontë, and George Eliot – none had a child and two never married.

Writing, however, is part of life, an overflow of it, and luckily, unlike Erica Jong, I have never found domesticity and imaginative thought incompatible:

'The demands of life are nearly always antithetical to the demands of art. The crying baby does not exactly enhance the day-dreaming state needed for writing poems. The trip to the vet or the pediatrician does not exactly prepare one for writing a chapter describing palazzi in 16th-century Venice. Or does it? They had cats and dogs and babies in those 16th-century palazzi and doubtless they felt about them the way we feel about our cats and dogs and babies. Even the most unexpected occurrence at the pediatrician's or the vet's, turns out to fuel the book one is writing. The look of an animal in pain. The feel of a wet baby. How can any artist believe that by excluding the clutter and commotion of life he is somehow enhancing his art ... Whatever one loses of concentration, one gains immeasurably in the richness of observation.'

This is borne out by the fact that George Eliot left her work to nurse her father, Charlotte Bronte put down her pen to 'pick the eyes out of the potatoes', and Mrs Gaskell tells us that she wrote in a room with six doors, thus enabling her innumerable children to interrupt her freely, while through further doors came requests for dinner and plans for the day. It took a man, Leo Tolstoy, to see how futile it was for a woman to wait until she has peace and quiet:

'Peace with six children was next to impossible. One would fall ill, another would threaten to fall ill, a third would be without something necessary, a fourth would show symptoms of a bad disposition, and so on and so on...'

It did not occur to me then, as it does not occur to me now, either to question or analyse my motivation for writing, the necessity for which is as essential as the necessity to eat and which, according to Roland Barthes, represents 'a way of being both passive and active, social and asocial, present and absent in one's own life.'

For Keats writing was a means of 'banishing the disagreeables'; for Anthony Burgess 'a hopeless attempt to heal the festering diseases of the soul'; William Burroughs called it 'a curse and evil spirit'; George Orwell was 'driven on by some demon whom one can neither resist nor understand', while for Leonard Woolf 'one of the best unfailing pleasures is to sit down in the morning and write'. Writing, an addiction which 'requires no capital, no special education, no training, and may be taken up at any time without a moment's delay'* seemed to

---

* Anthony Trollope

me as natural as breathing and despite the fact that it is often done at the expense of one's body, is as fundamental to my health. I was intrigued by the fact that human beings, like handsome edifices, are not always lovely beyond the exterior. Curious by nature, my inclination has always been to look behind the façade.

The short stories were set down in longhand at the dining-room table. I sent them to a random selection of fiction editors who lost no time in sending them back to me. There was no one to tell me that the magazine market was one to be studied for form and content, or to acquaint me with the writer's Bible, the *Writers' and Artists' Yearbook* (the authors' equivalent of Delia Smith's *Cookery Course*), which was, and is still, published by A & C Black. Within the red covers were listed the major periodicals, together with their precise requirements, names of literary agents, chapters on how to prepare a manuscript and correct a proof, and information on such useful topics as copyright, income tax, and social security benefits.

I stumbled across the threshold to my future life in an evening class at the City Literary Institute: 'Writing for Pleasure'. I have said that creative writing cannot be taught. Not so technique. 'If you want to be considered a poet, you will have to show mastery of the petrarchan sonnet form or the sestina. Your musical efforts must begin with well-formed fugues. There is no substitute for craft ... Art begins with craft, and there is no art until craft has been mastered.'*

Although writers are born and not made and a 'voice' of one's own is innate, for the untried writer there is sometimes much to

* Anthony Burgess

be gained from group discussion about work in progress – in the course of which the writer's strengths and weaknesses will be revealed – and the dissemination of useful information about matters such as narrative, structure, and the question of the author's omniscience. In the UK, in contrast to the USA where universities, such as those of Indiana and Iowa, offer masters' degrees in creative writing, the writer's garret has a longer tradition than the writers' group. The University of East Anglia's successful writing course set up in the 1960s by Professor Malcolm Bradbury, has however spawned such household 'names' as Booker Prize winning Kazuo Ishiguro and Ian McEwan.

There is a difference between doing something, and doing it well. Michelangelo didn't suddenly decide to have a go at painting the Sistine Chapel, he worked as an apprentice for seven years. Beethoven studied under Haydn. De Maupassant learned from Flaubert ('the novelist's novelist'). On Tuesday nights at the City Literary Institute, at the feet of a patient and gifted teacher, I learned that accurate observation is the *sine qua non* of the accomplished writer.

A man in shirtsleeves runs along a beach. His tie flaps behind him. He leaves footprints in the sand. We can all picture him. He is a figment of our slovenly imaginations. If, however, we apply what Anthony Trollope called 'the elbow grease of the mind', come a little closer, take the trouble to stand for a moment on the sea wall, we will *hear* the jingle of coins in his trouser pocket, see how the sweat-soaked shirt cleaves to his back, smell the fear, feel the exertion which goes into each thumping stride, identify the trailing shoe-lace that trips our hero up as his city shoes crunch indiscriminately over cans and crab shells. Of what is he frightened? From whom is he running? Where is he going?

21

THE WRITING GAME

A minibus overturns on a motorway. From our armchairs it is no problem to imagine the crumpling of metal, the tinkle of glass, the appearance of the police and the wail of ambulance sirens familiar from TV and cinema screen. From his vantage point *inside* the minibus, the true observer will see that the seats are crammed with university students. They are singing a popular song. One of them knits. Her wool is blue. On impact the singing stops. In mid-verse. In slow motion, as in a silent movie, the bus rolls over. The students panic. Covered with blood, they clamber over each other to reach the buckled doors. One of them smashes the back window and they try to extricate themselves. *Their arms and legs are entangled in cats' cradles of blue wool.* Flaubert, of course, was a master of close scrutiny. Not content with merely describing the tightly closed carriage in which Emma Bovary and her lover ride, he adds a gem of accurate observation which ignites the scene: 'Once, in the middle of the day, when they were right out in the country ... an ungloved hand stole out beneath the little yellow canvas blinds and tossed away some scraps of paper, which were carried off on the wind and landed like white butterflies in a field of red clover in full bloom.'

We must beware the stereotype. A dumpy, middle-aged 'housewife' in an amorphous coat and a skinny young girl with freaked-out hair sit opposite you in a tube train. Their belongings are on the floor between them. A tartan shopping trolley stuffed with plastic carriers emblazoned with the names of Oxford Street stores. A violin case. You have composed their stories. The train stops. The 'housewife' gets out. She takes the violin case.

We are left with the girl. There is a tattoo on her arm and a ring through her nose. Her jeans are frayed, her tee shirt, with its defiant slogan, unironed, her hair unwashed, her nails bitten. What is in her carrier bags? Where has she come from? Does she live in a squat? Is her bed a mattress on the floor? What lies beside it? Did she have breakfast? What school did she attend? What job is she going to? She gets out at Earls Court. To work, study, meet a friend, 'sign on'? Is she alone in London? Does she smoke, drink, do drugs? Has she got a steady date, a live-in lover? Does her mother know?

I learned to carry a notebook. To jot down seemingly irrelevant snatches of conversation – observations, from the seeds of which, perhaps after many years of gestation, stories, novels, plays, scripts would be born – often when there is no writing material to hand other than a scrap of paper or used envelope. My working notes, interspersed with shopping lists and other *aides mémoires*, make bizarre reading. The ideas must be your own. You learn to parry the Ancient Mariner who detains you in the certain knowledge that once you have heard his story you will drop everything to write it for him. His experiences may indeed have been fascinating, but the mere recording of them will never add up to a book. A work of art is not *about* this or that kind of life. It *has* life.

Reading out my work in the evening class and listening to the silence that followed, as it does the final notes of music which has reached the heart, confirmed that I had some aptitude for writing.

I bought a copy of Pitman's *Teach Yourself Typing* and on an antedeluvian Remington typewriter began a convoluted full-length novel in which the characters spent many pages getting themselves into and out of rooms. The afternoon hours proved insufficient for this labour and I soon learned that *le monde appartient à ceux qui se lèvent tôt*. Getting up early did not come easily but seemed the only way to combine my duties in the practice, writing, and the demands of family life.

Domestic and creative life do not always mix easily. Women are torn between their artistic and their human responsibilities in which their days are squandered in response to the demands of others on their time, energy, and psychic space. Simone de Beauvoir considered herself lucky to have escaped most of the usual kinds of 'female slave labour'. Vita Sackville-West longed for 'places where no one will want me to order lunch or pay house books', while Virginia Woolf declared: 'How any woman with a family ever put pen to paper I cannot fathom. Always the bell rings or the baker calls.' E. M. Delafield, a pillar of the Women's Institute and author of *Diary of a Provincial Lady*, describes the frustrations of trying to write at home:

'. . . I carry chair, writing materials, rug and cushion into the garden, but am called in to " 'ave a look at the pantry sink, please, as it seems to have blocked itself up". Attempt to return to garden, frustrated by arrival of a note from the village concerning Garden Fête arrangements, which require immediate answer; necessity for speaking to butcher on the telephone and sudden realisation, that Laundry List hasn't been made out and the van will be here at eleven.'

When men want to diminish women as artists, they point out that not only are they inferior in intellect, but too preoccupied with domesticity – reflected of course in their work – to compete with them in either scope or quality of output. They do not really consider literature to be a valid concern of women and the more they are engaged in their 'proper' duties, the less time will they have for it. To dismiss the domestic setting as 'limited' would be to deny the talents of Jane Austen and Virginia Woolf not to mention those of Ibsen, Strindberg and Beckett. It is not the subject matter of a novel which is important, but its execution. What matters is the imaginative truth and the perfection and care with which it has been rendered.

When my novel was finished, I had it professionally typed and bound and naïvely sent it to the first publisher on the list I had compiled, from the spines on the fiction shelves of the public library, by Special Messenger. Little did I know that due to the unprecedented number of unsolicited manuscripts publishers receive each week, it was the practice then, as indeed it sometimes is now, to keep any submissions which land on the 'slush-pile' for weeks, if not months, before reading them. I was not, at this point, familiar with Doris Lessing's writers' manifesto:

'Without me the literary industry would not exist: the publishers, the agents, the sub-agents, the sub-sub-agents, the accountants, the libel lawyers, the departments of literature, the professors, the theses, the books of criticism, the reviewers, the book pages – all this vast and proliferating edifice is because of this small, patronized, put-down and underpaid person.'

It was my first intimation that the role of the author came so far down in the pecking order as to be almost indiscernible. The rejections, once they started to arrive, were courteous. In the days before Thomas Tilling took over the Heinemann Group and sold it on to BTR – who sold it to Octopus who in turn sold it on to Reed International who sold the trade publishing arm to Random House – and 'pass the parcel' became the fashionable game amongst publishing houses, publishing was still, as it had been since the 1930s, 'an Occupation for a Gentleman'. A direct line existed between the man who loved books and the man (the senior ranks of publishing were always occupied by men) who ran the company, who *pace* Fred Warburg's bestselling account of the period, were by no means always gentlemen. Sometimes it was the same person, and the leading publishers (Collins, Longman, Murray), were either the successors of a long line or, in the case of such household names as Jamie Hamilton, Michael Joseph, Sir Stanley Unwin and Victor Gollancz, eponymous with the name over the publishing house door.

Although unbelievable now, in those days civility was the name of the game: 'We cannot anticipate a sale for the book in our lists which would satisfy either you or ourselves'; 'Unfortunately we have decided against publishing it'; 'We are sorry to have to give you this disappointing decision'; 'Since you have been so courteous as to send this work for our consideration, we will take careful reports on it, but we think it only fair to warn you that we can only add to our lists, which are very full at the present time, if our reports are quite outstandingly enthusiastic. We hope therefore, that you will not be unduly disappointed if we have to decide that we cannot proceed further in the matter of publication.' Needless to say their reports were not 'quite outstandingly enthusiastic'. Neither, despite the fact that over a year went by between the first and last of these missives, was I unduly disappointed.

Sooner or later every artist encounters a rebuff – even the most renowned. One hundred and fifty years ago a succession of publishing houses turned down *Jane Eyre*, a novel about a young governess by a Yorkshire vicar's daughter. Fortunately for us its author, Charlotte Brontë (who wrote under a male pseudonym), was depressed but undeterred. Those disheartened by rejection should take heed of George Bernard Shaw: 'I finished my first book (*Immaturity*) seventy-six years ago. I offered it to every publisher on the English-speaking earth I had ever heard of. Their refusals were unanimous: and it did not get into print until, fifty years later, publishers would publish anything that had my name on it...' In 1911 Marcel Proust had completed the first 800 pages of what was to become *Remembrance of Things Past*. After his manuscript had been refused for the third time – with the comment that it took the author 30 pages to tell how he turned over in bed – Proust decided to pay for publication himself.

Shaw and Proust were by no means alone. *Moby Dick* ('very long, rather old-fashioned') was at first rejected as was *Barchester Towers*, *The Razor's Edge*, *Lolita* (it will not sell ... I recommend that it be buried under a stone for a thousand years'), *Lady Chatterley's Lover* ('for your own good do not publish this book'), *The Rainbow* ('disgusting'), *The Good Earth* '...the American public is not interested in anything on China', *Animal Farm* ('animal stories don't sell in the USA') *Wind in the Willows* 'an irresponsible holiday story', *Lord of the Flies* (an 'absurd and uninteresting fantasy which was rubbish and dull') and *Watership Down* ('older children wouldn't like it because its subject matter was babyish and younger children wouldn't understand it because its language was too difficult'). Three subsequent publishers and three literary agents also passed on this worldwide bestseller because they failed to see how adults could possibly want to read a novel about rabbits.

Stella Gibbons was told by her publishers that she would have to hawk *Cold Comfort Farm* about on a wheelbarrow before she sold any copies, John le Carré (*The Spy That Came in from the Cold*) refused to believe that he 'had no future' and Ian Fleming that 'James Bond will never sell'. Booker Prizewinner Iris Murdoch, together with Jilly Cooper (Lifetime Achievement award), began her writing life – as did Joyce Cary, Samuel Beckett, Norman Mailer, Kingsley Amis, Georges Simenon,

27

Evelyn Waugh, Joseph Heller, Toni Morrison, William Boyd and countless other authors – on the receiving end of rejection slips, while Catherine Cookson's early novels were offered to several short-sighted paperback houses who strongly advised the author not to take up writing as a career! One Chinese publisher wrote to an author: 'We have read your manuscript with boundless delight. If we were to publish your book it would be impossible for us to publish any work of a lower standard. And as it is unthinkable that in the next thousand years we shall see its equal, we are to our regret compelled to return your divine composition and beg you, a thousand times, to overlook our short sight and timidity.' This was perhaps better than the apocryphal: 'Many thanks for submitting your manuscript. We shall waste no time reading it.'

Amongst the many brush-offs my first novel received was one ray of hope. Mr H. P. Guttmann, managing director of Hammond, Hammond & Company Ltd, 87 Gower Street (now defunct), apologised that owing to holidays he had kept my manuscript – which he liked very much in the first half but was regretfully returning – longer than he should have, but following his reader's report, wondered if I could spare the time for luncheon over which a talk might be of some value to both of us.

I doubt if this would happen today when the face of British publishing has changed for ever, the wheeler-dealers at the helm use 'manufacturing profits' as an excuse to justify advances that haven't a hope in hell of being earned out, and the first consideration is not 'is it a worthwhile book' but 'how commercial is it? Sales figures, rather than artistic merit, are the paramount concern of today's publishing houses whose finances dictate a more hardbitten approach. Consumed by conglomerates, and spending 80 per cent of promotional budget on 10 per cent of 'sure-fire' titles, no one can any longer afford to foster talent by 'carrying' a first novel (unless 'written' by a sportsman or pop-star) even were they perspicacious enough to see it as the forerunner of a successful *oeuvre*. Fortunately for the writer there are still some independent publishers willing to take risks. Breakaway editors such as Ian Chapman (ex-Collins), dissatisfied with multinational companies in whose portfolios the 100,000 books published each year are merely an item, and in which the personal touch is non-existent, have set up their own imprints. There are hopeful signs that the pendulum, in grave danger of 'killing the goose which lays the golden eggs', is at last about to swing.

There followed several civil letters from Hammond, Hammond & Company setting up our luncheon. They conveyed Mr Guttmann's relief that I was not offended by his reader's report, and begged me not to hesitate to telephone him if I was uncertain how to reach Gower Street.

The greater part of the luncheon passed in silence. Mr Guttmann, an elderly and gracious gentleman, spent a great deal of time minutely examining his Dover sole from which he extracted every bone with a meticulous delicacy. When he wasn't dissecting his fish he was puffing on the inhaler which relieved his asthma. My novel, he said when he had a moment to spare from his activities, definitely 'had something', but he was not sufficiently enthusiastic to make an offer for it. His suggestion was that I regard the novel as a kind of literary limbering-up exercise, and that I go home and write another which he would then be happy to consider.

I did go home, not to write another novel but to alter the

whole texture of reality, change the shape of the world, by having another child. Perhaps I would never have written another book at all had I not, whilst pregnant with my third daughter, sold a short story.

'The Magic' – about an elderly spinster who ostensibly ran a bookshop but was the secret and pseudonymous author of torrid romances – was accepted by *Woman's Journal* which not only offered a fee of 18 guineas but asked for more. The story was published in the same issue of the magazine as an excerpt from Rebecca West's *The Fountain Overflows*.

Although when I wrote 'The Magic' I had never met another writer, I must have realised when I described my 'bookshop lady' that writers do not look like writers, any more than child molesters or axe-murderers look like criminals. Anita Brookner can do her shopping in Marks and Spencers, and P. D. James mingle happily with the crowds in Oxford Street, without fear of recognition.

Short stories must be 'received'. Unlike the novel there is no starting with an amorphous lump of clay or stone, no hacking, sculpting, moulding, adding, subtracting, infinite possibilities of ultimate shape and form. Triggered by a person, a remark, an event, an idea, they arrive, like bolts of lightning, at unexpected moments, in a flash and 'all of a piece', their cast immutable and needing only polish and refinement. They are exciting to write but deceptive in their apparent ease of execution. 'Each word should be weighed carefully as for a telegram to be paid for by the author'.* There is little room in the short story for self-indulgence, for excess.

Flushed with success (I sold rights in 'The Magic' to France

* Ernest Hemingway

and Scandinavia) I began another novel. Using my everyday world of a general medical practice, I wrote swiftly and to the point. Once more, among the rejection slips from such now defunct houses as Rupert Hart-Davis Ltd and The Cresset Press, I received a glimmer of encouragement. Once again I was invited to lunch with a publisher. My manuscript, he said over the *coq au vin*, was not without merit. The problem, as he saw it, was that the story was written on two levels, the light-hearted and the tragic. It fell, he explained kindly, between two stools. It was an expression that I was to hear many times over the years and I once toyed with the idea of setting up 'The Between Two Stools Publishing Company', a kind of *Salon des Refusés* for novels. I think it would attract a great many writers. The publisher's advice, as he signed the bill, was that I make my novel either entirely a work of comedy, for which I had a natural gift, or wholly serious. When I had rewritten it in accordance with his suggestion, he would be happy to have another look at it.

I did not take his advice. Laughter *and* tears have been ingredients of practically every popular success since Dickens, and I decided to try one more publisher before reconsidering the situation. I sent the novel to Hodder & Stoughton and two days later (13 November 1956) received the following letter:

'We have safely received the typescript of your novel, No White Coat, and will give it a careful reading. We hope however that you will not be too disappointed if we have to decide that we cannot make you an offer for its publication, as our lists are so full for many months to come that we have to be extremely selective in adding to them.'

I heard nothing more until 5 February (my birthday) 1957.

31

THE WRITING GAME

Hodder & Stoughton liked my novel for its qualities of 'kindness, feeling and humour' and enclosed a Memorandum of Agreement to publish it. I had submitted the manuscript under a male pseudonym, 'Robert Tibber', and the covering letter, from the chairman of the firm, Ralph Hodder-Williams, was addressed 'Dear Sir'.

CHAPTER THREE

Do You Write Under Your Own Name?

<hr style="width:30%"/>

'Unless one is a moron, one always dies unsure of one's own value and that of one's works. Virgil himself, as he lay dying, wanted the Aeneid buried.'

Gustave Flaubert

Why a man's name? There was a simple answer to a question frequently put. *No White Coat* revolved around a young house physician who had abandoned his 'white coat' and left the privileged world of hospital medicine. The doctor's account of his first year in general practice would, I thought, sound more authentic if the reader were to believe that the author of *No White Coat*, and the narrator, were the same 'man'. Some male readers will not even pick up a book which is written by a woman. Do women write differently from men? Is there such a thing as a 'woman's book'?

THE WRITING GAME

As long ago as 600 BC Sappho and her contemporaries were turning out poetry on their Greek island, but from that time on – with certain notable exceptions – there was a deafening silence from female writers in England until the end of the eighteenth century. Given the fact that women at that time were not only denied education, but were frequently knocked about by their husbands, this is not surprising. The circumstances were hardly favourable to creative expression. It was not until women had a little money, a little leisure and, if they were lucky, the proverbial room of their own that the well-springs were uncovered and the talent gushed forth. Was women's situation apparent in their writing? Consider the following examples:

'During the interval between dinner and the arrival of the guests, she felt as a young soldier feels before going into action. Her heart throbbed violently and she could not keep her thoughts fixed on anything.'

'Although it was busy work to look after all the children and restrain their wild pranks, though it was difficult to remember whose were all those little stockings and drawers, not to mix up the shoes for the different feet, and to untie, unbutton, and then do up again all the tapes and buttons ... she was never happier than when bathing with all the children.'

The above two passages were written not by a woman but by Leo Tolstoy! They clearly demonstrate the hazards of 'labelling'. The novelist must be androgynous, capable of *becoming* at will male or female. The ability to empathise, to put oneself inside the skin of one's characters, to think, to react, to suffer, not in one's own way but in their way, is the hallmark of a good writer.

I have not been widowed, as was Kitty Shelton in my novel

34

Do You Write Under Your Own Name?

Rose of Jericho, nor have I known what it is to be a concentration camp inmate, like Maurice Morgenthau in the same novel. Yet *Rose of Jericho* is recommended by bereavement counsellors to give consolation to women who have lost their husbands, and Holocaust survivors have testified to the accuracy with which I have described not only their experiences, but their *feelings*.

Male writers have it easy. Many of them have dedicated wives who free them to serve the Muse without domestic or secretarial burdens. Anthony Trollope worked with a pencil then '... Rose made a copy in ink afterwards. In this way the greater part of *Barchester Towers* was composed.' Bernard Shaw publicly acknowledged his gratitude to Henry and Clara Higgs '... without their friendly services, I should not have had time to write my books and plays nor had any comfort in my daily life.' When Count Nikolai Tolstoy described his writing day for a Sunday broadsheet he included the give away sentence: 'Georgina brings me Ovaltine at 11'!

That grand old man of letters, Victor Pritchett, confessed: '... four hours writing have washed out all sense of time – my wife calls me down for a delicious lunch. She has spent the morning typing what I wrote the day before ... knowing that she'll have to do the whole damn thing over again two or three times because I cover each page with an ants colony of corrections ...'

Carrie Balestier took over Kipling's household to 'protect him from visitors'; Anthony Burgess's wife drove him round Europe while he got on with his novel in the back of the Dormobile; Mario Vargos Llosa's wife brings his food on a tray which she leaves outside his locked door; Danielle Smith (who has now become a writer herself) freely admits that she stood at the ready from 9 am to 3 pm each day to receive and process Wilbur's jotted requests for information. Vera Nabokov, however, out-wifed them all. She guarded her husband's privacy, typed his manuscripts, answered his letters, drove his car, attended his classes, replaced him at the lectern when he fell ill, marked his students' exam papers, translated *Pale Fire* into Russian, learned Italian in order to correct Vladimir's verse, saved the manuscript of *Lolita* from the incinerator, and earned money for them both as a tourist guide when the going got tough.

To be sure Muriel Spark has the loyal Jardine who '... takes care of the house, the finances, the travel, the cooking, the shopping, the correspondence, the filing. She keeps the outside world at bay', but this is the exception rather than the rule.

Authors tend to resort to pseudonyms either to place distance between themselves and their work or to separate two writing persona. 'Dan Kavanagh' is the name under which Julian Barnes publishes detective stories (he is married to literary agent Pat Kavanagh), and Ruth Rendell does likewise under the pseudonym 'Barbara Vine', while 'Caroline Harvey' is none other than the bestselling Joanna Trollope. In my use of 'Robert Tibber' (Tibber was my maiden name and Robert the nearest I could get to Rosemary) I was in the best of company. George Eliot (Mary Ann Evans), George Sand (Amandine Aurore Dupin Lucie), George Orwell (Eric Blair), Samuel Longhome Clemens (Mark Twain), Aleksei Maksimovih Peshkov (Maxim Gorky) and John le Carré (David Cornwell) all preferred, for one reason or another, to write under pen names.

I had signed the contract for *No White Coat*, and received my first advance of £75 before Hodder & Stoughton realised, as I walked into St Paul's House, Warwick Lane, that I was not a man. My deception was taken in good part, and was later exploited on TV when I was billed as 'Robert Tibber' and – unknown to me – the camera homed in on my ankles and worked its way upwards.

I had no idea as to the equity of the terms offered by Hodder & Stoughton for the publication of *No White Coat*. I signed the Memorandum of Agreement (which I believed to be standard because it was so nicely printed) and sent it back by return of post. I was to receive 10 per cent of the published price (12*s* 6*d*) on the first 3,000 copies sold, 12 ½ per cent on the next 4,500 copies, and 15 per cent thereafter on all copies sold in Great Britain, Northern Ireland and Eire. These figures were not inconsistent with those in today's contracts: 10 per cent to 2,500 copies, 12.5 per cent on the next 2,500 and 15 per cent thereafter. Other clauses, in which the author was held to ransom, have now been superseded by those of the Minimum Terms Agreement protecting his or her legitimate rights, to which the more enlightened publishers have signed their names. I agreed to leave 'all details as to the manner of production', to the publishers as well as giving them 'first refusal' on my next two books. I was to be paid annually each July, the royalty figures having been made up to the 31st day of the preceding March. I signed away my rights to be consulted on jacket design, blurb and publicity and, no matter how poor a job Hodder & Stoughton made of publishing *No White Coat*, no matter how few copies they sold, I dutifully promised not to go elsewhere with subsequent books. In addition I granted them free use of any moneys accrued from the sale of my books for 15 months before I saw a penny of it!

Although, like many another first time author, I was exceptionally compliant and eager to please, the above arrangement was not as naïve as it sounds. The unilateral contract was standard for the time when publishers were more or less able to dictate their own terms. As a result of strenuous efforts by the Society of Authors and the Writers' Guild however, many of them have now signed the Minimum Terms Agreement. This agreement is a code of good practice, under which the publisher undertakes (with minor individual variations) to offer 20 year licences rather than seek rights for the full duration of the copyright, to give the author the opportunity to ask for the terms of the contract to be reviewed after 10 years, and to offer him a share of the income from the subsidiary rights. The publishers concerned have also agreed that the author will as of *right* be consulted over matters such as illustrations, editorial changes, the jacket, the blurb, the publication date, publicity, and all major sub-licences and will guarantee to publish his book within 12 months of the delivery of the manuscript.

Those who are not writers themselves imagine that an author is entitled to unlimited free copies of his books. While these same people would not dream of asking a motor manufacturer for a free car or a dress designer to hand over a dress, they are deeply hurt when an author tells them that her book is on sale at the bookshop round the corner. The author gets, at best, a dozen free copies, with the opportunity to purchase further copies at a discount of 45 or 50 per cent. Under the Minimum Terms Agreement the publisher must also make up accounts six monthly, disclose the print run, and pay the author any moneys due in respect of sub-licences within *one* month of receipt of same.

In 1957 there were still publishers who considered that the main purpose of producing books was to bring to the public outstanding works of literary and human value rather than mere fictive publications. They understood very well that the qualities that give a book merit are not necessarily the same as those that make it a commercial success. They were happy to invest time, energy, and cash in a novel which they liked, even if they knew in advance that it would lose money. 'Name' authors could be bought for £1,000 to £1,500 pounds, and print runs were a modest 1,500 to 3,000 copies in hard cover. Today, authors are sold to the highest bidder, confident in the knowledge that publishers who have paid vast sums to acquire them will spend equally vast sums on promoting them. International conglomerates pay as much as $20 million in advances (frequently unearned) for world rights of books, and print runs can be anything up to 500,000 copies in hardback. In this climate fewer and fewer punters can be found who are willing, or able, to nurture the first-time 'author of promise'. Because of this, and despite their faithful readership, many well established authors in the publishers' 'mid-list' (commercial death) category are now unable to find anyone willing to publish their books and have sadly gone to the wall.

The advance which I was offered against royalties for *No White Coat* was £75. With it I bought the *Encyclopaedia Britannica* from a salesman who had had his foot in my door for so long that when I succumbed he nearly fell through it with surprise.

When John Milton sold *Paradise Lost* to the bookseller Samuel Simmons he was paid £5 and his widow £8, making the rate of pay for the greatest long poem in the English language slightly over a farthing a line, not a good deal even in the seventeenth century. Fifty years later Alexander Pope made £4,000 from his translation of Homer's *Iliad* (worth £100,000 today), while in 1995 Martin Amis, in an unprecedented breakthrough, demanded and received the then unheard of sum of half-a-million pounds (£350,000 of which was unearned) for his poorly received novel about literary envy *The Information* (together with a book of short stories), from HarperCollins. The difference between the deal made by Amis and those of the poets, is not only several hundred years but the fact that fighting on Amis's behalf was his New York literary agent Andrew 'the jackal' Wylie, renowned for negotiating huge advances for authors such as Philip Roth and Salman Rushdie.

I did not have an agent, and did not feel the need of one, until *after* I had signed my contract with Hodder & Stoughton. I did not know any agents and had no idea how to go about finding one. In the era of the stable and independent imprints – not yet swallowed up by international corporations – who did not make much money but did so in a gentlemanly manner, it did not seem necessary to employ an intermediary to act on one's behalf. Now, however, with the rise of the red-in-tooth-and-claw world – in which editors are in perpetual orbit – that publishing has become, the agent with her finger on the pulse of exactly who is devouring whom is essential. As the tide of unsolicited manuscripts swells, publishers rely on accredited agents to protect them from badly presented offerings such as the motley collection of notes and photographs of lions, rejected by Heinemann, and rescued from the slush-pile at Collins, to be published as *Born Free*. Today it is almost as hard to get a reputable agent to act for you as it is to find a publisher for your book.

Joyce Weiner was introduced to me by chance. She was a friend of a friend who persuaded me that if I was to be a writer I *must* have an agent. He gave me her address and somewhat diffidently I sent her the manuscript of *No White Coat*. Her verdict on the novel was 'lively and accomplished' (she always chose her words with utter honesty and great care) and on the author 'a writer of distinct talent and ability'. *Faut de mieux* I authorised her to act as my agent which she did for 14 happy years until her retirement in 1971.

Miss Weiner, as I called her in those days (she always referred to me as *Mrs* Friedman) was not only physically formidable but a law unto herself. A graduate of Lady Margaret Hall and one-time acquaintance of Thomas Mann, Miss Weiner lived and worked in a book-lined flat in St John's Wood, together with her younger sister, Margery, novelist, historian, wartime member of MI5, and founder of the *Daily Telegraph* Information Bureau. The two sisters formed a unique partnership. Margery was the fast talker, the wit, the cook, the nurse, the house-keeper; Joyce – to the end of her life totally impractical and unable to hold a needle or boil the proverbial egg – the breadwinner, the academic, the *grande dame*, the *materfamilias*.

Neither of them had married (I sometimes caught veiled hints of romances which had come to grief) although Margery must have been a great beauty in her youth. The two sisters were as close as any married couple and when Margery died of a heart attack in 1982, the stricken Joyce, although she made a brave attempt to survive without her lifelong companion and helpmeet, managed to outlive her by less than a year.

Miss Weiner, *my* Miss Weiner, was extremely short, extremely fat, extremely near sighted, and extremely ugly. She was an immensely hard working and sympathetic agent (rising at 5 am for the whole of her working life) and was prepared to go to almost any trouble for clients who included Georgette Heyer, Compton Mackenzie and Naomi Jacob. She was a loyal and affectionate friend, an honest and fearless counsellor – the best gift any writer can have – and her standards were uncompromisingly high. To have her act on one's behalf was to employ a tigress and I have known eminent publishers (to whom she was fond of giving 'pep-talks') cower in her path. If she wrote a letter (on her familiar blue letterhead) she insisted upon a prompt and written reply from the recipient himself, no matter how exalted. She would have no truck with underlings, no author of hers was ever allowed to languish on a slush-pile, and if a manuscript was returned she disregarded the standard rejection slip which accompanied it and insisted upon knowing the exact reason why it had been turned down. For the privilege of her protection I agreed to give Miss Weiner 15 per cent of my literary earnings. The going rate for agents was then, and is now, 10 per cent, with 15–20 per cent for foreign rights. When I had the temerity to bring this to my Miss Weiner's notice I was told brusquely that these terms applied to 'ordinary' agents and that she did not increase her commission for overseas sales. It was a case of take it or leave it and I was too intimidated by her to leave it.

All in all, with hindsight, although I was aware from time to time of some resentment at her *chutzpah* in demanding more than the market rates, I think that the championship, the advice, the loyalty and, later, the friendship which I enjoyed from Joyce Weiner over the years were well worth the extra 5 per cent.

My family was delighted that I had become a *bona fide* author rather than a dining-room table philanderer with aspirations. There had never been a writer in our midst. Their pride, however, was as nothing compared with my own amazement at the fact that my novel was to be published. It seemed too easy. I was doing I what I wanted to do, what I was happiest doing, and someone was willing to pay me for it.

Do You Write Under Your Own Name?

Despite the fact that a personal letter from Ralph Hodder-Williams, the chairman of Hodder & Stoughton, had warned me that they would not be able to bring out my novel until 1958, *No White Coat* was published on 3 October 1957, eight months after the acceptance of the manuscript and less than a year after its submission. This promptness was a reflection of all my dealings with what was to be the first of many publishers.

Not knowing either better, or differently, I took my relationship with Hodder & Stoughton, and their continuing interest in my career in general, and future titles in particular, for granted. I thought that every author was taken to lunch at a coveted table in the Savoy Grill, every author invited to meet the sales manager of his publishing house in person over a glass of sherry, every author allowed to comment on, and assist with, jacket design (no matter that he had signed away his rights to the contrary), every author received a yearly, scarlet, tooled-leather bound copy of his 'own book in seasonable dress' with 'every good wish for Christmas and the New Year from his 'publishers in the City of London'.

Hodder & Stoughton were gentlemen publishers personified and I enjoyed a long and happy relationship with the eccentric Robin Denniston (later of Oxford University Press), Eric Mackenzie, the personable Scots, piano-playing sales director, and the eager young Dick Douglas-Boyd (later chairman of Pelham Books) who was responsible for publicity.

The period between submission of manuscript and publication went smoothly. The role of the publisher's editor ('one who separates the wheat from the chaff and prints the chaff'*) had not as yet become sacrosanct, and he was certainly not king. In

* Robert Benchley

43

my time with Hodder & Stoughton I was not even aware that there were such rarefied beings as editors from whose attentions not even Flaubert was immune:

'...let us take full charge of your novel (*Madame Bovary*) in the *Revue*; we will make the cuts we think indispensable... My personal opinion is that if you do not do this, you will be gravely compromising yourself, making your first appearance with a muddled work to which the style alone does not give sufficient interest. Be brave, close your eyes during the operation, and have confidence – if not in our talent, at least in the experience we have acquired in such matters and also in our affection for you. You have buried your novel under a heap of details which are well done but superfluous: it is not seen clearly enough and must be disencumbered – an easy task... You may be sure that in all this I have only your own interest at heart.'

With my first novel, there was no hassle, no urgent, last-minute biking of page proofs (which *must* be returned *immediately*, the printer was waiting) when one was deep in some domestic crisis or poised to leave for foreign parts. I received a polite letter from the production manager, Mr Haydn Stead, on 21 May. 'Under separate registered cover we have today sent you the typescript and three sets of page proofs for *No White Coat*. We would be glad if you would correct the marked set of proofs and return it to us at your earliest convenience.' The other two sets of proofs were for me to keep and are still in my possession. Today, proof copies are like gold dust and each set is jealously guarded, even from the author. A further, equally civil letter from Mr Stead arrived on 12 June: 'It just so happens that we had a request this morning from our printers asking for return of the press proofs of *No White Coat* in order for them to keep to their printing schedule. I should be grateful, therefore, if you will complete the press reading and correcting just as soon as you can spare the time.'

Publication day brought not only the then statutory six free copies of my book, but an extravagant congratulatory bouquet of flowers from Hodder & Stoughton. It was about all it did bring! Like every new author, I had expected, if not the heavens to fall, at least that every bookshop would be piled to the ceiling with copies of my book. I did not anticipate even having to go into the shop and ask for it, for it would surely be prominently displayed in the window. The curious non-event of my first publication day was my initiation into the harsh realities of the literary world.

I was one of the lucky ones. Hodder & Stoughton printed 4,500 copies of No White Coat (which eventually sold 6,500 in hardback). A first-time author today would be lucky to get a print run of 1,500. My novel was published in a paperback edition by Hodder in 1957, reprinted in 1958 and again in 1964, and published by them in paperback in 1957 (reprinted 1958 and 1964) and by Corgi in 1959 (reprinted 1960). A German language Swiss edition was produced by Benziger Verlag (1961), and a Dutch version by Zuid-Holland Uitgevers (1964). Large print editions appeared in 1970 and again in 1974. In the same year an excerpt from No White Coat was included in Einzunehmen Dreimal Täglich, a collection of best doctor stories, together with such illustrious names as A. J. Cronin, Frederick Dürenmatt and Heinrich Böll. The book was published in condensed 'mini-book' form in Woman's Illustrated, serialised on BBC Woman's Hour and repeated by them by popular request. My reaction to all this was minimal. I was of course pleased as success followed success but, in my ignorance of the ways of the publishing world, I considered the entire process run-of-the-mill. As far as reviews were concerned, *No White Coat* did not make the national press but was well, and largely favourably, covered in the provinces. Newspapers such as *The Irish Times*, *The Weekly Scotsman*, *The Sheffield Star*, *The Liverpool Evening Express* and *The Nottingham Evening Post* variously found 'Mr Tibber's' first novel 'amusing', 'tragic', 'shrewd', 'autobiographical', 'entertaining', 'competently handled', 'delightful', 'easy-to-read', 'harrowing', 'a pleasant bromide'. The comments were nothing to write home about but my book was at least acknowledged.

The bookshops were a different matter. I refused to enter them alone in case I was recognised. I would walk nonchalantly into the back of the shop while my companion enquired of the salesperson if they had a copy of *No White Coat* by Robert Tibber. 'Robert who?' Robert Tibber. A blank face. 'T-I double B-E-R.' A shake of the head. 'When was it published?' A week ago. 'Do you happen to know the publisher...?' Meanwhile, over the street-maps and the cookery books, I died a thousand deaths. It was a mystery to me then, and it is now, where all the published copies go to. With the exception of the bestseller, for an author to find his book stocked by any but the largest bookstores is rare. Finding the book is marginally worse than not finding it, and is like exposing oneself in public. Furtively, one removes a copy from those on the shelf and displays it, full frontal, in the hope that it will attract attention. Connoisseurs of this practice say that you can always tell when an author has been into a shop because every copy of his latest book will be displayed at eye level, with the front of the dust jacket to the fore. Catherine Cookson never had the nerve to rearrange her titles, but Barbara Cartland cheerfully confesses, particularly at

Do You Write Under Your Own Name?

London Airport, to shifting piles of other authors' books the better to reveal her own. Booksellers, especially in the Hampstead and Camden Town areas of London where writers are two-a-penny, are well used to these devices and turn a blind eye. By the following day the strategically repositioned books will have been returned firmly to their places.

Thirty odd years later it still disconcerts me to see someone reading one of my books – it is as if they are reading my thoughts – and I am diffident about going into bookshops and asking for them. Few writers are household names and only a minority of the population will have heard of you. When you admit that you are a writer (almost as shameful as admitting to prostitution), rather than a dental nurse or a trapeze artist, people ask you to tell them the names of some of your books. Recited aloud the titles sound so fatuous you wonder how you ever came to choose them.

CHAPTER FOUR

Act of Creation

'If you let the reins loose the horse will find its way home.'
Graham Greene

Writing, like cooking, is in part *l'art d'accomoder les restes*. My medical material, of which I had a fresh and gratuitous supply daily, was by no means exhausted with the completion of *No White Coat*. I immediately started work on my second novel, *Love on my List*, which once more had a background of general practice. Strange as it may seem I managed to write five books around the same central character without once mentioning his name. The omission was not deliberate and I only became aware of my young doctor's anonymity when it was pointed out to me some years later. I have never been able to explain this phenomenon, although I suspect that it is not without psychological significance.

Anthony Trollope wrote to an unknown correspondent: 'Pray know that when a man begins writing a book he never gives

over. The evil with which he is beset is as inveterate as drinking
– as exciting as gambling.' In common with Anthony Trollope,
and unlike many other authors, I do not need a rest or fallow
period between projects. I finish a novel one day and start a new
one on the next.

Creativity is the capacity to express directly those feelings
which have been experienced and understood at all times; like
the works of Bach and Beethoven, Mozart and Schubert, they
must be simply there for everyone. For Anthony Storr creation
is 'the ability to bring something new into existence' while
for George Steiner '...the creative act, which unleashes such
obvious, felt communion between artist and audience, echoes
the original moment, creation...'

The aim of every writer is to produce a masterpiece. Although,
like the juggler, he or she will always have more than one idea
in the air at a time, new ideas cannot be conjured up on
demand. Short stories and plans for novels are apt to make their
appearance either during the night, in the bonus hour between
sleeping and waking, or in response to something one sees or to
a chance remark. This brief moment of conception will be
followed by a period of gestation during which the unconscious
mind will keep the concept on the agenda while the conscious
mind is occupied with routine tasks.

A writer doesn't proceed in an orderly fashion from one piece
of work to the next. The incubation period for a novel is long
and ideas jostle for position in his head. The one which refuses
to go away, which elbows its way to the front of the queue, is
the one which the author will work on next. A writer knows
more than he knows; he has a subconscious ability to read signs
and never ceases to be amazed by his knowledge when once he
has started writing. A finished novel is a finished novel. Whilst I

am engaged on a book it occupies every waking thought as well as every waking moment. Every other daily activity, by comparison, fades into lesser significance and I am more anxious about getting on with my work than about anything else in the world. Although no highly creative person is ever satisfied with what he or she has done, once the final words are on the page, the umbilical cord is severed. The fiction becomes inanimate, impersonal. Unlike Virginia Woolf, who worked with a 'kind of tortured intensity' and 'excruciating effort' and when she came to the end of a book was terrified to let it go, I have no qualms about leaving it. For this reason I am able to adapt my own novels for other media, to wield the scalpel with the detachment of a surgeon.

Creative people, for whom writing is a form of begetting order from disorder, are usually reticent about work in progress and often find is hard to write while someone else is in the vicinity. Through bitter experience they learn to be secretive. 'New ideas are tender plants and are better not exposed too soon to comment. They wither under criticism and are often dispelled and diluted by premature revelation.'* In common with Virginia Woolf I do not show my manuscripts to my husband until they are 'hard and fast finished' and not only shut myself away when I write but put a hand over the paper or turn off the computer screen as soon as anyone comes within earshot. Writing a novel is an intimate activity, an unshareable process: that is why '...one can never be alone enough when one writes, why there can never be enough silence around one, when one is writing, why even night is not night enough.'†

* Anthony Storr
† Franz Kafka

Act of Creation

The writer is lucky. She has only to take up her pen and the burdens of life evaporate. She is cast adrift in a universe of imagination and, on her return to reality, she is astonished at what *she* has produced. As if someone else has written it. Thackeray was surprised at the observations made by some of his characters. It was as if an 'occult Power' was moving his pen. For Nabokov the creative act was like being given an undeveloped film: 'All I had to do was develop it', while William Burroughs – who considered writing a curse but regarded himself as a medium – simply let the 'words pass through him'.

Creation is not simply a matter of a gifted person sitting down, thinking hard, and then writing, composing, or painting something. There are times when more is accomplished by passivity than activity. Bertrand Russell:

'After first contemplating a book on some subject, and after giving serious preliminary attention to it, I needed a period of subconscious incubation which could not be hurried and was if anything impeded by deliberate thinking. Sometimes I would find, after a time, that I had made a mistake, and that I could not write the book I had in mind. But often I was more fortunate, having, by a time of very intense concentration, planted the problem in my subconsciousness, it would germinate underground until, suddenly, the solution emerged with blinding clarity, so that it only remained to write down what had appeared as if in a revelation.'

Luckily I have never suffered from the 'blank sheet of paper' syndrome, neither do I think with Scott Fitzgerald that 'writing is a miserable business' and jump at any excuse to be doing something else. While many writers long for structure to their lives and find it easier to work to a deadline, I organise my life by means of self-imposed routines and once I have tuned in to the magnetic field of concentration, the listening attitude of mind which is the necessary prelude to the creative process, have no trouble in getting started. What I am going to write is already there, and I am sometimes surprised at where my characters lead me. Balzac was so taken aback when Goriot, a figment of his imagination, died, that he opened his window and shouted: '*Le Père Goriot est mort! Le Père Goriot est mort!*' When *I* get bored, I know that the reader will be bored. Only then do I pull on the reins, and use my heels to kick my creations in another direction.

My creative peak is at its zenith in the mornings and declines steadily throughout the day. Some psychological tests indicate that people whose body clocks are adjusted in this way (slow) are shyer and more anxious than their (fast) counterparts who find rising an ordeal but have no problem staying awake until the small hours. I have always been interested in patterns of time and have developed techniques for setting priorities in relation to my own goals, rather than someone else's. In order to get the maximum benefit from the minimum investment of time, and to treat it as the limited resource it is, I have learned not only to protect myself from unwarranted intrusions which threaten to usurp my day, but to delegate, to plan, to concentrate on what is important to me, and to disregard trivia.

It makes sense for me to plan my key tasks around the best hours of the morning, and to reserve less demanding work for the afternoon. I use this early morning, or 'prime time' for my imaginative writing when I will produce something that did not hitherto exist. One knows that one has done it well if one can move about freely in the world one has created, touch one's inventions, communicate with the figments of one's imagination. Sometimes, off guard, I look up from my desk and quite expect to see my characters walk through the door. This prime time lasts for from three to five hours. During it I try to defer all other activities (although unlike Charles Dickens I cannot afford the male luxury of putting everything else away from me 'for months at a time') which, on another day, may become priorities in their own right. I cannot think what to have for dinner and write, organise a meeting with friends and write, make travel plans and write. When I am in full flood it is with the greatest reluctance that I give up my creative hours to these and other pursuits.

'Secondary', or standard time, is given partially to the work in hand, but now the external world is liable to intrude. What do we need from the shops? Do the houseplants need watering? Should I telephone the plumber? I am not unique in this. Harriet Beecher Stowe, writing in 1850, also had plumber trouble:

'So this same sink lingered in a precarious state for some weeks, and when I had *nothing else to do*, I used to call and do what I could in the way of enlisting the good man's sympathies in its behalf ... nothing but deadly determination enables me ever to write; it is rowing against wind and tide...'

From years of practice, from writing – often with a child on my lap – in the teeth of the disruptions of domestic life, I have learned, like Mrs Stowe, to switch my imaginative flow on and off at will, even when the flood-gates are fully open. During this 'standard time', when the pressures of the early hours are off, progress is slower. I correct and amend. I make notes of matters arising from what I have written, organise my work, read round my subject, research.

THE WRITING GAME

'Tertiary', or off-peak time, generally towards evening, is devoted to living. Concentration on the real world, however, paying bills or tidying the house, does not mean that one is not working. The writer writes *all the time* even when she appears to be otherwise engaged. Ideas, thoughts, revelations, come to her at unsuspecting moments, which is why she often appears to be distracted or does not pay attention when addressed. Because she would rather be writing than doing anything else, the writer may not be exactly a bundle of laughs to live with. She is there, yet she is not there, and while she cannot exist entirely in her imagination she is aware that the more fully she participates in life the less able is she to see it clearly.

The first words of *No White Coat* were: 'It was spring; a delicate, lilting spring of a hundred forgotten smells and pink, pink almond blossom, when after an anxious and sterile winter, I was finally chosen by the Executive Council to run a general medical practice.' While this opening paragraph cannot perhaps compare with George Orwell's 'It was a bright cold day in April and the clocks were striking thirteen' or the immortal: 'All happy families are alike but an unhappy family is unhappy after its own fashion' of *Anna Karenin*, it tumbled out as spontaneously as a river at source.

I have never had any terrors about starting a novel which is like setting out on a voyage into the unknown: an act of faith. My particular nightmare does not arrive until about half-way through the book. Becalmed in mid-ocean, I cannot see where I have come from, and nothing lies ahead but the horizon. Panic sets in. I have exhausted my material. There are not enough words to fill the remainder of the pages. I have dried up. I am used up. I wallow in self-pity, am odious to those around me.

Act of Creation

Despairingly I pick up my paddles and make futile and desultory movements. My boat gathers momentum. I am impelled by the stiff breeze of my second wind. I am going to make it. Once again the miracle has happened. Land is in sight.

Love on my List was published two years after *No White Coat*, once more on my birthday. During this time I had short stories accepted by *Good Housekeeping*, *Housewife*, *Woman and Beauty*, and *Saturday Evening Post* (USA). The rights for these were sold, by Miss Weiner, to Europe and Scandinavia. My second novel brought even more kudos than my first. In a paragraph in the *Manchester Evening News*: 'What Manchester is Reading' (compiled in collaboration with Sherratt & Hughes, Boots Library, and Manchester Public Library), *Love on my List* was ranked above Alastair Maclean's *The Last Frontier*, Boris Pasternak's *Dr Zhivago*, and John Braine's *Room at the Top*. In addition to complimentary reviews, magazine condensation, and radio serialisation, I was interviewed on television and in the evening newspaper *The Star* the front page of which carried a photograph of myself with two of my daughters. Again I thought all this par for the course

The television interview (for which the fee was 15 guineas) was on an ABC Television Ltd programme *The Book Man*. It was transmitted live from a Birmingham studio, and because we had no television set in the house (my views on TV were the same then as they are now), the children watched at a neighbour's where, unimpressed by the sight of their mother on the screen, they switched channels to the cartoons. The interviewer was Simon Kester, himself a writer of thrillers, who for the benefit of millions of viewers put me through the catechism which over the years has become depressingly familiar (and is as nonsensical as asking a dancer how she manages to get up on her points and keep time to the music). 'Why do you write under a man's name?' 'How do you manage to run a home, bring up a family and write?' I often ponder this last question and to this day have to make up the answers. The truth is, I don't know. My physical energy, often depleted by minor ailments, has always left much to be desired. My health, like George Orwell's '...is wretched but it has never prevented me doing anything I wanted to...' I do have mental energy. It is one of the secrets. Talent is useless without energy, and energy without talent. When the children were young, I rose at dawn – like Mrs Trollope – and did my stint before the family woke up.

'How long does it take you to write a book?' 'How quickly do you write?' In the early years I averaged a book or a child every two years. In terms of conception and gestation the two acts have been compared. A book is easier: giving birth to it is the end of the matter.

Apart from the creative effort which goes into a novel, writing demands discipline and perseverance. 'Novelists do not write as birds sing, by the push of nature ... there should be much routine and some daily stuff on the level of carpentry.* It is the physical act of writing which stimulates the flow. When the imagination is warm, good writers work fast. Unless you work at speed your imagination flags and your invention runs out of steam.

People who talk about 'waiting for inspiration' generally do not understand the effort involved in writing. For Joseph Conrad writing a book was '...a horrible, exhausting struggle, like a long bout of some painful illness'. You must be prepared

---

* William Golding

to sit for long periods, to concentrate the brain, strain the neck, tense the shoulder muscles, tax the eyes. Whilst you are writing none of this is apparent. Time contracts, and you have no sooner sat down at your desk in the morning than it is time for lunch. It is only when you put down your pen, or finally press the 'save' button on the computer, that you realise hours have passed during which a power other than yourself seems miraculously to have composed what you see before you. In my own case, on a good day, this is usually about four pages, or 1,000 words.

Anthony Trollope, who held down a job in the civil service for 33 years (as well as inventing the pillar box), thought that for 'all those who live as literary men – working as literary labourers ... three hours a day will produce as much as a man ought to write. But then, he should so have trained himself, that he shall be able to work continuously during those three hours – so have tutored his mind, that it shall not be necessary for him to sit nibbling his pen, and gazing at the wall before him, till he shall have found the words with which he wants to express his ideas.' On his own admission Trollope started work at 5.30 in the morning with his watch on his desk, and wrote 250 words every 15 minutes for the self-prescribed three hours – a prodigious total of 3,000 words a day – while Balzac, a close rival in literary output, turned out 40 pages in a night.

Arthur Hailey aims for 600 words a day, Wilbur Smith for 1,000, and Barbara Cartland 10,000! Kingsley Amis regarded 300 words as good, 600 as wonderful, and 750 as terrific, while the prolific Georges Simenon – who at the age of 29 complained that he had published *only* 277 books (which took one day to think about and 14 days to write) – was in a league of his own.

THE WRITING GAME

Work that is produced quickly has often been brooded upon for a very long time. Darwin was 20 years contemplating *On the Origin of Species by Means of Natural Selection*, while poor Thackeray, who spent 30 years preparing to write his first novel, described himself as 'sitting for hours before my paper, not doing my book but incapable of doing anything else'. Fantasy (James Bond), and romantic fiction, tend to be produced at higher speed, while novels which provide not only a 'story', but which enrich the human condition by means of the characters' or the authors' reflections, tend to take longer. Michael (*Jurassic Park*) Crichton withdraws to the back room of his house and after six or seven weeks, during which he sees nobody, a draft manuscript is produced. Consistent with the fable of the tortoise and the hare, Flaubert beats all comers for slowness:

'It will have taken me from July to the end of November to write *one scene*.' 'Since you saw me last I have written 25 pages in all (25 pages in six weeks) ... I have gone over them so much myself, copied them, changed them, shuffled them, that for the time being I see them very confusedly ... Sometimes I don't understand why my arms don't drop from my body with fatigue, why my brain doesn't melt away...' 'Last week I spent *five days writing one page...*'

There are as many different approaches to the *methods of writing* a book as there are writers. According to at least one authority, Shakespeare 'never blotted out a line', while Smollett and Johnson wrote rapidly (also without revision) and Simenon – an instinctive worker for whom the 'music' ran and ran – wrote, once the mechanism had started, as one possessed. Some writers (the wizards) will not set out at all unless they have a route map; the plans for their novels are as detailed as any

58

architect's drawing, and they can tell you exactly at which point in the story they will be on any given page; the *dramatis personae* are not only sketched but fleshed out, storylines are meticulously plotted, nothing is left to chance. Others, such as Bernard Shaw (the bumblers), insist that they begin at the top of a page without the slightest inkling of what was going to happen by the bottom of it. Plot comes of course from character but as E. M. Forster has pointed out 'you may create the most scintillating characters who will sit about and be too lazy to involve themselves in a plot at all. You may be able to write the most brilliant dialogue and descriptions so vivid that the reader may feel able to touch the furniture, or smell the cooking; but all this, if you have no plot, is but sounding brass and tinkling silver. Plots, however much they may now be despised, are the motor engines of a book; they carry the reader through his experience and discover the theme. They are, as every practitioner knows, extremely hard to come by. So elusive are they that our greatest dramatist rarely invented his own but acquired them on the second hand market then transformed them.'*

For myself, I start with the merest trickle of an idea or theme which has made its way from the subconscious to the conscious mind, and dive in. *Plus je vais plus je trouve.* All I need are my protagonists and console myself with the fact that when we conjure into memory the novels of Jane Austen or of Dickens what springs to mind is not so much the story as the richness of their characters.

In all my years of writing I have luckily never suffered from 'writer's block', that miserable condition in which one sits before the blank paper in an agony of literary inertia which has

* E. M. Forster

been known to last for years. The psychoanalyst, Otto Rank, linked writer's block to the writer's 'earliest relations with the world'. Every novelist fears that it will happen to him but he usually has the confidence to assume that the block, if it does occur, will pass. E. M. Forster's silence was not resolved by time. Unkind critics assert that his failure to produce anything after *A Passage to India* was due not to the fact that he was blocked, however, but to the fact that he had nothing further to say. Mark Twain's affliction ('when the tank runs dry you've only got to leave it alone and it will fill up again in time') was only temporary. A costive Joseph Conrad, who at best produced only 500 words a day, gives his view of the condition:

'I sit down religiously every morning. I sit down for eight hours every day – and the sitting down is all. In the course of that working day of eight hours I write three sentences which I erase before leaving the table in despair ... It takes all my resolution and the power of self-control to refrain from butting my head against the wall. I want to howl and foam at the mouth but I daren't do it for fear of waking the baby and alarming my wife.'

One classic symptom of writer's block is a neurotic compulsion to revise every word. To rewrite – even your name – for no reason. According to Anthony Burgess, writer's block is 'not calculated to impress British writers who have to regard literary paralysis as a luxury' which probably endorses Freud's view that inhibitions are likely to occur 'as soon as writing ... assumes the significance of copulation'.

Malcolm Bradbury (who admits to having jettisoned several novels in his time) believes there can be a whole litany of reasons for writer's block: 'Some blocks are to do with the book itself – you realise that maybe you'd never wanted to write it, you picked the wrong subject, it's turning into a sort of mistake. Sometimes you haven't done enough research – emotional as well as historical – so you just aren't into the story deep enough...' Bradbury's cure is to work on something else for a while – 'It's one reason why I like to have more than one book on the go at any time' – while for novelist Michèle Roberts, a trip to Sainsbury's usually does the trick.

Every writer has off days. Times when the words are dredged up as from some primeval swamp from which they emerge lumpen and banal. If he manages to keep going, however, and is fortunate, the muse will generally return.

The novelist does not know what he wants to write until he/she has written it: it is the physical act of writing which liberates the thoughts. Although at the end of each day I write a note to myself, a jumping off point to get me started, I never know exactly what is going to happen next. A reader once confronted Charles Dickens with the question: 'What will happen to Pickwick next week?' 'I don't know, madam,' was the reply, 'I haven't written it.'

There is another matter which takes care of itself; the aesthetic, pattern-making aspect of the creative act which is not altogether conscious. I neither plan the length of my chapters nor calculate in advance the number of words in a book. Writers and artists not only have slide rules in the belly but what Ernest Hemingway referred to as 'a built-in, shock-proof shit detector'. The chapters fashion themselves according to some inner logic, and together they invariably combine to form a work of the appropriate length. If the writing process is one of listening, it is also one of obeying; of sensing with one's entire body – even to the fingertips and down to the toes – what is 'right'.

THE WRITING GAME

My mode of writing, again idiosyncratic, is to write the book straight through, giving it everything I have, freely and abundantly from page one to 'The End'. I stop for nothing. Getting the 'bare bones' down on to the paper is the pain, *fort et dur*, of writing. This first creative flush happens quickly, then comes the real work, making sure that the meaning conveyed is that which was intended. Returning to the beginning, I fill in the gaps, correct and polish, hone and rewrite. Using this method I find that I do not generally have to alter the basic structure of my novel all that much. The first draft, produced in white heat, is the freshest. Other writers proceed differently. They will not leave a word until it is exact, a sentence unless it is flawless, a page before it is to their satisfaction. By this painstaking means they reach the end of the manuscript which is by then, with no further alteration, ready to submit to the publisher.

Although the relation between creativity and the obsessional character is of considerable interest, there is no more futile task than studying the working habits of other writers some of which have taken on a talismanic importance.

If Wordsworth sat with a pen, it made him perspire and brought on a pain in his chest; Somerset Maugham bricked up his writing room to shut out the Côte d'Azur; Carlyle needed absolute quiet, while Thackeray preferred to work in a tavern and Trollope was quite happy in a railway carriage. Truman Capote composed supine; Bennett Cerf pondered deeply on the lavatory; Thomas Mann could not write without his tortoise-shell tobacco box; Balzac required coffee and Schiller sniffed his drawerful of rotting apples.

P. G. Wodehouse used to pin paragraphs of work in progress round his study; Virginia Woolf wrote on a large plywood board on her knees which had an inkstand glued to it; George

Act of Creation

Orwell pounded his typewriter from 6.30 am until midday, pausing for a cooked breakfast; Oscar Wilde would spend an entire day removing a comma from his proofs and another putting it back; Nabokov composed his novels on 4 inch by 5 inch index cards (1,075 of them for *Pale Fire*), Muriel Spark writes with black Biros, a new set for every book, which she throws out of the window should anyone dare to touch them, while Anita Brookner, on her own admission, just sits down and gets on with it.

An athlete can run, a painter can paint: a writer is someone who is born with a gift. If a paragraph has to be torn apart, wrestled with on the carpet, it may be that he is not doing his job properly. Shakespeare, Freud, and the Bible, are all easily accessible without constant recourse to the dictionary. Somerset Maugham stressed the importance to the novel of lucidity, simplicity, and harmony, and there are a great many writers – whose works are bought but not always read – who confuse obscurity with profundity.

Simplicity is achieved by economy in the use of language. Style is the moment of identity between a writer and his language. It should attract as little attention as possible since it is an organic aspect of the work and never something 'decorative' and the reader should be unaware of what it is which carries him from page to page and prompts him to say of a book 'I couldn't put it down until I'd finished it.'

A good prose sentence should be as lyrical, as harmonious, as a good line of poetry. Euphony is paramount. Flaubert's quest for *le mot juste* led him sometimes to recast a sentence twenty times 'in an agonised pursuit of the uniquely appropriate cadence'.

'Writers only write well when they listen to the music of what they are writing – either on magnetic tape or in the auditorium set silently in their skulls.'*

I read aloud everything I write. It is a stringent test. If it does not *sound* good the words are not the right ones. 'Sentences must stir in a book like leaves in a forest, each distinct from each other despite their resemblance.'†

Flaubert, a stickler for sonority, was deeply distressed when he realised that proposed changes for which he was asked by his publisher would be aurally detrimental to his text. 'That is going to break the rhythm of my poor sentences. This is a serious matter.' It was equally serious to Kipling, whose ear was superb and who paid more attention than any other writer to the problem of making people talk on the page. It is because of this desire to give prose the cadence of verse that it is often distressing to hear one's work serialised, or abridged, when adapters who have no feeling for the exigencies of resonance and precision in the written word, allow discordant phrases and clumsy sentences to creep in.

As far as milieu is concerned, I am a creature of habit. I can only write in my own lair. Writers write in bed (Proust, Truman Capote), in restaurants (Jack Higgins), or gazebos (Marie Corelli); standing up (Thomas Wolfe), or lying down (Barbara Cartland). Rudyard Kipling could not produce anything unless it was in black Indian ink, John Steinbeck was unable to write without a six-sided pencil, D. H. Lawrence had first to scrub the floor, while Isaac Asimov confessed that the only fixed routine he had before he started writing was to make sure he was close enough to the typewriter to reach the keys.

* Anthony Burgess
† Gustave Flaubert

Act of Creation

It does not much matter what arcane ritual is invoked, as long as the words get on to the paper. At which point the writer will be paid, as Robert Benchley succinctly put it: 'Per word, per piece, or perhaps'.

CHAPTER FIVE

Do You Do Much Research?

———————⋙•◆•⋘———————

'If you steal from one author, it's plagiarism; if you steal from many it's research.'

Wilson Mizner

After *Love on my List* I decided that I had, for the moment, had enough of doctors. I had published half a dozen more short stories and was now ready for something different. About this time some important domestic changes took place. The house we lived in was both unheated and decidedly cramped, and we embarked on a programme of extension and modernisation precipitated by the ambivalent relationship we had with the Ideal boiler – a misnomer if ever there was one. The 'Ideal' stood in the corner of the kitchen like a recalcitrant child, demanding constant attention. Each morning, in all weathers, anthracite had to be shovelled from an outside coal bunker. With the help of an iron ratchet, one had to remove the circular plate from the top of the boiler, and replenish the beast from a

66

hod with a perpetually rusting bottom, which sifted a fine cloud of black dust on to one's feet. Before going to bed, one had to riddle the glowing embers with a poker, remove the dead ashes, extract the clinkers with the finesse of a surgeon, refuel the stove to the brim, and pray that it would survive the night. If it did not, one was faced the following morning not only with cold baths, as a despairing cry of 'boiler's out!' from the first one up filled the house, but with a solid mass of dead coke which must be manually extracted from the stove's maw before the stove was relit with a cunning arrangement of paper and sticks. The days of scraping the ice from *inside* the windows on a winter morning, of getting undressed before the coal fire in the sitting-room at night, were numbered.

According to Samuel Butler: 'It is questionable if all the mechanical invention yet made has lightened the day's toil of any human being.' We installed central heating and replaced the wash boiler and the mangle ('A machine for rolling and pressing linen and cotton clothing after washing: consisting of two or more cylinders working one upon another.' OED) with an automatic washing machine. The boiler-stoking and mangle-turning gave way to the anxieties of remembering to order the heating oil, and the time consuming task of chasing elusive repairmen for the maintenance of the mean-spirited washing machine. Samuel Butler could indeed be right.

Building, I discovered, was like writing, creating something out of nothing. The house 'extension' was only another bed-room and a second bathroom over the surgery, but had it been the Taj Mahal, the construction of which took 28 years and is said to have cost £3 million pounds, I could not have found it more satisfying. Architects' plans, with their pristine diagrams, their fine lines and rectangles, their etched figures and arrows, their minuscule legends promising rooms and services, are as heady as the outline for any book. I even enjoyed the upheaval. Shrouded staircases, the spatter of paint, the white mist of plaster dust, possessions in cardboard boxes, represented the chaos from which order would ultimately emerge. The process is the same as in novel writing. Half-revealed thoughts, the fine haze of ideas, the jumble of experience, and from this confusion, in the fullness of time, the bound copy. I could, and still can, look at a plan and from it not only furnish a room but people it; in my mind's eye I could ascend a staircase, open a cupboard, light a lamp, turn on a tap. I did not even mind the team of muscle-bound magicians, in their paint-spattered overalls, who with their hammers and their brushes, their mugs of tea and cigarettes, their tuneless serenades, and their raucous ghetto blasters, appropriated the house and who would, admittedly after many months, work the miracle.

The other change we made, justified by my small financial success, was to employ extra domestic help. '...the house seems to take up so much time ... when I have to clean up twice or wash up unnecessary things I get frightfully impatient and want to be working. So often this week I've heard you and Gordon talking while I washed dishes. Well, someone's got to wash dishes and get food ... I walk round with a mind full of ghosts of saucepans ... and "Will there be enough to go round," and you calling (whatever am I doing) ... and " ...isn't there going to be tea? It's five o'clock?" as though I were a dilatory housemaid.'*

Domestic life and art do not *always* mix easily. When the family is young and dependent, one is apt to wake worrying

* Pamela Hansford Johnson

about coughs, colds and other minor ailments, rather than about the progress of one's current chapter. There are, however, compensations. A sink full of washing-up or a pile of potatoes waiting to be peeled, frees one's mind marvellously for imaginary explorative excursions, whilst cooking, in which I have always been interested, can be positively therapeutic. When characters refuse to budge, forsaking the word processor for the food processor will often reactivate them; when a scene will not gel, the aroma of a soup, the innovation of a sauce, the ordered *mise en place* of biscuits on a baking sheet, are often enough to coagulate it. I was not sorry to delegate some of the more soul destroying aspects of housekeeping – the cleaning, the vacuuming, the shifting of the dust from place to place – and apply myself to my new novel.

We All Fall Down germinated from a newspaper headline which had stuck in my mind: 'City Tycoon drops Dead'. Deferring to interior reason, I had many years earlier clipped the article and stowed it away in my cuttings file. By the time its number came up the newsprint was crisp and yellowed. A writer can learn a great deal from the *faits divers* in newspapers through which the world was revealed for Isaac Bashevis Singer as 'a combination of a slaughterhouse, a bordello, and an insane asylum'. The habit of cutting snippets out of newspapers is ingrained. While this is irksome to others who have to read them after one it is extremely useful. The cuttings appear to be unrelated. You have no idea exactly *why* you need an article about *grands crus* and *petits châteaux* or a harrowing picture captioned *Battle to Save Boy down Well*, but you can be pretty sure that sooner or later you will be writing a novel in which fine wines feature or for which you need an 'inciting incident'. The secret is to tear out the relevant passage selfishly and at once! If you leave it, even for a day, you will have forgotten exactly where it was you saw the piece and all will be lost.

'Always carry a pencil and paper,' was Hardy's advice to Robert Graves. I am more likely to go out without my door keys, and of course keep notes, although at the moment of note-taking I have little idea of how useful the scribble might be. My notebooks are not so much 'books' as the backs of envelopes and cheque books or torn fragments of (French) paper table-cloths. The contents are chaotic and often, having been written whilst in motion or on foot, largely illegible. They are interspersed with recipes and shopping lists, and are incomprehensible to anyone other than myself. Journeys abroad posit new, spiral bound 'reporters' notebooks', but in them you will not find travelogues of routes and distances, climate and history, art and architecture, flora and fauna, but fragments of conversation, details of smells and sensations, faces and facets, quirks and impressions, unobtainable from the most informative of guide books.

'Note it in a book, that it may be for the time to come for ever and ever.' Taking the advice of Isaiah, I keep a commonplace book (unimaginatively called *Things*), the true pleasure of which is the randomness of its nature, which now runs to six volumes and several thousand entries. In it I record anything and everything which touches a chord, which strikes me and sets me thinking, either in the course of my eclectic reading or on my daily round. Paragraphs, sentences, lines of poetry, mottoes, notions, half-formed ideas and *bons mots*. Unlike Trollope, with his penchant for lists and systems, whose commonplace book was arranged alphabetically, these jottings are entered indiscriminately but none the less constitute a rich seam of information. If I have to give a talk, or write a chapter, on 'writing' or 'wit' or 'women', I dive into my commonplace books and come up with pearls. If I have referenced the entries carefully (which I am more liable to do now than when the collection was first started), I can access the sources and in this way am launched on my research for the subject. Sometimes, when I am jaded, I flick through the books, which is stimulating and rewarding. In the frontispiece of Volume One are two quotations in addition to the passage from Isaiah. The first defines the collection:

'A personal notebook in which the owner copies passages from the writings and speeches of others, or in which he writes his own compositions.' And the second, deeply sentimental, is for my daughters: 'This book by any yet unread,/I leave for you when I am dead,/That being gone, here you may find/What was your living mother's mind./Make use of what I leave in Love,/ And God shall bless you from above.*

Although I am not a chronicler, I also keep a diary which, like Kafka's – 'Germany declared war on Russia. Swimming lesson in the afternoon' – is more an *aide mémoire* than a document for posterity.

Research, which is central to the writing process, is not merely a question of checking facts. It has been an important part of fiction writing ever since Daniel Defoe boned up on Alexander Selkirk for *Robinson Crusoe* and Arnold Bennett sat by the bedside of his dying father secretly making notes for Darius Clayhanger. Too much research and the writer is accused of regurgitating facts, too little and 'The poor fictionalist ... catches salmon in October; or shoots his partridges

* Anne Bradstreet

in March. His dahlias bloom in June, and his birds sing in the autumn.'*

In order to wear research lightly it is necessary to do a lot of it, and preferably from primary sources. Computerisation of indexing, in which you need to know exactly what you want, can be counter-productive. It is wandering idly along the stacks on the way to finding the book you *think* you need, that will lead to the chance discovery of some completely other book the existence of which you were unaware.

Research falls into two categories. 'What you know' and 'what you don't know'. 'What you know' is not something that you specifically have to do before getting down to a book. It is a ragbag of remembrance, of places recalled, of conversations recollected, of relationships explored, of random and unrelated occurrences added over the years to the compost heap of the writer's mind. By the time a new novel is started the matter is well rotted, and all that he has to do is turn it over with his spade.

The second type of research is more specific and for some writers is the fruit of experience. Albert Camus realised 'that even after a single day's experience of the outside world a man could easily live a hundred years in prison. He'd have laid up enough memories never to be bored.' A. J. Cronin (*The Citadel*) and Somerset Maugham (*Of Human Bondage*) – both of whom were doctors – drew upon their medical knowledge, and Ernest Hemingway (*The Old Man and the Sea*) upon his skills as a fisherman. Ian Fleming used his training as a secret agent to establish the credibility of James Bond. 'The best part of Conrad's novels would be destroyed if it had been impossible

---

* Anthony Trollope

Do You Do Much Research?

for him to be a sailor. Take away all that Tolstoy knew of war as a soldier, of life and society as a rich young man whose education admitted him to all sorts of experience, and *War and Peace* would be incredibly impoverished.'*

Some novelists set out on their voyages of discovery with the minimum of physical effort. Shakespeare had no need to go to Denmark in order to write *Hamlet*. Elizabeth Barrett Browning rarely left her bedroom. She certainly never worked in a factory. She lay on her sofa, with R. H. Horne's report on child labour, and came up with *The Cry of the Children*. Harriet Beecher Stowe was confined to the North with her large family. She immersed herself, however, in contemporary accounts of the brutality of Southern slave owners, and not only astonished the world but precipitated the American Civil War with *Uncle Tom's Cabin*.

Arthur Hailey spent months in hotels, airports, and factories, before embarking on the bestselling *Hotel*, *Airport* and *Wheels*. Frederick Forsyth mastered small arms for the *The Day of the Jackal* and never describes a street unless he has actually walked down it. Experience derives from what we feel rather than what we see, but there are few authors who are able accurately to invoke unfamiliar worlds without leaving their desks.

Research, an aid to imagination rather than a substitute for it, can be divided into 'before' and 'after' a novel. Even after one comes to the end of several hundred odd pages there is still work to be done, for it is in scrupulous attention to detail that authenticity is found, hence James Joyce's constant letters of enquiry to Dublin: 'Are there trees (and of what kind) behind

* Virginia Woolf

73

the Star of the Sea church in Sandymount?' In answer to the question would *Ulysses* have been a lesser book had Joyce got the trees wrong, I believe it would. We have only to look at the howler made by Nobel prizewinner William Golding in *Lord of the Flies*, when he carelessly made Piggy's *short sight* or concave lenses concentrate the rays of the sun and start the fire on the island, to see why.

The best research is talking to people. Most people are happy to have their routine interrupted and flattered to think (usually mistakenly) that you are going to put them into a book. While for some novels I have made use of the 'ground beneath my feet' (*Proofs of Affection*), my own research has taken me, amongst many other places, into a New York police precinct (*Rose of Jericho*), behind the 'Chinese wall' of a City bank (Golden Boy), into a judge's inner sanctum (*An Eligible Man*), to the major chateaux on the Bordeaux wine route (*Vintage*), and to the transplant unit at Harefield Hospital (*The Gift of Life*). When I am asked how I know so much about US police procedure, hostile takeover bids, the Crown Prosecution Service, *coulure and millerandage* or lung transplants, the answer is that I don't. The writer knows, or appears to know, the whole world. The success with which she does this is in direct proportion to the meticulousness of her research.

Novels are about extraordinary people in ordinary situations, or about ordinary people in extraordinary situations. *We All Fall Down* was to be the latter. It had to be contemporary. Any attempt to evoke a past, in which the rhythms of speech cannot be heard, is as far as I am concerned a non-starter. Like Mrs Disraeli – who was never sure whether the Greeks came before or after the Romans – I have always had problems with history.

Researching the 'tycoon' of my newspaper clipping 'City

Do You Do Much Research?

Tycoon drops Dead' was not difficult. I had a friend who was chief executive of a toy business and it was no problem to sit in at his office, to follow him round with my notebook and micro-cassette recorder and discover how a captain of industry spent his day. To complement my cast I also needed a barrister, a beach-café proprietor, and a striptease dancer. The fact that I regarded my assembly of characters as a 'cast', the *dramatis personae* of a drama to be enacted on the wide screen of my mind, was perhaps indicative of the turn my career was later to take. The barrister was easy. I had only to follow my brother from chambers to court, court to chambers, chambers to case conference, and case conference to late-night sessions over his beribboned briefs. Since there was no professional stripper amongst my acquaintance, I set out for a Soho club, which was infinitely more disconcerting than infiltrating a police precinct. Joining the shifty lunchtime queue outside the narrow doorway, I paid £5 (this was 1959) for my compulsory year's subscription and was ushered upstairs through the bar and into a large room filled with a semicircle of white-clothed tables from which vantage point – the only female amongst a roomful of men – I sat through 'Welcome to the Paris Striptease', 'Nudes on the Town', 'Ladies Only' and 'The Girl with the Swinging *Derrière*'. After the show I made the acquaintance of one Tracy Goss from Epping (who divested herself of her clothes as nonchalantly as if she had been beeping the barcodes in a supermarket checkout), later to become the template for Honey DuPont in *We All Fall Down*.

Researching the beach café was more difficult. At the time we had a seaside house in Birchington, Kent, and having staked out my ground I approached the owner of the promenade café. Luckily Herbert Smith had been a film producer before his retirement. When I explained my needs he was only too willing to co-operate. For three weeks I worked behind the counter in his café, filling trays and selling candy-floss. Starting at dawn, when the sands were empty and only the gulls broke the silence, I learned how to brew tea in a half-gallon teapot, how to set apples in toffee (which would only adhere to fruit of a certain variety) and line them up on a buttered marble slab, how to slice ham thin, from the freezer, and how to brew coffee in an urn. To while away the time, as we prepared for the daily onslaught of damp and sandy customers queueing at the counter with their tin trays, Herbert Smith played music on his gramophone. One morning he asked me what I thought of a particular record. I listened carefully but was unable to distinguish anything extraordinary about the enthusiastic noise and repetitive lyrics which filled the shuttered café and spilled out on to the promenade. 'You mark my words,' Herbert said. 'You are listening to the future.' The record he had put on was by the Beatles; the beat the 'Mersey sound'!

CHAPTER SIX

Where Do You Get Your Ideas?

<hr>

'L'art c'est une idée qu'on exagère.'

André Gide

They used to be delivered by the milkman –
'Two pints please and a brilliant idea' –
But they began to vanish from the doorstep
And I was only getting three a year.

I tried the shop – the big one down in Norwood,
I-D-R-Mart. I wandered down an aisle
Where Nature was displayed in great abundance,
Trees, flowers, sunsets, dead sheep (by the pile) –

The usual stuff. I hurried past Domestic,
Domestic pets (BE TENDER! MOURN YOUR CAT!),
And Politics (GREAT VALUE! EEZEE TARGETS!),
And paused at Love. But I was sick of that.

THE WRITING GAME

It's difficult. It's worse than buying trousers.
They have to be just right. They're hard to find.
No luck for weeks. Then someone asks a question
And gives me one I like. How very kind.

Wendy Cope

Novices in the arts think you have to start with inspiration to write or paint or compose. The truth is that all you have to do is start. 'I write fifty pages until I hear the fetal heartbeat' Henry Miller used to say.

'Where do you get your ideas?' is the $64,000 question for the writer. The answer is simple. You don't. The writer doesn't choose his theme, the theme chooses the writer. Creativity has been defined 'as the ability to bring something new into existence'.* The creative writer does the same thing as a child at play. He creates a world of fantasy which he takes very seriously and invests with a great deal of emotion while separating it from reality. At an adult level he regards these fantasies as shameful and ignominious, which is why when he is occupied with them he hides them from other people.

There are two ways of being a writer, painting powerful, tragic frescoes like Shakespeare or, like Chekhov, describing in detail the minutiae of life. Great novels begin with tiny hints: the much maligned sliver of madeleine melting in Proust's mouth; the shade of louse-grey Flaubert had in mind for Madame Bovary. Robert Louis Stevenson claimed his plots were delivered gratis, by some kind of elf, while he slept; Henry James concocted his novels from little scraps, other people's talk, chance happenings which he called 'the jog of fancy's elbow'.

* Anthony Storr

Where Do You Get Your Ideas?

New ideas cannot be conjured up voluntarily, they come to people.

The catalyst for *Anna Karenin* was the suicide of the mistress of a neighbouring landowner who threw herself under a train near Count Leo Tolstoy's home; Kafka translated the dilemmas of his own life into the paradoxes of his fiction; the plot of *Dr Jekyll and Mr Hyde* appeared to Stevenson in a dream; Graham Greene was sitting at his daughter's Christmas dinner table watching his grandchildren pull crackers when the idea for *Dr Fischer of Geneva* came to him; Ruth Rendell's best ideas happen during her post-prandial walks; Barbara Cartland simply asks God to give her a plot and he does, and Shakespeare never bothered to think up a plot at all.

The novelist's choice of subject matter is an existential decision made without rules and without external guidelines. Many authors start with neither plot nor outline but with only the idea of a character whom they merely allow to make contact with other characters (in the manner of real life). Although the world is perpetually in a state of flux, the human condition remains constant. The only thing worth writing about is the human heart which must be attached to a human being, and the human being must belong to a particular time and place and have to do with other human beings and to be involved with them.

According to Zelda Fitzgerald, Scott 'couldn't write anything he didn't know'. Only the dilettantes try to be universal. Imagination is the re-arrangement of material already in the mind, and most successful novelists tell their own stories (although some insist they are writing not about the experience they've had but the experience they're going to have). We have in our lives no more than two or three really great or moving experiences which we present time and again – each time in a different guise – for as long as people will listen. Whether these incidents occurred 20 years ago or yesterday is immaterial. The true artist repeats himself. Someone once asked Picasso why he was always to be found on the balcony painting the same view: 'because every moment the light is different, the colours are different, the atmosphere is different'.

Writers dislike being asked what their novels are 'about'. A novel, in its totality, is bound to express ideas, but in ways not easily formulated, other than in writing that particular novel. You might as well produce a brick to show someone what your house is like.

Like Lawrence, for whom the daily lives of his protagonists were more important than the plot, the only thing I need to know before starting a novel is the characters. It is not the ability to invent a plot that makes a novel good, but the ability to get inside the skin of others, to think, to react, to suffer, not in one's own way but in their way that really matters. If the characters live, the book will write itself and the 'plot' will follow.

Novelists who deliberately choose their subject matter with the idea of making money, or because they think that something is 'politically correct', may enjoy commercial success. Their books are unlikely to be of lasting interest because they are written to conform to short-term expectations. A book will not hold together unless it has some of one's own blood mixed in it. There is no copyright in ideas, so when the novelist has a book incubating she is well advised to keep her idea to herself. It is perfectly legitimate to draw on the day-to-day experiences of an acquaintance, or the anecdotes of a stranger, for material. The circumstances in which these ideas are disclosed are not confidential and cannot give rise to a claim in breach of confidence.

Where Do You Get Your Ideas?

As far as my own novels are concerned there are various 'inciting incidents'. My first novel *No White Coat* began, as do many novels, with the title. It came to me out of the blue and seemed to encompass the dilemma of the young doctor who lives the (in those days) rarefied world of hospital medicine in which he is surrounded by devoted nurses prepared to tie his shoelaces, for the realities and hands-on experience of general practice.

A Loving Mistress – in which a young professional woman sacrifices her career for the love of a married man – was inspired by the covert trysts I observed in a health farm (where I had gone to recuperate after surgery) which is where my fictional protagonist meets her lover.

The Long Hot Summer of Lorna Brown, the story of an ostensibly well off but unfulfilled wife and mother who kicks over the traces, was inspired by a mixture of my observation of the isolated lives led by suburban housewives and mothers – before the raising of women's consciousness – the unprecedented heatwave of 1976, and the first stirrings of my own mid-life crisis.

For *Proofs of Affection* I had only to use the atavistic ground beneath my feet, while its sequel, *Rose of Jericho* – concerning the realisation by a widow of her own potential – hit like the flash floods in the Sinai desert where I found the eponymous dried up 'rose' which opened up fully only when immersed in water.

Having explored the possibilities of widowhood, I made a conscious decision to turn my mind to 'widowerhood', a very different, and inequitable cup of tea, the result of which was *An Eligible Man*.

Golden Boy, in which a high-flying executive bites the dust

81

with devastating consequences for himself and for his family, was inspired by the impact of the 1987 recession on the banking world, and *Vintage* was the fallout from the research for a commissioned television drama which was, in the manner of so many commissioned dramas, ultimately scrapped.

The compost heap of material on which I was to draw for *We All Fall Down* had been rotting since childhood when I had observed my father setting off for work at the same time each morning, and returning, similarly predictably, at night. Intrigued by the notion of life as a 'treadmill' I speculated what would happen if the quotidian round (*metro, bulot, dodo*) were to be wilfully sabotaged. What would happen if a spanner were to be thrown into the works.

We All Fall Down was published by Hodder & Stoughton in 1960 and received encouraging reviews: 'A very human novel'; '...the story assumes a vitality that carries the reader intently from page to page'; 'A good yarn'; 'This is an interesting and unusual novel and the theme is handled with sympathy and insight'; 'This splendidly written book holds the interest throughout'; 'Well worth reading'; 'Shows a marked maturity in style and workmanship and a broader sympathy towards the frailties of human nature'. In accordance with the publisher's self-fulfilling prophecy *We All Fall Down* sold moderately well in hardcover. It took 30 years before I understood about 'self-fulfilling prophecies'. The writer perennially expects his latest novel to occupy major review space and to fill the bookshop shelves. *Unless the publisher decrees at the outset that it will do so he might just as well forget it.* When costing your book he allows a certain sum for its promotion and, as Martin Amis commented, 'even a child knows that if they don't spend money on it they're not going to sell it.' Long before a book appears in

Where Do You Get Your Ideas?

the shops, the marketing department reach certain decisions concerning its fate. Will money be spent on a poster? Will there be advertising in the newspapers or on the sides of buses? Will the author be sent on a book tour? Will there be dumpbins in shops or a free 'covermount' (paperback) given away with glossy magazines such as *Elle* or *Marie-Claire*? If the publisher spends a modest amount, your book will sell modestly. If he gambles heavily he will stake his all on recouping his outlay, and will put his considerable clout behind getting your book mentioned in the media and boosting the sales. It is neither coincidence nor the private initiative of an individual book-seller, but the outcome of a rigorously orchestrated, often hugely costly, campaign on the part of the publisher which fills bookshop windows with a novel and makes absolutely sure it catches our attention. Apart from winning a major literary prize (for which your novel must be entered by your publisher) there is *absolutely nothing you can do to alter this state of affairs. We All Fall Down* was published as a Hodder paperback but, despite the good reviews and the determined efforts of Miss Weiner, no foreign rights were sold.

At this point in my career I was invited by Granada Television to write an episode for their popular weekly series *Knight Errant*. Going to Red Lion Square to be interviewed by Granada, for one who spent her days filling the maws of washing machines and children, operating the school run, and minister-ing to the paramedical needs of the patients, was quite an adventure. The producer of *Knight Errant* explained to me that they were trawling for new writers. He was familiar with my work, which he liked, and invited me to submit an hour long episode for his series. I turned the offer down almost before the words were out of his mouth. I had never seen *Knight Errant*, I had never written for television. I did not own a TV set. I had no idea that, unlike in novel writing, there would be story editors and others about one, and that although for me it was an untried medium, I would by no means be alone. Paralysed with fear, I told the producer that I was quite incapable of what he suggested, and made my escape. I know now, of course, that it was both naïve and foolhardy to reject a proposal for which most of my colleagues – had I known any writers at the time – would have given their right arms.

Although, looking back, my life seems always to have been action-packed in terms of having to juggle the calls of being a writer with the demands of my housewife/doctor's-wife/mother/ daughter role, the years following the publication of *We All Fall Down* were particularly fruitful.

The patience of a saint was what a GP needed when trying to look after 4,000 patients, single-handed, 24 hours a day, under the exacting terms of the National Health Service. It was hardly surprising that *Patients of a Saint*, in which I returned to the familiar world of medicine, was the title of my fourth novel.

It is by sitting down to write *every day* that one becomes a writer. Those who do not do this are amateurs. My working methods at this time seem, by today's standards, quaint. Having learned to type (with the help of Pitman's *Teach Yourself Typing*), I hammered out my novels on my manual typewriter. There were certain words, such as 'the' and 'himself' which brought on an attack of dyslexia – 'hte' and 'himslef' – and it never quite became touch-typing. Chapter by chapter I showed what I had written to my husband at night. He was then, and remains now, my first and best critic (not to mention copy editor) and I feel sorry for authors who have no one in their lives whose opinion they respect and from whom they can get instant feedback.

Although I am unable to identify with the writer (familiar from the cinema screen) who angrily rips sheets of paper from his typewriter, crumples them up and hurls them towards an overflowing bin, there are certainly off days in which one's writing seems maudlin, banal, plodding, worthless, and one's lacklustre pages covered with meaningless symbols. At such moments it is invaluable to have a fresh eye cast over them, to be told that there is some gold amongst the dross. Each morning in those days – as indeed I still do – I reread the previous day's output, which I then correct in pencil, inserting and crossing out, before continuing with my story. Every day it is an act of faith. You sit down at your typewriter. *Pizzicato* you approach the keys. Letters become words, words become sentences, sentences become paragraphs, paragraphs become pages, until at last you are up and away on a glorious crescendo of creation.

'One simply has to tell a story with the same kind of application as a cabinet maker at his bench. The miracle will either happen or not happen, and the rest will follow'.* The pleasures of writing are hard to describe to those who have not experienced them. Your fictional characters beckon you to follow them and the world recedes. The process of creation, of bringing forth something which hitherto did not exist, is an out-of-body experience which Flaubert equated with the sexual: 'Save your priapism for style, fuck your inkwell.' For the film maker, as for the novelist, film is always more real than life. When Steven Spielberg's girlfriend interrupted him on the set, he told her to

* Georges Simenon

go away. 'Don't you understand, I'm fucking my movie.' This degree of involvement is felt only by the true artist to whom it is always a shock to abandon the make believe and return to the real world.

When the 300 odd pages of my manuscript of *Patients of a Saint* were finished, they were legible only to myself and the initiated. One of these was Mrs Pilgrim, a retired civil servant who now came to the surgery twice a week to help with the secretarial work. The earlier novels had, for their final draft, been sent out to a typist who took many weeks transforming the overwritten pages, which had then very often to be retyped because of further errors. It was a time-consuming and expensive process yet one on which I was not prepared to cut corners. I am – and this is by no means always a good or comfortable thing – a perfectionist. I was not prepared to submit anything but a clean, legible, professional-looking manuscript to my publisher. Proust's 'manuscripts' consisted of small pieces of paper, glued together, and covered with so many crossings-out and amendments that there was scarcely room for an additional comma. I was no Proust however (although I could certainly have done with a few days in bed being waited on hand and foot by a devoted Albertine), and it was not my way.

Mrs Pilgrim took my chapters home and laboriously retyped them. It was in the days before the photocopier eliminated the anxiety associated with the single copy of one's manuscript. Every moment that my reams of deathless prose were out of my sight was torture. Would Mrs Pilgrim leave my manuscript on the bus? What if her house burned down and with it my immortal words? I could of course have made a duplicate copy on carbon paper as I worked, but inserting the flimsy blue sheets into the typewriter (managing to get them the right way round) was not only impractical, particularly when it came to corrections, but slowed down production and inhibited the imaginative flow.

Patients of a Saint was published in 1961 and the now familiar sequence, of paperback, large print edition, and serialisation by the BBC (as well as by Polish and Hungarian broadcasting stations) was repeated. By the following year I had written and published several more short stories, attended a variety of evening classes (largely, I think, in order to get away from domesticity and out of the house), finished a three-act stage play, written my first book for children, and given birth to my fourth daughter. Even writing about all this activity now makes me tired. When you are young and energetic you don't think about it.

The play, a new departure for me, was called *Visitor from Seil* – lies in reverse – 30 years later to be rewritten and staged as *Home Truths*. Stacy, a 17-year-old girl, who has grown up on a remote island where only the truth is told, is sent to England where her philosophy plays havoc with the conventional English household with its double standards. Learning quickly that dissembling is an integral part of the real world, and painted into a corner by dramatic events, Stacy lies for the first time in her life. As ill-equipped to live with deception as the host family is to live with the truth, the disillusioned *ingénue* returns to Seil.

If I were asked where I got my idea for *Visitor from Seil*, I would have to admit that I don't know, and to fabricate the answer. The theme had *to do* with our inability to communicate satisfactorily with one another, with the complicated manner in which we run our lives, with the artefacts with which we think it necessary to surround ourselves, and with our capacity for mutual destruction. Although it was any or all of these, the theme arose in its entirety from the unconscious.

William Golding tells an amusing story about the occasion on which he was forced to listen to a PhD student's theory of where the idea had come from to set fire to the island at the end of *Lord of the Flies*. 'Ah yes,' Golding says, when the student has finished his tortuous interpretation. 'I won't say I was able to follow you in all your exegeses, but the *real* reason why it happened was this: I wrote the book in my spare time as a teacher, and my wife grew very tired of finding me shut up in my study. Towards the end of the book I said to her late one night in a state of exhaustion – "I can't think what to do with the island," and she replied – "Why don't you burn the bloody thing!"'

Questioners will often not believe that the making of books is not something completely conscious. They suspect you of holding something back, and will probe away at your secret until they find what they imagine is the formula, which will then of course equip them to write their own books.

Visitor from Seil, my first play, *almost* made it. There was an offer to direct it from Charles Ross (Charles Ross Productions Ltd) and also serious interest from Linnet and Dunfee, the then doyens of the commercial theatre. A meeting was set up with two of the directors (the third one being in New York at the time) at which casting for *Visitor from Seil* was actually discussed. Unfortunately the man from the States turned out to be the one with the money and, with his return, my balloon of hope was pricked.

I can pinpoint the moment when the idea for *Aristide* (my first book for children) was conceived, although the details of the actual birth remain, as always, a mystery.

Where Do You Get Your Ideas?

The publishing history of *Aristide* is bizarre and, apart from being a recommendation for perseverance in the writing game, it is a cautionary tale for any author. When the manuscript was finished, the dedication on the fly leaf was to my second daughter, Louise. *Aristide* was written when she was eight years old. By the time it was published Louise was 15 and the dedication no longer appropriate.

Aristide was, and still is, one of my favourite, if not *the* favourite amongst the books I have written. I do not consider myself a children's writer. Writing for children requires a very special flair and it is not a *genre* which comes easily to me. My abilities, as far as entertaining the young is concerned, extend no further than making up well-received bedtime tales ('head stories') for my grandchildren.

In the year before the youngest of our four daughters was born, we took our three girls to a rented holiday villa in the south of France, a country with which I had always felt a great affinity and where we were later to have our second home. The notebook which I took with me on that occasion, and which I still keep in my cupboard together with a lifetime's collection of others, is a red 'sixpenny' Lion Brand Memo Book, measuring 6 inches by 4 inches. There is an 'A' (*Aristide*) scratched on the cover. Our villa was called *Notre Rêve*. I made a list of the names of other villas in the area, both in the interests of accurate observation and for future reference. *Lylou, Clopant Clopent, Gai Logis, Ma Lucette*. No matter how vivid one's imagination they were hardly house names one could conjure up from 800 miles away on a rainy morning in London. The list was followed, on the feint-ruled pages, by observations to do with our own villa and its kitchen: '...iron-gates (rusty lock), terrace, red/white tiles, green shutters, frilled curtains, veg. dishes and *frites* pans, pestle and mortar, moulds, fish kettles, salad bas-kets, wall-plates...' Brief shots are then taken, and sounds recorded, on the beach: '*Pan Bagnat* – sun oil, sea, sun, sun oil – matelas – parasols – cabines – glaces (pistaches, praline, moka) – "Location de Voiliers' – bikinis (locals) – one-piece (Americans) – stand-up, sit-down, check face, check time, walk, talk, kiss, comb, undo straps, touch, grin, smile, sun, turn, shake towel, adjust straps, read, young, old, infants, oars, fishermen, rocks, sky, bags, specs, hats, rings, lilos, paperbacks, newspaper vendors: '*Daily Hexpress, Hupserver!*' '*Marriettes! Marriettes!*' Overhead Caravelle (London bound) daily at 1 pm – sea-sounds – thwack of beach balls – cars – Chambords, Dauphines, Simcas, Renaults, 'Minxes', 'Zephyrs' (Fr number plates), Citroëns, Panhards, Frégates, Vespas, outboard motors. Laughs, music, song. Anxious children: '*Maman!*' '*Papa!*' Anx-ious parents: '*Françoise, Brigitte, donnez-moi ça.*' '*Jean-Pierre, mets ton chapeaux!*' '*Tais-toi, Dominique!*' '*Michèle, prends ton bonnet!*' *Reste tranquille!*' '*Dépèche-toi, Emile ... Micheline ... René ... Rolande ... Christiane ... Charlotte ... Marie-Hélène ... Anne-Marie ... Lulu ... Aristide ... Aristide ... Aristide!*'

Aristide. The name stayed with me. There were other notes in my book, seemingly unconnected: '1. Great men emerge during war. 2. Backward nations unfit to rule. 3. Misunderstanding due to language – lack of education. 4. Religious intolerance. 5. The wooing of backward states. 6. Banding together against the common enemy.' From this motley collection, six years later, *Aristide* was born.

CHAPTER SEVEN

If at First...

⬥

'The novelist is a man who writes novels. I insist on the "s".'

Simenon

Aristide, written at white heat and in three weeks, was about a small French boy who spends his summer holiday with his grandmother in the north of France while his parents take off for the *Côte d'Azur*. Aristide's grandmother buys him a lilo. While she is asleep on the beach, he goes out to sea on his lilo and is carried away across the Channel. Landing in England, Aristide joins a group of boys who are at war with a rival group in the next-door garden. By applying the lessons taught to him by his father, Aristide manages not only to stop the war but to demonstrate its futility. The story can be read on many levels.

Despite the best efforts of Miss Weiner, no one wanted to publish *Aristide*. The readers' reports (which Miss Weiner always insisted upon seeing) varied from the condescending – 'mixture of fantasy and realism' – to the downright rude. The most insulting of all came from the pen of Margery Fisher, wife of the naturalist James Fisher, and mother of six children: 'It seems to me that the story has been written for the sake of the moral... The character of Aristide is so lightly sketched that it is impossible to accept that he would suddenly stand up so nobly for a principle.' There were several things Mrs Fisher 'did not care for': 1. Explanation of long words (an insult to any child over four). 2. Tedious French phrases. 3. Use of italics for emphasis. 4. Aristide's inconsistent command of English. 5. The author talking down to children. 6. Aristide's tiresome relations.

The bottom line was that there was no way she could recommend *Aristide* for publication. Miss Weiner continued to submit *Aristide* to publishers of children's books. To a man they declined the offer. After three years had elapsed she wrote to me: 'I really think you will have to accustom yourself to the idea that this book will not be sold. It has been to a variety of publishers and simply not rung a bell anywhere. Sometimes one has to admit honourable defeat, and I confess that I do this with regard to this particular book ... I am sending the manuscript back to you...'

If *Aristide* had riled Mrs Fisher, Miss Weiner's letter annoyed *me*. I *liked Aristide*. My children liked *Aristide*. Other children, on whom I had tried it out, liked *Aristide*. I wrote to Miss Weiner requesting the names of the publishers who had seen the manuscript. Offended (it was not difficult to upset her), she got her secretary to reply. There were eight British and two American publishers on her list. I picked a ninth British publisher at random – Hutchinson and Co. – parcelled up

Aristide and sent it off. It was accepted by the children's fiction editor, Miss Tomlinson, almost at once.

I now had a problem. Should I allow Miss Weiner to handle the rights in a manuscript I had placed myself? Must I hand over 15 per cent of my earnings on *Aristide* in the interests of 'good relations? I belonged to no professional body, there was no one to advise me. I took the coward's way out.

Miss Weiner, predictably, was huffy about the turn events had taken. *Of course* she knew Miss Tomlinson of Hutchinson. She was a *very old friend*. Why, I wondered, had she not then sent her the book? Relationships between myself and my agent were strained for some time following this episode. To redeem her hurt pride Miss Weiner quarrelled with the advance offered by Hutchinson and Co., and nitpicked over the royalties. We are all human. I daresay Miss Weiner *was* fed up with submitting *Aristide*.

I tell the story only to demonstrate that the opinions of publishers' readers are, by definition, subjective. If the author has faith in his or her work, if he or she has a gut feeling for it, no matter how long it takes HE OR SHE SHOULD NOT GIVE UP!

Hutchinson and Co., manifested their belief in *Aristide* by engaging the renowned Quentin Blake (an accolade in itself) to illustrate it. His drawings were delightful, and on the strength of our combined efforts (although I never either met or talked to the artist, the arrangements were all made through the publisher) the book was bought by Collins for paperback, and by Dial Press for hardback publication in the USA.

The publication of *Aristide* in 1966 was by no means the end of the saga. The reviews were excellent and it was highly recommended by *The Times Educational Supplement* (so much for Mrs Fisher). In France the reception was equally gratifying: *'L'aventure d'Aristide est racontée avec une simplicité et une économie de style brillantes... Ce livre est délicieux. Il fera certainement tout autant plaisir aux jeunes français qu'à leurs parents.'*

I must now wind the clock forward to 1985, by which time *Aristide*, which had sold in respectable numbers, had been out of print for some years. My current agent, Ilsa Yardley, was unfamiliar with *Aristide*, children's fiction was not her province, but she could not see that there was any extra mileage to be got out of it. Again my hackles rose. I found myself an agent who dealt specifically with children's books, Caroline Sheldon, ex-Hutchinson, who had just set up her own agency. Caroline agreed to take on *Aristide*, to try to give it a new lease of life and to introduce it to a new generation of children. After a few false starts, Adrian Sington, of Grafton, made an offer for publication, provided I agreed to write a sequel! Again my persistence was vindicated. Terms were agreed and, although contracts were not yet signed, I had started work on *Aristide in Paris* when an unexpected spanner was thrown into the works.

A senior Grafton editor was strongly opposed to publication of the story on the grounds that *Aristide* represented a hazard to children. Aristide's fictional Channel crossing *might* encourage them to venture out to sea on their own lilos. Backed by child psychologists, I pointed out that *Peter Pan* had not resulted in generations of children jumping out of windows in the mistaken belief that they could fly, nor were *Alice in Wonderland* readers prone to hurling themselves down potholes in search of the White Rabbit. As the mother of four little girls I was the last person to want children to read a book that would in any way

94

endanger their lives. It was touch and go for some weeks as to whether Grafton would honour their contract. In the end they signed and *Aristide* was read by a new generation of children from whom I received a poignant and critical fan-mail: '...thank you for your everlasting gift of Aristide'; '...I'm really into Aristide's adventure on the air mattress'; '...it was my kind of story ... the best part was the sausage part and I loved the title of the book'; 'I like your story ... it's funny ... my name is Todd ... will you write some more...'; 'I really enjoyed the story *Aristide* that you wrote. How do you get your Ideas for your storys [*sic*]?' 'I read *Aristide* and *Aristide in Paris*, and they were very good. Are there any other Aristide books? if there are can you give me the titels please. Aristide's dad said that Jean d'arc was executed But really she was burnt But stile it was very good.'

Whereas *Aristide* had come from the heart, *Aristide in Paris*, written to order at the request of the publisher, came from the head. I was not particularly proud of it. An incident concerning its production did little to improve matters, and is once again a cautionary tale. Since Grafton were using Quentin Blake's original drawings for the republished *Aristide* it seemed a reasonable assumption that the same artist would be commissioned to illustrate the sequel. When the proofs of *Aristide in Paris* arrived I was surprised to find that the drawings were by Steven Appleby (an ex-pupil of Quentin Blake). Although the style was similar, and the pictures extremely competent, it was not 'Quentin Blake'. I conveyed my disappointment to Adrian Sington who told me that 20 years on, Quentin Blake was *the* children's illustrator and now 'far too expensive' for the Grafton budget. I accepted this explanation. Some months later I met Quentin Blake. I told him how sad I was that his fee had been too high. He was amazed. 'I would have been delighted to do the drawings,' he said, 'but nobody asked me. *Aristide* is one of my favourite characters and I would certainly have come to some arrangement with Hutchinson!' Once more I should have been ahead of the game.

Caroline Sheldon tried to get a French publisher for *Aristide* and *Aristide in Paris*. No longer either shy or willing to accept the received view that 'agents know best', I suggested that she approach the prestigious Gallimard. She did as I suggested and got a 'no' from Gallimard's London representative. Once more I persisted. I had a good friend in Paris, Plum Le Tan, who had some dealings with French publishing houses on behalf of her husband, artist Pierre Le Tan. I asked her if she would like to try to place *Aristide*, and she was only too pleased. Gallimard was the first house she approached. The Paris editor loved *Aristide*. Gallimard made an offer for the book and commissioned Plum to translate it into French. Even this small success was not the end of a long story of persistence. Twenty-four years after its original publication, a second edition of *Aristide* was published by Gallimard. At the end of the book there were games, puzzles, and questionnaires based on Aristide's adventures. Thirty-three years later it is still in print and I receive regular royalties!

'I hold my inventive capacity on the stern condition that it must master my whole life, often have complete possession of me, make its own demands on me, and sometimes for months together put everything else away from me.' Lucky old Charles Dickens! I bet he never had to queue up for 35 minutes in the post office on a Monday when everyone was drawing their pensions, never had to stand in a lunchtime line in the bank when the cash machine was 'down', never had to wait 20

minutes at the supermarket checkout to have the till roll snarl
up on him, never had to listen to the 'Ride of the Valkyrie' over
and over while the telephone operator put him on 'hold'. Like
the Brontës, who in addition to their literary endeavours had to
concern themselves with potato peeling and bread-making,
there was no way that for 'months together' I could 'put
everything else away from me' in the interests of 'my inventive
capacity', and I'm not at all sure, when push came to shove, that
I would have wanted to. If you are lucky enough to be able to
follow Trollope's dictum, to do his prescribed 'three hours a
day' without 'staring at the wall' or chewing your pencil, you do
in fact produce as much during this time as you are able to
write. Any attempt to create more is counter productive.

The birth of our fourth daughter was the apotheosis of my
attempts to juggle my many hats, and after this addition to our
household it became obvious that there must be certain changes.
Immediately prior to her birth we made a significant one.
Having held out for so long, and turned deaf ears to arguments
such as 'I'm the only one in the class who hasn't seen...' (the
implication being that we were cruel and uncaring parents) we
submitted to pressure, and the demands of the lady who was to
stand in for me during my absence in hospital, and – against my
better judgement – acquired that national pacifier and nepenthe
of the masses, a TV set.

'In this big white house are the Kreugers in their dark living
room, watching television poor things. They sit in the bluish
light and from their faces it's hard to tell if they're alive or in
a persistent vegetative state – maybe it's time to pull the
plug.'*

* Garrison Keillor

97

THE WRITING GAME

It is often said that television – which, like film, purveys life to those who do not live it – has killed the art of conversation which enriches understanding. Since this remark is characteristically made by individuals with the conversational talents of a telephone answering machine, society may well be able to stand the loss. What is disturbing is that TV has destroyed the habit amongst the young not only of amusing themselves but of reading, which fosters the ability to concentrate and to conjure up mental images from written descriptions which enable one to make connections, to speculate, to use one's head. Today, the teenager who reads for pleasure is rare. 'Not reading' is his way of alerting the intellectual establishment to the fact that he prefers to watch a flickering screen than to plough through a book. Reading is hard work and children no longer buy into the myth that something that takes effort is more worthwhile than instant gratification.

'We live in an illiterate country. The mass media ... pander to the low and lowest of the low in the human experience. They finally debase us through the sheer weight of their mindlessness.'*

As adolescent couch potatoes slump in front of TV screens offering round-the-clock entertainment, we have to accept that 'unliteracy' is their contribution to modern culture, a state of affairs tacitly endorsed by parents who themselves sit in nightly silence and relate better to the stars of their favourite 'soaps' than to their children. The cult of the media 'personality' – often someone of low intellectual calibre and famous for being famous – could well be responsible for the low self-esteem of many adolescents who downgrade themselves because no one recognises them. It is this obsession with personalities that

* David Mamet

If at First...

T. S. Eliot prophesied could lead to the cultural breakdown of the twentieth century.

As a medium for information, TV, which sees and hears selectively, is inferior to radio. Its reports, which are anecdotal, are often determined by the availability, or quality, of the visual image and they blanket-bomb our emotions into accepting the part for the whole. What is bad news for human beings whose sufferings are exploited by the camera, is often good 'news' for television which plunges people into noisy isolation and encourages an inertia frequently mistaken for relaxation. Experience derives from feeling – 'Some of the love passages make me cry' Thackeray said of *Jane Eyre* – rather than from seeing. Television, with its regular fixes of violence, its nightly disasters, inures us to grief and misery, and dulls our perceptions. Although it can transport us within seconds to the other side of the world and provide us with more information, more quickly, than the human brain is capable of processing, the paradoxical effect is sensory *deprivation* (the viewer is required to call neither upon his imaginative nor aesthetic responses) rather than *stimulation*. Even the sit-com is accompanied by prerecorded laughter, thus robbing us of one of the most significant clues to our existence.

Like most writers I am capable of holding two opposing views in my head at the same time. While having a TV is open to the above abuse, not having a TV as the millennium approaches is tantamount to declaring you know nothing of the time or country in which you live. While TV's proliferations of channels and 24-hour distractions may have dulled the craving for the 'open sesame' of the written word amongst teenagers, it has also, through its excellent dramatisations of such books as *Pride and Prejudice*, *The Mill on the Floss*, and *Moll Flanders*, introduced millions of viewers to the classics. Although today I

99

sometimes write for a medium capable of reducing the most significant events to wallpaper, and turning us into a nation of zombies who are spared the need to call upon either their imaginative or aesthetic responses, credit must be given not only to the succour the medium offers to the isolated, the bedridden and the housebound, but to the rich variety of programmes capable of transporting those unable to travel, to boil the proverbial egg, or to tend a pot plant, to the plains of Africa, the kitchens of the masterchefs or the gardens of the green-fingered. Historical reconstructions, while often leaving much to be desired in terms of accuracy, put the world into perspective and make up in some measure for the contemporary neglect of the history book. If you twist the arm of the brain-dead writer who readily confesses to relaxing with half an hour of mindless TV before bed, he or she will probably reveal that they also have their favourite – and sometimes addictive – programmes. My own eclectic viewing includes anything to do with cooking, hospital series (the gorier the better), general knowledge contests – masochistically pitting my score against that of the contenders – first-rate British comedy and any documentary concerning the lives of such *colossae* as Gandhi and Nelson Mandela which is just about the level at which I can assimilate the events of recent history. As far as the writer is concerned, television cannot be ignored. The medium serves the same purpose as did the novels of Dickens or Dostoevsky in their time and were these authors alive today they would probably (as would Shakespeare himself), be writing for the small screen.

Daughter number four was born at the height of a smallpox scare when the entire population panicked, and it seemed that a major part of it was queueing outside our house for the vaccine which was in extremely short supply. The telephone never stopped ringing with pleas for priority protection for the old, the young, and the infirm, the surgery was besieged, and we were completely unable to cope. It was with the greatest relief that I welcomed the onset of labour, left the family mesmerised by the sights and sounds of the new 'box', and escaped to the comparative peace and quiet of the labour ward.

The major change we made, having decided that we had had enough of living over the shop, was to move. The decision to 'go for it', in life as in writing, was prompted by the fact that a) my husband had taken on a partner to help him in the practice, b) his career was taking a turn in the direction of psychiatry, c) our corner house was bursting at the seams. I love looking at houses. Whilst the owners are extolling the virtues of kitchens redolent of times past, and of patently inadequate living-rooms augmented by happy memories, I am busy peopling their homes with my own family, adapting the vendor's space to my own needs. Many years afterwards I wrote a short story called 'Moving' eventually to be published in the bilingual literary review *Adam*. It embodied the sentiments – for which purpose I put myself inside the skin of both buyer and seller – of which I was conscious at this time. Our ideas, in the matter of houses, were grandiose. My parents, who belonged to a generation which believed in paying its way and regarded mortgages with horror, were appalled at the rambling properties with extensive grounds, which we could not afford but which we considered. If you are self-employed, at the peak of your earning powers, investing in bricks and mortar seems a good way to increase your capital assets and ensure the future of yourselves and your family. This is what we told ourselves as we trudged round folly after folly, ranging from a 1930s mansion built in the shape of a ship, to a pig farm. We settled finally for a low-built mock

Tudor house on the outskirts of London not too far from the practice, on a plot set well back from the main road and, according to the estate agent's blurb 'having a frontage of approximately 85ft with an area of approximately half an acre.' The house, 'an excellent family home entirely suitable for entertaining', was on the crest of a hill, facing a common. The attractions of the cricket pitch visible from our front windows were wasted on our exclusively female offspring. The house was large (later it was to be used as a location for a TV play by Alan Bennett with a young Stephen Frears as cameraman). We set about making it larger. We extended the ground floor into the 'rear garden mainly laid to lawn' which was to prove a paradise for dogs and children, enlarged and modernised the kitchen (later to become the model for Lorna Brown's 'prison' in *The Long Hot Summer*), and installed an additional bathroom for the exclusive use of our daughters who before long were to spend what seemed to be the major part of their lives in it. Although the transition was frenetic, and the upheaval significant, it was bliss not to be at the beck and call of patients knocking on the door at all hours, and to have my own space, if not yet a room of my own, for writing.

All the best artists are multi-faceted. I had, to date, tried my hand at the short story, the novel, the children's book, and the play. A new form of writing now came my way. I was invited to contribute a chapter to the *Great Society* series to be published by Anthony Blond Ltd. The series already included *The Computer in Society* (B. M. Murphy), and *Class* a symposium edited by Richard Mabey. My symposium was to be called *Confrontations with Judaism* (Ed. Philip Longworth) and my contribution to it 'The Ideal Jewish Woman in Contemporary Society'.

Here was a 'howdy-do' of the first order! My initial reaction

If at First...

(and indeed my second and third) was to turn down the offer. I was terrified by the illustriousness of the other contributors; Professor Henri Baruk, a distinguished French psychiatrist, Heinrich Guggenheim, professor of mathematics at the University of Minnesota, Raphael Loewe, lecturer in Hebrew at University College, London, and David Miller, fellow of the Institute for Higher Rabbinical Studies at Gateshead, amongst others. I knew nothing about the subject, and I had never tried my hand at non-fiction. It was Miss Weiner who coerced, bullied, and cajoled me into accepting the assignment and with hindsight I am extremely glad that once again I was persuaded to go for it. 'He has not learned the lesson of life who has not every day conquered a new fear.' Emerson was right. Once you manage to overcome the panic at contemplating unfamiliar projects, for which you consider yourself both inadequate and ill-equipped, you wonder what all the fuss was about.

Although I had been brought up in an orthodox Jewish home blindly and obediently to observe the tenets of Judaism, my intellectual understanding of the long and ancient history which informed our literature, influenced our actions, and permeated our blood, was decidedly limited.

Having agreed, with more than a little trepidation, to make my contribution to the symposium, I set out both to fill the gaps in my knowledge and to examine my heritage, a rewarding excursion and one on which I was glad to have been forced to embark. Although my approach to the subject was somewhat empirical, I enjoyed writing my chapter. I discovered the rewards of research, the bonus of the reference library, and the revelation of the fact that you have only to begin to look into a subject – to take the first step – for 'one thing to lead to another', an important consideration overlooked by those writers who employ professional researchers. As my chapter grew, so did my understanding of my roots. It was probably at this moment that the seeds were sown for my Anglo-Jewish trilogy (*Proofs of Affection*, *Rose of Jericho*, and *To Live in Peace*), to be published some 23 years later.

CHAPTER EIGHT

Cooking the Books

———⟫◆⟪———

'The history of a flea can be as fine as the story of
Alexander the Great: everything depends on the execution.'
Gustave Flaubert

One bonus of being a writer, rather than a performer, is that,
you have something to show for your pains. With the passage of
time the number of books with your name on the spine occupies
more and more space on your shelves, and in moments of self-
doubt, by taking them down and looking at them, you are able
to convince yourself that you exist.

By the time we had finally converted and settled into our new
house and, according to Parkinson's Law, expanded to fill the
available space, I had half a dozen titles to my name. The
'doctor' series, and *We All Fall Down*, had been joined by *The
Fraternity* and *The Commonplace Day*.

The Fraternity, set in England and the south of France, took
the dilemma of youth as its theme and the medical 'fraternity',

with which I was of course familiar, as its milieu. The novel was serialised on BBC Woman's Hour (an abridged version in which the author, of course, has no say) and favourably reviewed by both the provincial and the national press. Although by today's standards it performed extremely well, selling 4,500 copies in hardback, the paperback rights were not taken up.

Fortunately for the author, the blood, sweat, and tears that go into the writing of a novel, the sustained physical effort of producing it are, like the pains of labour, soon forgotten. Once the last word is written, the manuscript dispatched, it is as if it has never existed. The weight of its content, the burden of its construction, which you have been carrying around for so long, is eviscerated at a stroke, and the imaginative slate is wiped clean in anticipation of the next commitment. This is why authors often look blank when invited to enter into a dialogue about their work. Unlike painting or sculpting in which the results are immediate, or composing when you can at least *play* your tune, the period between the writing and the production of a novel is often considerable. By the time it reaches the bookshops and is read, a year or more may have elapsed, and the author is probably half way through another book and making plans for a further one. It is hardly surprising that he is unable to account for the behaviour of characters whom he only dimly remembers, and he frequently has to be reintroduced to his own creations. When, in an idle moment, he takes one of his books from the shelf, try as he will to associate with it, it is often as meaningless as if it had been penned in hieroglyphics, as dead as the proverbial dodo.

Many creative people tend to find conviviality exhausting. They can't wait to retreat into privacy where they can be 'themselves' again. They rationalise this by declaring that if one lives quietly one can put one's energy and imagination into one's writing rather than in socialising. There are, however, occasions when one has to pretend to be enjoying oneself, to be welcoming when one is tired, smile when one wants to groan, or put on an act – which is in itself fatiguing. There is always some discrepancy between an individual's public face and what he is in private, and nowhere is this more in evidence than at those dinner parties at which people one is unlikely to meet again sit around a table exchanging side-splitting stories and airing recycled opinions. Like Cyril Connolly I am not a professional diner-out and perhaps through some deficiency of my own fail to find 'other people's misfortunes uproariously funny'. Apart from the fact that, like most writers, I feel permanently ill at ease, many parties go on too late (which renders the writer unfit for work the following morning), and once the conversation has shifted from politics (sleaze in), TV programmes (explicit sex in), speculations about the economy and the calibre of the wines, the moment will come when your fellow diners, who have learned that you are a writer, will ask if they should know you (I've never thought of a satisfactory answer to this one) and what name do you write under? There's nothing quite so awful as repeating your name to people who have never heard of you and whose faces register nothing all. 'Tell me the titles of some of your books' they say. After you have been through the humiliating process of reciting them, the discussion will switch to your *latest* novel, the theme of which you are no longer able to recall. If you do manage to remember it, you will as like as not have moved on from the views expressed in it and even if you are not exactly ashamed of them, the chances are that you no longer agree with them. The writer – who like Kafka fears the external world, involvement with others, and loss of her own identity – dislikes exposure, other than through her work, and is inclined to shrink when the spotlight is focused on to her. Apart from not being able to recall her books, she feels a fraud for having hoodwinked people into reading them and mortified at having done nothing more worthwhile than produce them.

The frustration felt by artists in their latest achievements often leads them to disown or to disparage their work which disappointingly has turned out to be only a shadowy representation of that which was envisaged. Tolstoy repudiated his novels, and in the last five years of his life, Michelangelo said everything he had done was rubbish, a disaster – including the Sistine Chapel.

One cannot think well, love well, sleep well, if one has not dined well. Between writing *The Fraternity* and *The Commonplace Day* I enrolled in an advanced course at the Cordon Bleu Cookery School. Although I was interested in cooking (food defines the man) of the *grandmère* rather than the *nouvelle* variety, thinking what to prepare for my large family had become an onerous duty which far outweighed any possible creative pleasure in the task itself. The end product, after days spent staring blankly at cookery books as well as slaving over a hot stove, was often consumed with what appeared to be unseemly haste.

Food has always featured largely in my novels, one of which *To Live in Peace* even contains recipes, for *tzimmes* (an ambrosial dish of carrots stewed in brown sugar) and honey cake. Eating things in a novel is different from eating them in real life but can be almost equally satisfying. When Iris Murdoch won the Booker Prize for *The Sea, the Sea*, one of the judges

Cooking the Books

remarked that he liked everything in the book except the food which he found disgusting. John Bayley, however, Iris Murdoch's husband, is of the opinion that 'Food can make points for a novelist: it can dramatise a scene, provide irony, naturalise a character who is too artificial.'*

Whether it's Charlotte Brontë's fried chops, or Dickens's stuffed goose, a literary context adds zest to the palate. The partaking of the oyster (with its Freudian connotation) is a common literary ploy used to emphasise the connection between eating and sex; Rat, Mole, Toad and Badger (*The Wind in the Willows*) enjoy a 'simple but sustaining meal ... of bacon and broad beans and a macaroni pudding', while Virginia Woolf – who made use of food to emphasise her point – makes much of the *boeuf en daube* served up by Mrs Ramsay's cook (*To the Lighthouse*) and the restorative *crème de menthe* given to her by the principal of a women's foundation to compensate for the inadequate college fare:

'It is a curious fact that novelists have a way of making us believe that luncheon parties are invariably memorable for something very witty that was said, or for something very wise that was done. But they seldom spare a word for what was eaten. It is part of the novelist's convention not to mention soup and salmon and ducklings, as if soup and salmon and ducklings were of no importance whatsoever, as if nobody ever smoked a cigar or drank a glass of wine.'

Although I firmly believe that multi-generational gatherings round a table provide a history lesson not to be found in the national curriculum, and am convinced, like Proust that ... 'the shared partaking of food provides love, warmth, gourmandise,

* John Bayley

oral gratification and security. In the harmony of family dining the outside world, unpleasant fantasies, and other disruptive elements are kept at bay' – when I am writing I would prefer, like Kant, to have 'porridge for breakfast, vegetables for lunch and a boiled egg in the evening'.

Dis-moi ce que tu manges, je te dirai qui tu es. Sadly, even in France, with the drastic increase in the number of working women with neither time nor inclination to cook, and the insidious advance of the *four micro-ondes* (to which I still have not succumbed), respect for food is now rapidly yielding to *la restauration rapide*.

In the years preceding the takeaway and long before the high street emporia overflowed with beguiling boxes of chicken kiev, salmon en croute, and other *préparées* foods which could not hold a candle to the leek tarts, stuffed tomatoes and spit-roasted chickens of the simplest *traiteur* in the smallest French village – it was the remorseless dailyness of meals which vitiated. If I was going to have to cook, twice a day, seven days a week, for so many hungry mouths, I was, in accordance with my temperament ('when I dance I dance; when I sleep I sleep...*'), determined to do it properly.

My skills to date had been picked up from my maternal grandmother who – in the days before they were big business – had little use for cookery books, and from a domestic science teacher whose horizons extended no further than the statutory wartime rock-cakes (made from reconstituted dried egg) and macaroni cheese made with powdered milk and the meagre weekly ration of Cheddar. I did learn, from this same lady, how to turn a worn sheet sides to middle, to darn socks over a

---

* Montaigne

wooden mushroom, and put in an elegant patch. With the dawn of the post-war consumer society with its theory of obsolescence, these accomplishments – together with knowing how to boil odd nylon stockings in a saucepan to make them a uniform colour, and render down ends of soap for laundry purposes – were quickly to become obsolete.

At the Cordon Bleu School we worked in pairs, each couple responsible for producing one course. At the end of the morning the *entrées*, the main courses, and the puddings we had made were set out on a table. Since we were able to buy the dishes at a nominal price and take them home, my cookery days were extremely popular with the family. In a very short time the predictable meat and two veg, were being replaced by *Carré d'Agneau à la Portuguese* with a Julienne of celery and potatoes or *Poulet Véronique* accompanied by *Endives Braisées*. On Mondays and Fridays *Tonille aux Pêches* or *Salambos à l'Orange* would usurp my unimaginative syrup pudding (not such a popular move) and my inevitable fruit crumble (a very popular move indeed).

At the school, neatly prepared vegetables, minutely chopped herbs, elegant cuts of meat, fish with accusing eyes, and detailed recipes typed in mauve, waited for us each day on scrubbed wooden tables. As we stewed and stirred, battened and beat till our arms ached (no electric beaters or blenders), the supervisors in their pristine white toques assisted and advised, whilst at the corner sink, her hands perpetually in water, a *plongeuse* disposed of our used pots and pans. We learned to make *potages* and pilafs, *rôtis* and *ragoûts*, *galettes* and *gâteaux*. We sweated vegetables, tossed crêpes, attacked egg whites in copper bowls with balloon whisks. It was not so much the Cordon Bleu recipes that stayed with me however. The secrets of these dishes

111

were published in the estimable book which was to become my 'bible' *Cordon Bleu Cookery* by Muriel Downes and Rosemary Hume (founders of the school) which accompanied the course.

In learning to cook well, as in learning to write well, it was the small print, the accurate observation, that mattered. No recipe book could satisfactorily tell how to remove the milk solids from butter in order to clarify it, show the optimum degree of caramelisation of sugar, demonstrate how to mend mayonnaise (blend it into fresh yolks), crush garlic cloves (salt and a palette knife), remove the globules of egg yolk which had contaminated the whites (with half eggshells), extract zest from orange skins (with sugar lumps), trim a piecrust with a stroke of the rolling pin and knock up the edges with the back of a knife. As we concassed and cleared, blanched and reduced, tied thyme and bay and parsley and lemonrind for our *bouquets garnis*, the journey from raw ingredients to seductively presented dish, was as satisfying as a day at the typewriter and equally creative. Years later I was to sit at the feet of a very different cook, Claudia Roden (later to become a friend), to whom all the paraphernalia of the above was a huge joke. As I spent leisurely days in her aromatic Hampstead kitchen over minuscule cups of Turkish coffee (with cardamom seeds or cinnamon according to her mood), stuffing misshapen vegetables (which we had to first to scrub), and rolling filo paste, and listening to traveller's tales of Bedouin tents and Persian markets, I learned that the cool discipline of Cordon Bleu, and the warmth and colour of Middle Eastern cookery (in which precise quantities and oven temperatures were irrelevant), were two very different kettles of fish.

112

Cooking the Books

'Just as half the trick of being a good cook is knowing how to shop properly – which bits of meat and vegetables to choose from all the others – so a large part of being a good novelist is knowing which bits of experience to discard.'* The fact that my knowledge of the world was limited, both by my sheltered upbringing and the fact that I was more or less tied to the home by my young family, has never left me short of ideas when thinking what to write. Novels dealing with the feelings and preoccupations of women are often contemptuously dismissed as a dumping ground for the personal emotions.

'Although it was busy work to look after all the children and restrain their wild pranks, though it was difficult to remember whose were all those little stockings and drawers, not to mix up the shoes for the different feet, and to untie, unbutton, and then do up again all the tapes and buttons, Dolly, who had always been fond of bathing herself and considered it good for the children, was never happier than when bathing with all the children. To go over all those chubby little legs, pulling on their stockings, to take the naked little bodies in her arms and dip them in the water, to hear their squeals of delight and alarm; and to see these little cherubs of hers gasping and splashing, their merry eyes wide with fright, was a great joy.'†

'Women's writing'. You can just hear the reviewer, who has not read his *Anna Karenin*!

Most novelists, if they have any sense, make use of the world about them. *The Commonplace Day*, my seventh novel, was

* A. N. Wilson
† Leo Tolstoy

inspired by two thoughts of Ralph Waldo Emerson, whose essays were, and are, some of my favourite reading: 'No day is commonplace if we had only eyes to see its splendour.' And: 'Life consists in what man is thinking all day.' The book opens with: 'I woke at seven and thought stewing steak and ring about the cooker then turned over and went to sleep again.' You did not need to be a clairvoyant to see where I got my idea. 'Elizabeth Westbury,' read the blurb, 'happily married with two children, is typical of the contemporary middle-class young woman who has the vague but disturbing impression that life is passing her by. From behind the bourgeois bulwarks of her dishwasher, waste-grinder and washing machine, she follows the junketings of the famous, the notorious and the wealthy in the daily press and feels that somewhere, somehow, she has been cheated. Of what? She does not know. She is happy and cannot pinpoint what it is she misses.'

The Commonplace Day was born from my own experience, at that time necessarily preoccupied with the so-called trivia (often confused with the unimportant) of domesticity. In this instance I took the 'fix' for Elizabeth Westbury from myself, in a fleeting moment, on a bad day, in which I had felt entrapped and suffocated by the demands of children, the responsibility of a house (my passport still affirmed I was its 'wife') and the Orwellian menace of labour-saving machinery in the kitchen. 'In *The Commonplace Day*', the blurb continued, 'Robert Tibber deftly exposes the turmoil in the mind of a woman who lives in a world part real, part fantasy... We follow her attempt to retain her identity against the tedious, repetitive demands of every day.' Having stepped into the shoes of my Elizabeth Westbury, I let my imagination soar. *The Commonplace Day* is not a confessional however, and whether or not it is autobiographical is immaterial. What matters is the truth it contains, and the way that truth is expressed. It is what is inside the soul and mind that is important, what Thomas Hardy called 'the sadness of things'. In fiction the *feelings* of the characters cannot and should not be fabricated. This is why at the end of a day, although the writer will have appeared to have expended no more physical energy than the typist, he finds himself emotionally drained.

The Commonplace Day (later to be reworked as *The Long Hot Summer*) was received with delight by Hodder & Stoughton, in the person of John Attenborough the deputy chairman. 'May I offer you our very sincere congratulations on *The Commonplace Day* a most excellent novel, which it will be a very great pleasure to publish.' In leaving the social and external events of the 'doctor' books, and infiltrating the inner and psychological world of Elizabeth Westbury, my new novel was to reveal my true preoccupation as a writer and mark the end of my apprenticeship. *The Commonplace Day* was widely reviewed, this time making *The Times Literary Supplement* in addition to the national and regional newspapers. The subject of the book, 'a theme with a universality which is comparatively rare in contemporary fiction', was designated variously by the critics as 'adroitly and amusingly handled', 'a human and often humorous story', 'a skilfully drawn portrait'. The *Daily Mirror* pronounced *The Commonplace Day* 'a winner', whilst the *Yorkshire Post* compared and contrasted it with Margaret Drabble's *The Garrick Year*, which came out at the same time, had a similar theme, and was also written in the first person. Whereas Margaret Drabble, however, quickly became a household name, Robert Tibber, despite the best efforts of the publisher, widespread coverage, and excellent reviews, made little impression on the literary establishment. If one looks hard enough for excuses one can usually find them. *No White Coat* had had the misfortune to be published at the same moment as Richard Gordon's popular *Doctor in the House* (later to be successfully filmed); the confusion and lack of identity caused by my use of a man's name; my apparently unfortunate versatility (novels, plays, short stories), and the fact that I was not content like Picasso (or annually predictable novelists such as Anita Brookner) to stand on the balcony 'painting the same view over and over'. I am fortunate that I have never been 'seduced into thinking that that which does not make a profit is without value.'*

It was at about this time that I became aware of what is known in the trade as the 'rave rejection'. *Visitor from Seil* had provoked a rare personal letter from the great Binkie Beaumont (of H. M. Tennant) himself who 'regretfully' turned it down, whilst the Curtis Publishing Company of New York had favourably compared *The Fraternity* with the novels of Muriel Spark, although they could not see their way to publishing it in the United States. The 'near miss', in which one's work is warmly received but where the publisher does not put his money where his mouth is, is often harder to take than the harsh reality of the unqualified rejection, some of them downright offensive (Samuel Becket was once told 'I wouldn't touch this with a barge-pole') with which every author, no matter how illustrious, is familiar.

A letter from a script editor at the BBC, to whom I sent a play specially tailored for their 30-minute theatre slot – *The Special Occasion*, written between *The Fraternity* and *The Commonplace Day* – typifies the writer's dilemma: '. . . the only reason for

* Arthur Miller

116

this rejection is the length. *Fifty* minutes is now the length and I do not think this policy is likely to change for a long time...' The situation, particularly in the capricious world of TV, has not altered. If you suggest a 'series', the producers are looking for a 'one-off'. If you happen to have a 'one-off' handy, they are looking for 'soaps'. Despite the fact that in both fiction and drama it is often a no-win situation, it is useless to try to climb upon the current bandwagon. By the time you have provided the powers-that-be with whatever it was they were 'desperate for' at the moment of enquiring, by the time you have produced it, the bandwagon – in accordance with some mysterious and unfathomable principle – will have inexorably moved on.

Three Chimneys, our new house, with its half-acre of garden, proved an endless source of delight. My writing was done in an annexe adjoining the bedroom (originally intended as a dressing-room) in which I sat facing the leaded-light window in full view of a weeping-willow tree which I could also see from my bed. Romantically (I had read the Mazo de la Roche *Whiteoaks* series as a young girl) I imagined that I would die here (peacefully and in old age of course), within sight of it. We were so happy, and had so much space in which we could all move around, that it seemed no longer necessary for me to drive to Birchington each weekend in our estate car (my husband joined us later on the train), crammed to the gills with small children, large dog (a lugubrious collie later to play a major role in *The Long Hot Summer*), and carry-cots etc. We were sorry to leave Birchington and Little Stainton, our cottage 100 yards from the sea where, in the annual summer fête, one of our daughters had won the Beautiful Baby competition and another walked off with the Fancy Dress prize as 'Mrs Mop'.

THE WRITING GAME

One of the paradoxes of escaping – apart from having to worry about the plumbing – is that if you do it too often it becomes routine. For this reason I have always been ambivalent about second homes, especially when there were so many people who did not even have one roof over their heads. On the one hand it was a chore to load the car on Friday evenings with children, children's friends, belongings, and provisions in cardboard boxes, and transport them through the traffic to reinstate them in another place – in which some disaster, leaking roof or cracked pipe, had more often than not occurred since one's last visit – and to pack up the unappetising remnants of food in the selfsame cardboard boxes and reverse the process some 48 hours later. On paper this looked incredibly stupid. But magically, away from it all, stimulated by other sights, other sounds (other plates and teaspoons), as one's pace slowed and time expanded, life assumed another dimension the benefits of which were apparent in the energy and enthusiasm with which one faced the week ahead on Monday morning.

Sixties snapshots in the family album seem to be dappled with perpetual sunlight as work progressed, children grew and formed lifelong friendships, and our four girls developed imperceptibly into young women. Into this nirvana, uninvited, crept every writer's most feared enemy, the black dog of depression.

CHAPTER NINE

Enter the Black Dog

<hr/>

'Those who have become eminent in philosophy, politics, poetry and the arts have all had tendencies towards melancholia.'

Aristotle

When depression arrived, apparently from nowhere, struck with the velocity of a cricket ball, and stayed around to blight my present and bedevil my future, I joined what fellow author, William Styron, who came out of the closet of mental illness with *Darkness Visible*, referred to as 'the legion of the damned'.

In Freudian terms, artistic creativity is a form of sublimation; both art and the artist are pathological phenomena. Georges Simenon, outwardly a prolific and financially successful author, wrote that 'Writing is not a profession but a vocation of unhappiness'. Doris Lessing thinks that 'if you are a writer, by definition it seems to me you are pretty neurotic', whilst Proust, a self-acknowledged neurotic, alleged that 'Everything great comes from neurotics. They alone have founded religions and composed great masterpieces.'

Imagination, originating from dissatisfaction, may produce fears and anxieties but from these are born music, art and literature. 'I live in a constant state of over-excitement. So much do my work and conception thrill me it is almost too much for me and I am always feeling rather ill. One seems to work at the expense of one's body and there is no other way of doing it.'*

'Nervy, insecure and self-absorbed, first-rate writers are all too rarely first-rate people. The moral grandeur of Tolstoy's writings can be found only intermittently in his life; and the strength, humanity and elegance of Proust's masterpiece provide a piquant contrast to the invalidism, malice and occasional sadism which marked his increasingly hermetic existence.'†

Many great artists have had to 'pay' in some measure for their gifts. Milton was blind and Beethoven deaf, Flaubert, de Maupassant, Baudelaire and Gauguin suffered from sexually transmitted disease, Coleridge and Elizabeth Barrett were hooked on drugs, Keats and Chekhov had consumption, Dostoevsky was epileptic and the Brontë sisters never in perfect health. Anthony Burgess suffered from 'extreme depression' and George Orwell spoke of the 'prolonged illness which is the labour of writing a book'. While not all creative people are notably disturbed, it seems clear that if you are in perfect health and have nothing to worry about, you do not write great plays or

* Mark Gertler
† Francis King

compose great symphonies, make discoveries or uncover the unconscious. Although it is acknowledged that creative work often protects the artist from mental breakdown, there is a high rate of suicide (Virginia Woolf, Sylvia Plath, Romain Gary, Jean Seberg, Ernest Hemingway, Primo Levi) amongst writers.

In a recent study of British writers and artists selected for their eminence by their having won major awards or prizes, it was found that 38 per cent of them had at some time received treatment for the mood disorder, of whom 75 per cent had had antidepressants or lithium prescribed or had been hospitalised. These findings were not without precedent. Charles Lamb, Samuel Johnson, Goethe, Balzac, Tolstoy, Conrad and Ruskin all suffered from affective disorders; Kafka was schizoid, and Dostoevsky, de Maupassant and Nietzsche had organic brain disease. Boswell's account of Dr Johnson (who looked upon himself as thoroughly useless) depicts a writer dogged by depression throughout his life:

'He felt himself overwhelmed with a horrible hypochondria, with perpetual irritation, fretfulness and impatience and with a dejection, gloom and despair which made existence misery. From this dismal malady he never afterwards was perfectly relieved and all his labour and all his enjoyments were but temporary interruptions of its baleful influence.'

George Painter traces Proust's mental instability back to the time when his mother forgot to give the impressionable seven-year-old his customary goodnight kiss. Kafka's frequent 'sense of nothingness' arose from his father's indifference which led him to doubt his own validity as a person. Proust's view of the world was coloured by the impossibility of love, whilst Kafka's was dominated by a sense of helplessness.

THE WRITING GAME

'To be treated as if one hardly existed, as if one counted for nothing, is to live in a world in which, since power is in the hands of others, there is no way of predicting what is going to happen. Although the human infant is entirely dependent upon those who care for him, he is equipped with means for indicating his needs. If those needs are met in a way which is rational and considerate, he will grow up to conceive of the world as likely to be rational and considerate. Thus, if he is fed when he is hungry, allowed to sleep when he is tired, played with when he is lively, and cleaned when he is wet and dirty, there will appear to be a firm connection between what goes on in the external world and what he himself is feeling. But suppose that the infant's feelings are not considered; that he is fed when adults happen to think of it; that he is kept awake when he wishes to sleep, and put down to sleep when he wishes to be played with; that he is picked up and moved around at the whim of adults, without reference to his protests. For such a child the world will seem incomprehensible and unpredictable. Because what actually happens is unrelated to his feelings, it will appear to him that the world is ruled by capricious giants whom he cannot influence. Moreover, one can see that such a dislocation between the inner and outer worlds of the child must lead to an intensified preoccupation with fantasy and a sense of despair. If one can neither understand the world nor gain any satisfaction for one's needs from it, one is bound to be driven in upon oneself.'*

I have said earlier that my rigid and paternalistic upbringing in which *my* needs were neither considered, nor thought to be important, was responsible for my later breakdown. The above

* Anthony Storr

appraisal by Dr Anthony Storr who has made a study of depression amongst creative people, confirms this view.

It is not easy to describe clinical depression to someone who has not experienced it. It has nothing to do with the feelings of being down-in-the-dumps or unhappy – the inevitable consequences of a bad day at work or the breaking-up of a relationship – but is a biologically based state of hopelessness and paralysis affecting the mind and personality, in which one's entire perception of the universe suddenly, and for no apparent reason, becomes alarmingly distorted.

Those who have experienced this altered state – 'that ghastly lack of vitality that makes action impossible and utterance hard'* – which is as much an illness as coronary artery disease or arthritis, neither of which will respond to well-meaning advice such as that to take a hot bath, to 'cheer up' or 'snap out of it', will confirm that it is far more devastating, far more incapacitating than many physical ailments.

For the writer, one of the worst manifestations of depression is psychomotor retardation which inhibits coherent thought and effectively dries up his pen (Virginia Woolf stopped writing her diary, a sure sign of danger). It *is* possible to carry on working, to go through the motions, but since the symbols on the page become meaningless, and concentration difficult, if not impossible, one might just as well write out the list for the supermarket. In accordance with the writer's acknowledged habit of collecting every crumb from the table of his life and transforming it into a line or a story, I was able, some 20 years later, to make use of my own encounter with depression by dumping it on to the shoulders of pathologist Dr Jean Banks in A Second Wife:

* Cyril Connolly

───◆•◆───

...I was no longer Jean Banks, content, successful, but a dead and empty husk whose public image walked and talked and functioned, afraid that it would be found out for the hollow pastiche that it was. I lived in constant fear. That my paper-thin shell would be broken and it would become apparent, to my eternal shame, that there was nothing inside: not Sophie's friend, not my father's daughter ... not Jennie's sister, not even my own self whose facsimile discharged the obligations of the day and lived the terrors of the night, but did not exist. I thought I was ill. Physically I mean. Wearing my merry, coping mask, I conned my doctor into referring me for X-rays to establish a cause for the fatigue and chest pains, the cramps in my stomach, and the weight which I was losing. He prescribed alkalies to be taken before the meals I could not eat, when what I needed, although I did not know it then, was a sense, derived from loving and being loved, of my own worth.

I was a classic case. I did not communicate except on the most superficial level. With no one to define me, to reassure me of my existence, I became a robot, with no sense of reality and little grip on life. I was incapable of making the simplest decisions. Did not open my letters, let alone reply to them. I could not make up my mind what to put on in the mornings and when I did, changed it ten minutes later. It took me a lifetime to get dressed and I could not summon up the energy from my meagre resources to pick up my clothes from where, exhausted, I let them drop at night.

Craftily, at work, unaware how I had managed to transport myself, I went through the motions required of me. I picked fights over the most minor aberrations of my staff, causing them to stare at me open mouthed in consternation. When they spoke I listened but their words stopped short of the nimbus which surrounded me, and I did not hear. I walked nowhere for my legs were weak. I told my doctor who tested my plantar reflexes, scratching the soles of my feet. There were times when I became so inert that I could not, I swear I could not, get out of my chair. I sat alone in my consulting room with tears pouring down my face. Making telephone calls was a problem. Having mustered the energy to pick up the receiver, I would discover that I was unable to recall numbers I had thought engraved on my memory. When I did connect, my voice registered in apathetic whispers for which I blamed the line.

In my brighter moments, for there were times when the cloud lifted, I instigated projects, but when the time came to implement them my interest had gone. I arranged for tests on patients but was indifferent to the results; luckily I did not harm them. On bad days, pleading a cold, flu, migraine, backache, a host of nebulous complaints, I stayed at home where, sometimes for days, I did not leave my bed. It could not go on. I could not.

It could not go on. I could not. It was at this point that I sought help. The psychiatrist to whom I was referred asked me to describe how I felt. It was not easy when one's vocabulary had suddenly shrunk to that of a child's. I told him about the routine tasks and the difficulties I had in performing them; about the loss of self-esteem and the inertia precipitated by a heavy sense of gloom and hopelessness; about my guilt for something which was beyond my control – as if I had wished it upon myself – and my consequent self-loathing; about the resonance of voices, the garishness of colours, the grotesque distortion of familiar faces for which it was hard to find expression. Jean Banks explained it better:

I did not bother to cook. To bring food into the house. It was too much effort. The butcher, where you had to state your requirements, loud and unequivocal, to engage in dialectic be it about the liver or the weather, was out of the question. The supermarket was no better. I tried to explain how I had stood mesmerised before the display counter, blocking the path for other shoppers, trying to confer some sort of meaning onto quarters of chicken and pounds of mince. I had reached out for one of the film-covered plastic trays then put it back as furtively as any shop-lifter; tried again with another, but unable to endow it with any edible status from the recipe book of my blank mind, similarly replaced it. The delicatessen section did not help. Rosy mountains of taramasalata – no longer caviare to the general – ready-made salads, cheeses in a variety of textures from a dozen countries, strings of preserves, sausages, olives small and large and stuffed with pimientoes and green and black, and cooked meats. It was too much. When I was hungry I boiled an egg from the half-dozen left weekly by the milkman. When he rang the bell for his money and overcharged, the other Jean Banks, the one who functioned, did not argue. I let it go.

Clad in black, as if in mourning, which I was, although I could not identify my loss, I told the doctor, who had heard it all before, about the leaden weight I carried within my chest, about the sleepless nights, about the early waking, about the tears which sprang from nowhere, about the memory loss, about denting the car, about almost getting run over and not caring, and about the fact that *I could not write*, would never write again.

The treatment of depression has been revolutionalised in recent years by the introduction of antidepressants which alter the complex chemistry of the brain in a process which is not yet fully understood. The doctor assured me that my condition would respond to drugs, but in accordance with the truism that depression, while it lasts, is permanent, I did not believe him. I was not an easy patient. The smallest doses of the tricyclics I was prescribed produced intolerable side-effects whilst not alleviating the condition; monoamine oxidase inhibitors were worse. With dry mouth, trembling hands, and eyes unable to focus, I dragged myself reluctantly from the bed I had once been so enthusiastic to leave, for my weekly visits to the doctor. It was a long job. I got better. And I got worse. One step forward and two steps back. When I decided that the nightmare was no longer worth living and decided to do something about it, I was admitted to hospital. Twice. I wept and slept. What had gone wrong with this busy, efficient, fulfilled, competent, happy, productive, comparatively successful writer? It took me several years and a king's ransom to find out.

The drugs, by a long process of trial and error, did eventually work. They transformed me from a slim, miserable, mal-functioning sloth, into a fat, happy, malfunctioning sloth. I was writing, but the pills, which I was not allowed to stop, seemed to be doing it for me, and on quite another level. They saved my life on more than one occasion, but they were not the answer.

THE WRITING GAME

According to William Faulkner 'nothing can injure a man's writing if he is a first class writer', a view endorsed by Ernest Jones when considering the vexed problem of whether psychoanalysis is likely to impair or enhance artistic achievement:

'Many artists, both first-rate and second-rate, have now been analysed, and the results have been unequivocal. When the artistic impulse is genuine the greater freedom achieved through the analysis has heightened the artistic capacity, but when the wish to become an artist is impelled by purely neurotic and irrelevant motives the analysis clarifies the situation'.

When considering psychoanalysis, I was, like any creative person, fearful. If I poured out my innermost thoughts to a stranger would there be anything left to write about? What if I excavated my psyche to such an extent that nothing remained for my books? The drab analysts in their drab rooms to whom I would not have divulged my date of birth without a struggle, and the odd-ball analysts from whom I made a hurried escape, all sought to reassure me.

After a patient search for a therapist with whom I would be happy to embark on the search for my *id*, my *ego*, and my *superego*, I found a pleasant, middle-aged, *mittel* European lady, living in NW3 (where else?) upon whose eclectic couch I committed myself to lie, for one hour, every weekday afternoon, for as long as it took.

'Psychoanalysis', strictly speaking, refers only to those techniques evolved from the work and theories of Freud. These techniques have recently been rubbished by the pill-pushing school of psychiatry – which explains depression purely in physico-chemical terms – and have in many cases now been replaced by shorter term treatment methods such as behaviour therapy (desensitisation and flooding), light therapy, cognitive therapy (changing negative patterns of thinking), interpersonal therapy (dealing with relationships), and a host of other therapies. I was as unaware of any of this as I was of the rituals of psychoanalysis itself – the quiet room, the couch, the analyst's seat behind it, the omission of greeting, the immutable length of the session – designed to help the patient to get in touch with his inner world. Unaware of what I was letting myself in for (other than in terms of time and money), I made my pilgrimage to Belsize Park, five times a week, for seven years, with no time off for good behaviour.

Bearing in mind all my other commitments, it was not easy. That I found it beneficial was testified to by the fact that no matter how often I was tempted to, no matter how arduous I found the journey, how impatient I became with my analyst, how difficult I became at times to live with, how impossible it seemed to continue to find the time and the money, I did not give up.

We never emerge the same from any experience. It is hard to quantify the results of psychoanalysis, which is partly the reason why it has, in some quarters, fallen into disrepute. During the course of the analysis one pours one's innermost thoughts, fears, feelings, anxieties, hopes, into the ears of a non-judgemental listener, confident that one's confessions will never be divulged. 'What mattered about talking,' Freud said, 'was not only what the patient says, but who he or she says it to.' It is not the catharthis which cures, but the voyage of understanding (on which one is gently guided by the analyst) on which one embarks, which leads eventually to the healthy fusion of the external world and one's own feelings.

The Life Situation (1977) was, significantly, the first novel I

wrote under my own name. Although psychoanalysis was by no
means the subject of the book, in it I made full use of my daily
pilgrimage to Belsize Park. Oscar John is a writer in mid-life
crisis, his analyst the Viennese Dr Adler:

'Has anyone told you what psychoanalysis entails?'
'Partly. Long, expensive, and at the end of the day you may
well be exactly where you started.'
'Nobody comes out of analysis exactly the same as when
he enters it. You may still become depressed at times but
you will have learned the reasons which underlie it and
should be able to cope with it in such a way that it will not
last too long nor be so severe. Yes, it is time-consuming. I
would want to see you five times a week. Your session will
be at the same time each day and will last for fifty minutes.
At the end of each month I shall give you a bill. If you miss
a session other than through illness, you will pay for it.
That time is yours. I keep it for you and cannot use it any
other way. I take eight weeks' holiday a year, two at
Christmas, two at Easter, four weeks in the summer.'
'Suppose my holidays don't coincide with yours?'
Dr Adler shrugged. 'You will make them coincide ... If
you are late for a session you lose the time.'
'How do I know that you are going to be able to help me?'
'You don't.'
'For how long will I have to come?'
'Impossible to say.'
'You must have some idea. Do most of your patients come
for three weeks, a year, ten years?'
'It varies.'
'How will I know when the analysis has ended?'

'We shall decide that together.'
'About my writing. I think it will do it harm.'
'Are you writing now?'
'No.'
'In analysis a writer with nothing to say will come to realise it. A real writer ... can only benefit. Your wife will be better because you have learned to use your insight.'

My illness and subsequent analysis took a good chunk out of my life and, although it now seems incredible, almost no one knew about it. Depression is more common than diabetes, strikes indiscriminately, and is no respecter of sex, age, class or status, but it was not then done to talk about it. As mental illness has gradually became more acceptable and depression is no longer regarded as an admission of poor character or weak will or as self-indulgence (depressives feel they have no self to indulge), therapists have flourished and opinion about this disabling syndrome, now recognised as the disease it is, has changed. Writers, in particular, are no longer ashamed to admit to bouts of depression of varying degree, and I do not know one who has not at some point in his life experienced what Winston Churchill called the 'black dog' on his shoulder.

Depression can be cured, but paradoxically it rarely goes away. I have never had a recurrence of the condition in its most acute and intolerable form, but am frequently reminded, by unsuspecting moments of doom, self-limiting days of despair, that it is always waiting in the wings.

CHAPTER TEN

Who's Your Publisher?

'Live all you can; it's a mistake not to.'
Henry James

Despite the inroads made into it by my illness, life went on. Hodder & Stoughton published Robert Tibber's *The General Practice* (1967) and *Practice Makes Perfect* (1969), which brought to an end the 'doctor' books. Both of these titles were well received, serialised on radio, and translated. I was considered a sufficiently prestigious author to be taken by my publisher on a personal tour of Harrods' Book Department to meet the manager (Mr John Whiting), and the book buyer (Mr Van Danzig), and to Truslove and Hanson in Sloane Street to be introduced to their Miss Hawker. This was followed by lunch with the managing director of Hatchards, Tommy Joy, and another with the group director of John Menzies (which I learned to pronounce 'Mingies') Mr Norman Wilson OBE. I was courted by Hodder & Stoughton's fiction editor, Elsie

132

Who's Your Publisher?

Herron, over lunch at the Mermaid Theatre, and by Robin Denniston – who outlined exciting plans for my future writing career – at the Caprice. After all this, it came as a considerable shock when in 1974 – almost *two months* after I had delivered the manuscript of *The Life Situation* – I found the door of Hodder & Stoughton, with whom I had had such a good relationship for over 20 years, slammed in my face.

These days, when most publishers are part of huge conglomerates which are run by accountants swayed by cash-flow rather than literary considerations, such cavalier treatment of respected authors is commonplace and writers have had to shift (as did Anthony Trollope) between a variety of firms. That there are too many books published is (according to T. S. Eliot) one of the evils of democracy, but there are many household names who have been loyal to one publisher for all of their long writing careers who suddenly find themselves dismissed and as 'mid-list' (the kiss of death) authors have considerable difficulty in finding a home for future books. Barbara Pym, summarily rejected in 1963 by Cape after four books, is a case in point, but at least she had her friend, Philip Larkin, to pick her up and dust her down.

I can see now, after a lifetime of hacking my way through the dense undergrowth of the literary jungle, that I was lucky to have had so many years of carefree writing behind me before coming face to face with one of the many disappointments which, for many novelists, are par for the course.

It was not so much the rejection which hurt, but the manner of it. Coming from Hodder & Stoughton, whom I would have said were incapable of treating their authors in such a way, I was taken aback.

The bombshell arrived in the form of a letter from a lady of whom I had never heard and whose status within the firm was not indicated. The gist of it was, that whilst agreeing that my new book was 'very professionally written, touching and humorous at times', there were various elements which 'detracted' overall. The sum of these elements led to Hodder & Stoughton regretfully declining the offer to publish the novel, a decision based on the changes which had overtaken the publishing world and the rising costs of producing a book, as a result of which the 'general novel' had gone to the wall. Had I not lost my *fidus achates*, Joyce Weiner, I firmly believe that the matter would not have been allowed to rest there.

It had been a great disappointment, on 1 February 1971, to receive a letter from Miss Weiner announcing her retirement. The decision had been taken on the advice of her doctors – because of poor health – and she was anxious to give up work *before* she became unable to maintain the high standards she had set herself throughout her professional life, or to retain the personal touch, which had given her literary agency its individual character for the past quarter of a century. The letter continued:

'Though this agency will cease to function on the above-mentioned date, its work will be carried on independently on her own account, and under her own name, by Mrs Deborah Owen at 78, Narrow Street, London E14 8BP. Mrs Owen, though young, has had considerable agency and publishing experience on both sides of the Atlantic, comes from a well-known American publishing family and is married to Dr David Owen, MP for Plymouth, Sutton Division. She is serious and enthusiastic and possesses both charm and efficiency, and I have every confidence that she will take care of your interests sensitively and energetically.'

Who's Your Publisher?

I remained with Deborah Owen (whose husband was later to become Foreign Secretary) for nine and a half years but she was not Joyce Weiner (they don't make agents like that any more). When the rejection of *The Life Situation* came from Hodder & Stoughton, Miss Weiner would not only have demanded to know the reason they had seen fit to treat one of their authors in such a manner, but would have insisted on a meeting with the managing director whom she would confront on my behalf. Although Deborah Owen sympathised with my feelings, she accepted the publishing decision.

Taking the matter into my own hands, I wrote to Michael Attenborough. His prompt letter in reply was apologetic. He was sorry not to have kept in touch in with me since publishing *Practice Makes Perfect* in 1969, but there had been many changes at St Paul's House. Robin Denniston had left Hodder & Stoughton in the spring of 1973, and Elsie Herron had retired the same year. The person who had written to me was one of their senior editors, and although her decision on *The Life Situation* rested, she would 'value the opportunity to meet with you and talk over your future work'.

I did not take up the offer. Although my hurt pride was somewhat mollified by the courteous communication from Michael Attenborough, which I should have received in the first place, I had to face the fact that after so many years of being cocooned from the harsh realities of publishing, I was out there, holding the manuscript of *The Life Situation*, on my own.

I did not want to leave my baby on the first doorstep. The imprint on the spine of a book is to the practised reader (as well as to literary editors) as significant as its title. The publisher's logo, like the brand name on a tin of beans, is an indication of what manner of book you are likely to find inside the covers.

THE WRITING GAME

You would not expect – and probably would not get – romance from Methuen, science fiction from Cape, literary biography from Mills and Boon. Today, when musical chairs in the corporate boardrooms has played havoc with publishers' identities, the boundaries, though less well defined, are still observable to the cognoscenti. There is an elitism (which has been known to disintegrate in the face of an unrefusable advance offered by an editor) amongst authors. A Cape author considers himself a cut above a Weidenfeld & Nicolson, a Faber & Faber above a Bloomsbury, a Bloomsbury above a Hodder Headline. When it became obvious that it was not a question of which publisher I would have, but which publisher would have me, I consoled myself with the fact that if you took a poll of serious readers, I doubt if a single one of them would be able to tell you the name of George Eliot's, or Jane Austen's, publisher.

The 1970s was a decade not only of a giant leap for mankind, but of changes for me in both my writing and my personal life. Between the writing of *Practice Makes Perfect* and *The Life Situation*, both my parents died, with very little fuss, and unexpectedly (fortunately for me whilst I was still in analysis), in the prime of their early 60s. I say 'with very little fuss' with some surprise, because in life both my mother and father verged towards the neurotic end of the spectrum of fussiness. It was not my first experience of death, having lost the three grandparents that I knew, but when one's parents pass on leaving one ostensibly at the head of the line for the great party in the sky – all receive invitations, refusals not accepted – Death requires more serious consideration. It assumes a capital letter.

My father died first, from leukaemia. It seemed no time at all between the evening he came home from the golf course with a large, unexplained bruise on his arm, to the February day when

136

we huddled sadly at the graveside to lay him to rest beneath his blanket of snow. Today, with the advance of medicine, it is possible that he might still be alive; leukaemia is one of the diseases we are in the process of licking. Neurotically as my father had responded, throughout his life, to every cough and cold, every minor ache and pain, he bore the wretched treatment, which included monthly bone-marrow biopsies, like a trooper. Although he knew, must have known, what he was suffering from, he never acknowledged the true nature of his illness, and in the face of his denial no one was ever brave – or cruel – enough to confront him with the name of his complaint. Taking the lead from him, throughout the long months of therapy, the attendances at the clinic, the frequent admissions to Bart's Hospital, those about him kept up the fiction of 'pernicious anaemia'. Despite the daily family vigil at his hospital bedside, he died alone in the night, a pathetic shadow of his former self fortunately no longer aware of the pain and indignity of his condition, hooked up to the loops and tubes that infused the failing mechanism of his unconscious body.

It would be poetic, but untrue, to say that my still youthful and pretty mother, who had borne the brunt of the past months, succumbed from grief. My parents' had been a pre-women's consciousness-raising marriage in which my mother, the proverbial woman of worth, was content to occupy herself solely with the 'ways of her household'. The two of them had been as inseparable, as interdependent, as their roles in the partnership were clearly defined. My gentle mother did not know how to live without her partner, and I suppose that in a way it was fortunate that she was not called upon to do so for more than 13 unhappy and bewildered months.

If my father's death had been an object lesson in denial – he never once mentioned the possibility of his untimely death – my mother's was an even greater one. To this day I have not fathomed the mysteries or strengths of it. She had always had a subjective interest in medicine and when she came to visit us she could not wait to settle down with my husband's *British Medical Journal.* She knew the difference between *hypo-* and *hyper*glycaemia, angina and infarct, haemoptysis and haematemesis, and having assessed her real or imagined symptoms against those in the journal, she would arrive at a diagnosis. Five years before my father's death, a pigmented mole on her leg, the plimsoll line by which she had always measured the length of her dresses, had been excised, and was found to be malignant; by the time of his burial, metasteses from the initial growth had invaded her mouth and defaced her body. Although she must have realised their significance, she chose to ignore them. The word 'melanoma' was never mentioned.

My mother had always been slim, but with what seemed unseemly haste she rapidly became slimmer. During her decline (she was not as my father had been, ill or in pain) our eldest daughter became engaged to be married, and my mother was determined to make the wedding. In accordance with the precedence of the last grisly year, her imminent death was never mentioned. We did not know if she was afraid of dying. We never discovered her views on the matter. As the dress she was having made for the wedding had to be taken in more and more with each fitting, her three children went along with the charade, and no one mentioned the weight loss, the fact that our mother was fading away before our eyes. She did not go into hospital, except for one blood transfusion, a week before her demise, during which she applied her nail strengthener. She had always been proud of her nails.

Who's Your Publisher?

'My mother's death was a beautiful experience for me. Death had only to smile at her and take her by the hand.'*

One week before her granddaughter's wedding, with her family around her, my mother died, at home and in her own bed, as quietly, as neatly, as elegantly as she had lived. It seemed so easy.

Even for those who are no longer dependent upon their parents, losing them is probably the most psychologically catastrophic event in life. The weeping of the aged for predecessors they scarcely remember, the cries of the demented for their mothers, are firm indicators that the adult is also always the child, and that the psyche knows no age.

There were other 'life situations' to enter this fraught period of my life. As I left my father's grave I found myself pregnant for the fifth time, a circumstance which led not only to decisions concerning a woman's prerogative over her own body, but to poetic thoughts upon the presence of life in death. After the events of the past year, aware that the next one was to be even more traumatic, and in the face of the fact that my existing family was at long last growing up, I took the view (endorsed by my husband and, I suspect, by my analyst who never gave a firm opinion about anything) that, with the best will in the world, another child was more than I could cope with. In theory I was a supporter of the rights of the foetus. Circumstances, however, significantly alter cases, and I elected to have an abortion. I have never ceased to be grateful that nature, in its infinite wisdom, intervened, and I did not have to go through with it.

During my mother's last months I became ill myself, an iatrogenic illness in which I almost bled to death (the story of

* Jean Cocteau

which would make a book in itself), which resulted in a major operation (removing the risk of further pregnancies) at a time when I was already debilitated by events. I was scarcely recovered in time to hold my mother's hand as she lay dying, and to stand by the wedding canopy beneath which my eldest daughter was the ethereal bride.

I mention all this because, although it is not war or revolution, insurrection or siege, it is human life, the fabric of the finest fiction, the stuff that books are made from.

The seeming 'unfairness' of my parents' deaths, they had sown but by no means fully reaped, added to the poignancy of it. I dealt with my bereavement, and immortalised my parents, by internalising their lives – I still hear their voices – and using their deaths in my work; Dr John in *The Life Situation*, Sydney Shelton in *Proofs of Affection*, Caroline Osgood in *An Eligible Man*. A more concrete monument to them was the small house I bought at the seaside with the legacy they had left.

I have always been a gambler. On my mother's side of the family one cousin was a well-known boxing referee, another a frequenter of casino tables and his son an international backgammon player. Since, at the age of six, I learned to roll pennies down a chute at Dreamland, the erstwhile amusement park in Margate, to watch them land clumsily on lines (you lost), or neatly in squares (you won), I have always been fond of having a fling (I have to be forcibly restrained from the roulette tables), of chancing my arm.

When G. K. Chesterton and his wife decided to buy a country home they had no idea where to look. Getting on a train at Paddington (which happened to be going to Slough), they tramped round all day until they finally came to Beaconsfield where they meekly bought a house.

Who's Your Publisher?

On one rainy day in Brighton, I watched labourers dig sodden holes in the ground on the site of the old Kemp Town brewery, on which there were plans to build a new square of town houses. Having nothing better to do, and probably to get out of the wind which is a permanent feature of that corner of the Sussex coast, I went into Bernard Thorpe, the estate agent, to inspect the architect's drawings. By the time I came out I had put down a deposit on 6 Seymour Square, and we became the quixotic possessors of a country house in town and a town house by the sea.

I loved Brighton, with all its sleaze, all its coach parties, all its winkles and warts, all its overflowing rubbish bins, all its dog-fouled pavements. To walk along the winter promenade, when the day-trippers had departed, zipped up against the stiff breeze, watched by the eyes of Georgian windows from the façades of decaying buildings – Brighton was in a permanent state of decay – was to hear the pounding of the sea against the shingle, the plaint of gulls, to feel the raw exhilaration of the elements, to throw off the slough of the working week, and to have time, and a head that was crystal clear, to think.

We kept Seymour Square, where from their balconies the neighbours looked out to sea with telescopes and everyone knew everyone else's business – a bit like *Under Milk Wood* – for seven happy years. We kept it until, every Easter, every summer, every Christmas, the little house would be filled with family, and dogs, and friends, and uninvited guests (with their sleeping bags) who would offer to help with the chores but were more trouble than they were worth. When the situation became ridiculous, and holidays a nightmare of catering and stepping over bodies in the living-room, we called it a day, and with some regret for number six with its Italian garden, for Brighton with its Victorian piers, its Lanes, its cosy Saturday nights in the plush seats of the Theatre Royal, we packed up the car for the increasingly tedious journey back to London, for the last time. We were left not only with happy memories of Brighton but, as a result of my precipitate action, with a tidy profit. We sold the house in the heady days of the upswing of the property market, during which the value of our little box – through the flimsy walls of which you could hear the neighbours blow their noses – had quadrupled.

'Once he reached Brighton he always followed the London Road right down to the promenade, enjoying his very first glimpse of the pier, which seemed to have endured forever, and the sea. Today the sun was shining and the sea was blue. One could almost kid oneself that it was the Mediterranean, until one got out of the car and into the biting wind – his mother called it "keen".'

This paragraph, in which I made use of my experience of Brighton, is from *The Life Situation* which no one was falling over themselves to publish, and which so far had come a cropper. Having tried several publishers, who were suffering the same difficulties and decline in the book trade as Hodder & Stoughton, Deborah Owen finally managed to place it with Barrie & Jenkins, publisher of the Flashman books. My relationship with Barrie & Jenkins, unlike that with Hodder & Stoughton, was not a happy one. They kept my typescript for several months before deciding that they would like to publish it. They delayed the publication for more than a year. They took for ever over the dotting of the 'i's and the crossing of the 't's and, at the very moment that my edited manuscript was due to go to the printers, they 'inadvertently' lost it.

CHAPTER ELEVEN

A Room of One's Own

'A woman must have money and a room of her own if she is to write fiction.'

Virginia Woolf

T. E. Lawrence, so the story goes, left the manuscript of *Seven Pillars of Wisdom* on Reading station; the first volume of Carlyle's *French Revolution* was accidentally burnt by a servant who used it to light the fire; the missing Boswell papers were later to turn up abroad as wrapping paper; Hemingway's wife lost a suitcase full of his unpublished work on the train from Paris to Lausanne where she was to join him on a skiing holiday, and Chatto and Windus had the typescript of Malcolm Lowry's *Ultramarine* stolen from the back seat of an open-topped 3-litre Bentley.

James Moore, editorial director of Barrie & Jenkins, wrote a letter offering his sincere apologies for losing the manuscript of *The Life Situation* which 'seems to have gone astray in our office'. He was, he said, the first to recognise that it was a 'most unsatisfactory state of affairs' and thanked me for my willingness to undertake the re-editing 'at such short notice'. What else could I do? At the time it seemed monstrous, not to mention time-consuming. Meticulous myself, I longed for the efficiency of Hodder & Stoughton who would never, I was sure, do anything as crass as lose a manuscript.

Patricia Parkin, my editor at Barrie & Jenkins, thought *The Life Situation* 'a very fine novel' about which she had few criticisms to make. From the point of view of selling paperback rights however, she felt that at 130,000 words the manuscript was too long. At her suggestion (in those days I still believed in the infallibility of editors), and in order not to reduce my chances of a paperback sale, I deleted 30,000 words from the text. Some months later Barrie & Jenkins' rights editor, Linda Shaughnessy, sent me the following letter which she had received from the paperback publisher, Coronet Books:

'Thank you so much for sending me Rosemary Friedman's *The Life Situation*, which I have enjoyed tremendously. It makes me very sad to turn down such a good novel, but I am afraid I just don't feel it's quite right for us. It has been a difficult decision to come to, especially as the novel makes compelling reading and I very much appreciated its blend of comedy and seriousness. However, I think it would be a difficult one to put over to the sales force and to package for the paperback market – at least, from our point of view ... Many thanks, though, for sending me such a very worthwhile book to consider.' I added this to the growing pile of rejections in my 'rave rejection' file.

My relationship with Barrie & Jenkins, if not sweet, was mercifully short. Whether it was the strain of losing my manuscript or not (it certainly told on *me*) I don't know, but having published my novel they promptly went out of business. Although after a few months in the bookshops *The Life Situation*, published in 1977 (hardback only), appeared to be dying the death, a letter received in 1989 from John Stretch, Drama Department Script Unit at Granada Television, testified to the fact that, even 10 years later, it was not quite dead:

'...our reader's report was very enthusiastic and when I read the book myself I found it much more subtle, interesting and entertaining than most novels of its kind. Furthermore I felt that it would work perfectly on television and recommended it to our Drama Department as either a film or a mini-series, but the sad reply was that there's no place for it.'

With the demise of Barrie & Jenkins, for which I felt personally responsible, I was once more, as far as my writing was concerned, out there on my own. I was to write one more book, *The Long Hot Summer*, before we packed our bags and moved house again, this time to the metropolis, but the history of this particular novel deserves a chapter to itself.

I have said that I do not like the country. Like Woody Allen I consider it a place to drive to for the day rather than sleep in, and like Anthony Burgess find little stimulation in the nature of Wordsworth, believing that 'only as a civic being does man ... fulfil himself.' Least of all I like the 'pseudo-country' – those far flung suburbs, with their high streets and supermarkets, pretentiously referred to as 'villages' – to which we had moved in order to be near the patients. Since my husband was no longer a general practitioner, but had, in a mid-life about turn, espoused psychiatry and hospital medicine, we were at last free to choose the energising and liberating air of city life.

Although I was determined to keep an open mind, I was not

really interested either in flats in which there was neither space nor privacy, nor town houses, where there was little freedom for children and which had none of the nooks and crannies needed by families to supplement the basics of kitchen and bedrooms. Town houses never had rooms, never had cupboards – by which I mean integral cupboards – never had anywhere to keep things. Modern designers, modern architects, rarely consider where you are supposed to do the ironing and the sewing and wash the wellington boots, never take into account the storing of photographs (and photographic equipment), the boxes of books and bundles of papers, the garden chairs and umbrellas, the picnic rugs and paraphernalia, the old dolls' prams and puppet theatres, the hockey sticks and golf-clubs and garden cushions, the coats and the satchels. It took me five years to find a house, by which time I had become a laughing stock, and my determination to move away from the delights of the cricket ground and the duck pond, suspect, but I did not care. I refused to be intimidated. As my stack of estate agents' particulars outgrew even my rave rejection file, determined to see everything, I trudged round flats (converted and purpose-built) and houses (mews and town), descended to basements and climbed to penthouses, peopling them in my imagination with ourselves and our possessions. Many of the properties I saw were 'suitable' but none of them came up to expectation. I did not know what I was looking for. As in writing, my search was dictated by some inner logic that would, in the fullness of time, indicate its satisfaction.

The signal, Very lights blazing, came at the end of a particularly traumatic day. Some weeks before, I had seen a small but intriguing picture in the property section of a glossy magazine, of a strange, Gothic looking property by the side of an elegant, grey, twin-spired church. The text beneath it was enigmatic. 'A house in central London...' (No indication of precise location). '...10 rooms'. An immediate call to the estate agent did little to elucidate. It was early days, they said. They could not tell me much about the house at that 'moment in time', least of all its address. They took my name and promised to keep me posted. My follow-up calls were equally non-productive and I had relegated the mysterious property to the back-burner when, out of the blue, I received a call.

I had spent all day in central London looking at houses and struggled home in the rush-hour traffic, to find a message waiting. The Gothic house was on view, and had been all day, and if I wanted to see it I must present myself before six o'clock! My children were waiting for their supper, my husband for his dinner. I was exhausted. There is nothing more enervating than house-hunting. I turned tail and went straight back to town. When you live by intuition it is futile to attempt to account for your actions. You carry them out because you 'have to'. There is no point trying to rationalise.

St Katharine's Precinct was constructed in 1827 to replace St Katharine's Hospital, a home and hospital for poor men and women of clerical connections, which originally stood near the Tower of London. The St Katharine's Dock Company, to whom the hospital had been sold, undertook to build a new chapel, and houses for the master, the brothers, the sisters and the bedeswomen, which became, by royal appointments, 'grace and favour' houses with a clerical bias. The new buildings, situated in Regent's Park, and designed by Ambrose Poynter (a *protégé* and hated rival of Nash), were Gothic in style and, being bare of stucco, bore no resemblance to the other houses in the park.

THE WRITING GAME

As I turned the car into the quadrangle with its central obelisk, its railinged lawn, its Cambridge-like *gravitas*, I knew that not only had I stumbled upon an exceptional situation but that my prolonged search for a house was over. That I had come home.

It was not surprising that the advertisement had not specified so many bedrooms, so many bathrooms, so many reception rooms, but had suspiciously referred only to 'rooms'. The lady from the estate agent's who grudgingly hurried me round the property – she had her coat on and was about to go home when I arrived – apologised for its decrepitude but said I must use my imagination. It was lucky that I had plenty of that.

The house was terraced, tall, narrow, and a rabbit warren of tiny rooms which clung like limpets to its five floors. It was dark, cold, damp, forbidding, unmodernised, and totally impractical. Crazed with desire, and without the blessing of my better half, I made an offer of the asking price and wildly undertook to carry out the renovations, which were way above our means, demanded by the Crown.

What sold it to me? Everything. Despite the inadequacy of the interior – I could not see it even housing our family – every window had a view (albeit sideways on) of Regent's Park. You could park outside your own front door – almost unheard of in central London. It had a walled garden, although in it, at certain times of day when the traffic raced round the Outer Circle, you could scarcely hear yourself speak. It had grace, charm, ambience, call it what you like, as soon as I saw it I knew that it was mine, that I could not live anywhere else. It was not so easy. I was a dreamer. I made plans, but like other Aquarians, was often incapable of carrying them out.

My husband liked St Katharine's Precinct as much as I did.

148

A Room of One's Own

Luckily he was born under Pisces. We are a good partnership. My five-year search for a house was over and he set about making my dream come true.

It was a long, long, haul. We had to sell our own house. We had to fend off other contenders for St Katharine's Precinct. We had to satisfy the Crown Commissioners of our intentions, spelled out on a million architects' plans, before they agreed to grant us a 60-year lease. Victorious, but homeless, we adopted a nomadic existence; for two years imposed ourselves, and our few possessions that were not in storage, upon accommodating friends. The house had to be replumbed, rewired, damp-proofed, protected against dry rot, wet rot and all manner of infestation.

Every floor had to be taken up, every ceiling had to come down, and every joist to be replaced. If the building firms (which came and went) did not carry out the renovations to the satisfaction of Her Majesty's building surveyor, who with his beady eye all but took up residence, they had to be done again. Friends came to look at us, freezing cold and grey with plaster dust, in our folly. They said that we were crazy. At times I thought they might be right. Our daughters hated the house and declared that they were not going to live in it. Determined, like William Morris, to have nothing in our new house that I did not know to be useful or believe to be beautiful, I put away my typewriter and set up a trestle table on which were plans of power points, and samples of tiles (for the bathrooms), and bits of marble for the hearth), and snippets of material (for the curtains), and patterns of paint. As it usually does, order, eventually, began to emerge from the chaos. The house, our house, began to take shape and I did not care that the decorator, in the moment in which I had turned my back, had hung the bedroom wallpaper with its intricate motif – so assiduously selected and after many months of delay imported from France – upside down.

It is said that the trauma of moving comes third on the scale of stress after bereavement and divorce. I can well believe it. But in the long run, in the very, very long run, it was worth it. Not least because, after more than 20 years of writing, I had acquired a room of my own.

Erica Jong speaks of '...the quintessential oddness of the writer's life: living one extravagant imaginary life in your study, in your notebooks, in the library stacks, while another quotidian domestic life revolves around it.'

My new study was at the top of the house. It was not very large but intriguing in shape because of two indentations at the far end, forming false windows outside, and enormous cupboards (ideal for files and boxes of stationery) within. I chose a dull red, the shade of warm terracotta, for the carpet and hessianed walls, which gave the room a womb-like quality, later to be experienced by others as welcoming 'vibes'.

These vibes, present but inexplicable, like those of a confessional, draw family and friends up the three flights of steep stairs to sit on my brown sofa with its cross-stitch cushions embroidered long ago by childish fingers, to swivel on my 1960s Heal's chairs which had come from the old house (their headrests reminiscent of dentists'), to pour out their hearts, disclose their worries, rid themselves of the *angst* of their various lives. A sign hangs outside the door, 'Not To Be Disturbed'. It has long become part of the furniture and nobody takes any notice of it.

To describe the room, in which of all the house I am undisputed monarch, captain of my own ship, is to disregard its charisma, to assume foolishly that, like a Rembrandt painting, it is no more than a sum of its parts.

'All writers arrange objects around them a way that means nothing to anyone except their owner. Then you feel safe and can set out on some sort of voyage of the mind, knowing you're going to find your way back.'*

Contrary to stereotype, the true artist is often highly organised. My own version of what Mrs Trollope referred to as her 'sacred den', is furnished mainly with books, while a mahogany counter-top, running the length of one wall, serves as a desk. At one end of this, flanked by the reveal of the false window, is my noticeboard from which flap drawing-pinned proclamations, of PEN meetings, and conferences (medical and literary), screenings at BAFTA, and concerts at the Royal Festival Hall. There is a *Verjaardagkalendar* (brought by a friend from Holland), the pages of which, if you remember to turn them, list birthdays, of family, friends, and acquaintances, so that there is no excuse for forgetting. Above the noticeboard, from a framed, sepia photograph, my great-grandfather, flat cap on his head and seated in his Windsor chair at a table covered with a lace cloth, reads his Bible and appears to keep a watchful eye on me. A grey metal (ex-surgery) filing cabinet, within extended reach, houses writing paper and envelopes, labels and elastic bands. In the drawer marked 'Bank' are old cheque books, envelopes for Rapid Deposit filched from the NatWest, and a box of Kleenex tissues for wiping both my nose and the surplus black ink from the nib of the chubby Mont Blanc pen used to sign letters with which I hope to impress. Files, holding material for work in progress, top the cabinet, together with personal correspondence secured

* Redmond O'Hanlon

151

beneath a blue-and-gold glass paperweight from the Venice ghetto. The computer comes next. The flat, humming box on which stands a Woolworth's desk lamp, a kitsch, soapstone paperweight depicting an Alaskan bear denoting, according to my inner logic, 'writing' as opposed to 'personal' documents, a wooden bookrest, and coloured copy-paper defaced with scrappy notes concerning the project in hand. The monitor and the keyboard abut the computer 'works'. The window of my room looks out on to both our own garden – shrubs in winter, the far wall covered with jasmine, honeysuckle, and my beloved rambling rose, Zefferin Druhin, in summer – and the formal gardens of Cumberland Terrace which front the forbidding Nash houses, but when I am working I find it advisable to face the wall.

To raise my eyes from the computer screen is to be confronted with things past. Between the flat top of the desk and the first bookshelf are photographs and postcards affixed with Blu-tack to the wall. My daughters as babies and as brides; my husband, camera round his neck, beneath the blue skies of Ephesus, in a boat against the backdrop of shadowy mountains rising like gentle ghosts from the mists of the Li river at Guilin; my mother with her grandchildren; my father about to speak. Further on, past Titian's *Assumption*, Pissarro's self-portrait, Chagall's *L'Anniversaire*, Picasso's *Grand Baigneuse*, are New York's 'Russian Tea Room', Pierre Le Tan's *Window*, Manet's *Déjeuner Sur L'Herbe*. This is not the random collection it seems. The pictures measure out my life in bromide paper. Each one is a catalyst, evoking memories of place or person, mood or event. I have only to glance at them to take myself back in time or space, to relive forgotten journeys, to remember bygone days.

A Room of One's Own

———◆◆◆———

'Isadora's desk appeared a random mess but like the novel in progress it had an inner logic apparent only to its begetter.'*

At my right hand, old Rombouts coffee tins (covered in a fit of enthusiasm with decorative Contact paper) hold a collection of Biros (most long dried up), blunt Chinagraph pencils, pens inscribed with the names of museums and art galleries, serving as memorabilia. A hand-thrown pot, once filled with Greek yoghurt, contains sticks of Pritt and bottles of Tippex, a green china Victorian shoe (a present from a nephew) Rapid Markers and text-liners, and a wooden vase, bought at a Shanghai roadside, my fountain pen. An olive-wood pencil holder, from the Holy Land, with self-contained sharpener, has outlived its usefulness since I was introduced (by LWT) to the throwaway Non-stop Paper Mate with its propelling lead. A pair of 'gold' Asprey's paper scissors (recalling a generous dinner guest), a plastic paperclip holder, and a Ryman's desk calendar each page of which denotes a birthday – *Guiseppe Verdi October 10th 1813*, and provides a motto: 'Tact is a method of putting your foot down without treading on anyone's toes' – are placed in front of a woven basket of old personal telephone books, school rulers and pink blotting paper. A sellotape dispenser, stapler, card-index box, pocket calculator, and a two-hole punch adrift on the sea of whatever it is I am writing, complete the 'random mess'.

A new laser printer (replacing the illegible dot matrix and the dilatory 'desk jet'), its maw fed from the banks of coloured paper stored at its side, quietly and efficiently, transforms my prose into print. Farther on (we are still on the desk), in the

* Erica Jong

153

family snapshot frame, a grandson in his dressing-gown practises the violin, four daughters – women now – pose on a former nursery bed for a group snapshot, a granddaughter plays on a swing. By the far wall, an *Observer* cabinet (I am a mail-order junkie) holds cassettes for the nearby radio and CD player, and see-through storage boxes my collection of floppy disks.

Books: when she is putting her reading in order, Virginia Woolf asks a great many questions about canon-formation, and insists that great books must be set in the context of inferior, ordinary, forgotten books: trashy novels, obscure memoirs, especially of women's lives, dust-gathering volumes of letters, mediocre biographies, minor plays.* 'A literature composed entirely of good books' would soon be unread, extinct; the isolation is too great'. We need 'trivial, ephemeral books': 'They are the dressing-rooms, the work-shops, the wings, the sculleries, the bubbling cauldrons, where life seethes and steams and is for ever on the boil.' They fertilise our minds and get them ready for the big masterpieces. We can't always be reading Keats or Aeschylus or *King Lear*, so she defends the pleasures of bad books, the historical importance of the rubbish heap. 'One has only to remember the tone of the references to Dickens in Cranford ... to realize that his serial numbers were considered the fiction of the uncultivated and inherently "low".'†

I see books as sources of material and of information rather than of objects to collect. T. S. Eliot saw 'three permanent reasons for reading: the acquisition of wisdom, the enjoyment of art, and the pleasure of entertainment.' Mine is a reading

---

* Hermione Lee
† Q. E. Leavis

man's library. I am no more a book-lover than a people-lover and agree with Philip Larkin that 'it all depends what's inside them'. Like Proust – never a great collector of books – I feel that in an ideal world books should be read, assimilated and discarded, but it was Arnold Bennett who put his finger on it: 'the man who does not read books is merely not born. He can't see, he can't hear; he can't feel in any full sense, he can only eat his dinner.'

The shelf above my desk, more or less within arm's reach, is for telephone directories and single volume reference books. The big stuff, the encyclopaediae, are housed in another room. Dictionaries (language, slang, quotation, synonyms and antonyms, Latin Tags), Roget's *Thesaurus of English Words and Phrases*, Horwell's *Modern American Usage*, Fowler's *Modern English Usage*, *The Oxford Writers' Dictionary*, books of Dates and Events and Lists, Companions (to literature) and Concordances, cut down visits to the library. After this, my books, spiked with leather bookmarks collected from my travels, are roughly classified in sections on the shelves which span the walls and cover them from floor to ceiling: Philosophy, Psychology, Anthropology, Essays, Music and Opera, Belles-Lettres, Biography, Literature, Poetry and Drama, Religion, Classics, 'Books About' – gardening, swimming, writing, film making etc., and Modern Novels. There is a horizontal stack of books to do with the book on which I am working, another of 'books to be read'. I buy the latter at random so that when I have a moment of leisure, or am going on holiday, I am never at a loss but have something lined up, chosen in tranquillity, to read.

A quick glance round the shelves reveals Dante and Milton, Homer and Shakespeare, Bacon and Montaigne, Nietzsche and Freud, Plato and Proust, Dickens and Dostoevsky, Wells and

Woolf. The *History of Tom Jones* and the *Journals of Dorothy Wordsworth* juxtapose a row of contemporary feminist diatribes. Volumes on Judaism (research for *Proofs of Affection*), legal books (for *An Eligible Man*), and Holocaust literature (for *Rose of Jericho*), emulate Flaubert's claim to have read and taken notes on 1,500 books before embarking on *Bouvard et Pécuchet*. There is a growing section of my own novels (Virginia Woolf used to 'shudder past' hers on the shelf as if they might bite her) in all their many guises, and another of books, signed, dedicated, and written by friends.

The tour of my study is almost over. There are shelves of photograph and press-cutting albums; cardboard boxes holding maps (buses and train) and guides, notes and newspaper articles; laminated wall maps (*Daily Telegraph*) of the British Isles, Europe, and the World; a medal and a signed certificate testifying that I have climbed the Great Wall of China; a long, narrow aquatint – Cairo to the temples at Philae – of the legend of the upper reaches of the Nile; a windowsill of lustre-ware souvenirs from English seaside resorts, and a lovingly tended container of pot basil. On an Italianate table of questionable origin (left by our predecessor in our first house), carved with leaves and heads of grinning lions (of great amusement to small children), an 'antique' vase from a sale of bric-à-brac, holds garden flowers, roses in summer, daffodils and grape hyacinths as precursors of spring.

'My study, lined with books, reflects my interests, confirms my identity as a writer, and reinforces my sense of what kind of person I consider myself to be.'*

---

* Anthony Storr

CHAPTER TWELVE

Writing for the Big Screen

———⟫·◆·⟪———

'When a producer says "trust me", that's the time to get it in writing.'

Like fellow writer, the late Sir Victor Pritchett (Mr Pritchard to the market traders) whose house was round the corner, it cheered me to live 'on the frontier of Camden Town and Regent's Park'. After so long in the wilderness – notwithstanding the Common with its duck pond and the cricket ground – the combination of one of the 'lungs' of London and the potpourri of the inner city was the Elysian fields. The suburbs, with their uniform houses, their pristine cars, their tended gardens, their mood of respectability and carefully planted trees, whilst paradise to some, have a consistency about them, a lacklustre predictability which had a stranglehold on my creative self.

Less than half a mile north of the smog and traffic of Oxford Circus, jerry-builder Nash's 'Crown cream' façades, topped

157

with Grecian figures (London's answer to the Rue de Rivoli), face the 250-odd acres of parkland with its lakes and prairies, its jungles and its wildlife – once used by royalty for game hunting – and the landscape turns magically from leaden grey to green. Our Gothic folly with which my family had rapidly come to terms, tucked away between two of the deceptively palatial terraces, represented the best of all worlds. Across the road, a short walk away, past winter football and transatlantic summer baseball, the Rose Garden, originally a nobleman's parterre, became not only my second home – I regarded it as a personal affront when it was infiltrated by seasonal visitors – but the breeding ground for a later novel, *A Loving Mistress*.

As I took my daily constitutional, round the children's playground, down the Broadwalk, through the iron gates of Queen Mary's Gardens, the ground beneath my feet was the catalyst for ideas and impressions fuelled by the kaleidoscope of foreign visitors, the Babel of tongues, the isolated balloons of conversation. 'As long as you've got a jelly you've always got a sweet...' 'It was hardly worth treating him. He was too old...' A dog? A cat? A relative? You could search the outer suburbs in vain for the sight of a dignified Nabob, raincoat over his white robes, red-checked kerchief round his head, inexplicably carrying a putter; for Japanese tourists pointing excited Minoltas and Nikons at everything that moved; for roller-skaters, skateboarders, joggers, pram-pushers, squirrel chasers, dog-walkers, bird-watchers, rose-sniffers, surreptitious flower pickers, pigeon fanciers, water-colourists, frisbee-players, kite flyers, newspaper and book readers, wheel-chaired invalids, frail convalescents, oblivious Tai Chi exponents, radiant Asian wedding groups, tandoori picnics, swotting students, Zimmer-framed elderly, distracted lovers, sybaritic sunbathers, pimply ice-cream vendors, muttering drunks, spaced-out junkies, enthusiastic players of hockey and rounders, pigeon-feeding pensioners and resolute families flowing amoeba-like towards the London zoo.

In my more reflective moments, as I carved my measured way between the mallards and pintails, the mute swans, the mandarin ducks, and the Canada geese, I thought what an agreeable gesture it would be if one of the wooden benches with their plaques – 'Emily Stevenson, who so loved this park' – were, after my death, named for me.

When I take my walk, it is always alone. Although I am alive to everything about me – the amorphous ladies, seemingly cast from the same grey-haired mould, with their '*Look* at this, Gladys...!' and 'O-o-oh, isn't that *bee-ooti-full*?' diminishing nature with their banal remarks – I am on automatic pilot, propelled as in a trance. If I am immobilised in a novel, the ideas come. If I am strapped for a story, I have only to open my eyes, to listen carefully: all the world is here.

Reality is even more in evidence in Camden Town itself – reached by a back gate behind the church – where, when the time comes for me to roam the pavements talking to my senile self, I shall not feel out of place. I do not feel out of place now. In the course of an hour's shopping in the cacophony of the street market or among the more sedate aisles of Marks & Spencer's Food Store (viz. *An Eligible Man*), I am likely, among the nose-ringed punks and the inebriates, to see Alan Bennett on his bicycle, Richard Mayne, Jonathan Miller, Dennis Norden, Derwent May, Hunter Davies, Ronald Hayman, Charlotte Hough, Beryl Bainbridge, Jean Lapotaire. When we first moved to St Katharine's Precinct, Parkway, our local shopping street linking Prince Albert Road to Camden High Street, was a shuttered waste. Now it is alive with jazz clubs, wine bars and pizza parlours. Boutiques, bookshops, launderettes and lighting emporia jostle sandwich shops ('Eat Here or Take Away'), wine-merchants, art galleries and video stores. Dry cleaners, Aeronautical Model and Orthoptic specialists intersperse the chalked pavement blackboards of the Trattoria Lucca (King Prawns and Pollo Dama Bianca), Chinese Food – Fish 'n Chips, and the Golden Grill. We have a multiplex cinema, a plethora of banks, estate agents (one functioning from a double-decker bus) and building societies; Indian, Greek, and Japanese restaurants; toy merchants, printers (personal fax), post office, and seductive stationery stores within easy reach. Within a half-mile radius of our house you can book your holiday, have your teeth filled and your ears pierced, and buy anything from a pin to a piano, from a poppadom to a talking parrot. No one will bat an eyelid as you do so.

'You could dance naked in Home Farm Close and no one would notice.' This was the plaint of Lorna Brown, trapped in her neo-Georgian prison in *The Long Hot Summer*. The failure of anyone to react to Lorna Brown's fantasy was due to the fact that in the streets of Home Farm Close there would not be a living soul: they were in their automated kitchens, their landscaped gardens, on the exclusive expanses of their striated lawns.

In Camden Town, at any time of the day or night, the entire population – bag-ladies in their slippers, dropouts prospecting for the euphemistic 'cup of tea', Rastas with their dreadlocks, winos with their bottles, weirdos anticipating the millennium – seemed simultaneously to be shuffling along the pavements.

The Long Hot Summer published in 1980, but written in the badlands, was the swan song of my sojourn in suburbia:

'What is ailing Lorna Brown? Her labour-saving life, with all its comfortable trappings – wall-to-wall carpets, double garages, au pairs, houseplants and health foods, burglar alarms and barbecues, clothes and commuting, Sunday supplements and Scrabble and en suite bathrooms, and the fact that at night you could dance naked in Home Farm Close and no one would notice. How could she explain to her husband? He would send her to a psychiatrist: "Women of your age..." He would say, and she would close her eyes and hold out her hand in the darkness for the bottle of coloured pills.'

Dissatisfied with the housewife/mother role in which life had cast her, and unsettled by the death of a friend, Lorna Brown welcomes the diversion provided by Armand, a contemporary of her daughter's, and in an apparently sudden decision walks away from her life in Home Farm Close to a squat in Regent's Park.

'The true writer doesn't write about the experience he's had but about the experience he's going to have'. *The Long Hot Summer*, with its Regent's Park squat, written two years before we had any idea of moving there, was an uncanny prognosticator of the future. It was not the first time. Long before Seymour Square, Brighton became a reality, the protagonists in *Practice Makes Perfect* moved to a similar town house. Kitty Shelton's New York mugging (*Live in Peace*), preceded by several years my own disagreeable encounter with a stalker on a dark night in St James's Square. In other novels, events and relationships, seemed to predicate the writer's crystal ball.

Although the sentiments of Lorna Brown echoed transient feelings of my own, *The Long Hot Summer* is not autobiographical. Personal experience (like the butter, eggs and sugar for a cake), is only the jumping-off point. For the finished product to be arrived at the components must be transmuted (the novelist's art) and the ingredients out of which the final work is constructed are not the fiction itself.

According to readers' letters from which I get my feedback, *The Long Hot Summer* is their favourite book. Words that come from the heart, reach the heart. It is perhaps for this reason that the novel has been a critical, if not a financial success. Its history is long and chequered. It marks my initiation into the never-never land of the movies into which such charismatic names as Glenda Jackson and Robert Redford were nonchalantly thrown.

The demise of Barrie & Jenkins left me, once again, without a publisher. Through the good offices of Deborah Owen, I fell into the capable hands of fiction editor Tony Whittome at Hutchinson, which had by that time gobbled up the Barrie & Jenkins imprint. Tony, a dedicated editor like so many of his ilk, liked *The Long Hot Summer* and, although it seemed to take for ever, my eleventh novel duly appeared. The book was nicely presented, and the jacket illustrated by Adrian George, an esteemed artist, and now a good friend of mine, whose work commands high prices. Hutchinson was well pleased with the novel, and subsidiary rights were sold to Arrow. Or so I thought. Having agreed to publish the paperback edition of *The Long Hot Summer* 'some time in 1981', Arrow decided, in February of that year, that owing to the recession and its aftermath – 'appalling conditions in the publishing trade at the moment have made unpleasant and stringent economies necessary' – they were delaying its appearance until the first half of 1982. This didn't seem too much of a disaster until, at the end of 1981, the tentacles of the 'stringent economies' embraced

Writing for the Big Screen

The Long Hot Summer and, much to Tony Whittome's embarrassment, Arrow reneged on their contract.

Sometimes I wonder why I did not give up and get a 'proper' job. It would surely have been easier. But the writer doesn't write because he wants to, he writes because he must. By the time Arrow's pusillanimous behaviour became apparent, I was not only well into *Proofs of Affection*, which marked a turning point in my writing career, but had had a movie 'nibble' for *The Long Hot Summer* which quite turned my head. It was in the days before I learned that a film company will tell you how wonderful your novel is and pay you peanuts for a year's option; that the property is then tied up for 12 months while they try to assemble a script, a cast, a director, some money and, most importantly, an outlet; that the best film projects never progress beyond the dreaded 'In Development' stage and are destined never to be made; that even if they do get made, clever accounting assures that they will never make a profit.

For a novel writer to receive an offer for film rights may seem at the time to be as exciting as winning a place in the Grand National. Before long, however, he will realise that not only is his horse an outsider but that it is virtually guaranteed to fall at the first fence.

When Debbie Owen told me that The Kettledrum Company had called from Hollywood 'absolutely knocked out with the film possibilities of *The Long Hot Summer*' and asking for an option on the book, the movie – to my unsuspecting mind – was as good as made. I shouted my news from the rooftops, and went about what I naïvely thought was my shortly-to-be-transformed life, in a state of euphoria. Little did I know that for the Americans to option a book meant *absolutely nothing*, that out of every 300 film scripts bought by the film industry, 15 are developed, and 5 made, that every single day 150 new scripts are registered with the Writers' Guild of America, or 'the nail-biting truth that 90 per cent of films that are, or ever have been made without a distributor punting up front, never ... get released.'* It was Peggy Ramsay, that doyenne of film and theatrical agents, to whom I went with my contract and good tidings, who cut me down to size. 'Has Kettledrum got any money, dear?' she said, looking at me from over the tops of her glasses in her Goodwin's Court hideaway. Money. Not only was the love of it the root of all evil, but it was the stumbling block, the shadow between the dream and the reality, of the movie business.

The Kettledrum Company, in the persons of Judd Bernard and Patricia Casey, had produced Glenda Jackson's first film, *Negatives* (Paramount Pictures); *The Marseilles Contract* (Warner Bros) starring Michael Caine, Anthony Quinn and James Mason; *Double Trouble* (MGM) with Elvis Presley; and the first Monty Python film *And Now For Something Completely Different* (Columbia).

Their proposition was to 'translate Ms Friedman's remarkable novel into a first class film made at a disciplined budget of $2 million...' that would 'touch the emotional nerve that generates massive word-of-mouth box-office business'. Because 'skyrocketing costs had forced major companies to re-evaluate' Kettledrum intended to finance the picture with private moneys, so that they would have the benefit of an unencumbered negative, which 'in today's market, with Cable Television looming on the horizon ... is tantamount to gold.' To this end they

* Alan Parker

hoped to lure Ed Asner and Glenda Jackson to accept the leading roles, and shoot the film on location in Chicago or Atlanta. Because of the current Hollywood writers' strike (which the Directors' Guild was shortly expected to join), they proposed Annette Olsen (a non-member) a Danish graduate of Poland's 'prestigious National Film School', as director. A masterly breakdown of my novel from Annette Olsen, indicated that she was not only a sensitive director, but that we were on the same wavelength and saw eye to eye on my book.

About this time we took a holiday, with two of our daughters, in a house, lent to us by friends, in Beverly Hills. Sitting in our backyard, round our kidney-shaped pool serviced daily by a pool-man, my husband and I played host to Kettledrum.

Patricia Casey and Judd Bernard were as enthusiastic about *The Long Hot Summer* in the flesh as they had been on paper. But they were not the Hollywood tycoons I had been expecting. The couple seemed far from prosperous and Patricia Casey had a large run in her much mended tights.

Notwithstanding the fact that Glenda Jackson had read *The Long Hot Summer* and agreed to play the role of Lorna Brown, I think it was the state of Patricia Casey's panty-hose that led me to lose confidence and, when the opportunity presented itself, to take another tack in the ongoing saga of my book.

On our return to England we were invited to dinner by our next-door neighbour, Jacky Hyer (Meteor Films). I took her a copy of *The Long Hot Summer*. Some months later, after Kettledrum's option had run out (they wanted an extension but no money was forthcoming) Jacky, who had liked the book, called to tell me that Stuart Lyons of Pinewood Studios, producer of the successful *The Slipper and the Rose*, was interested in

The Long Hot Summer and thought it had great potential as a film.

More than a year had now passed since Kettledrum had first endeavoured to get the movie off the ground. To give them credit they had tried. Annette Olsen was lined up (Robert Redford had been approached to direct but declined), Glenda Jackson was on 'hold', and Ed Asner was in the process of reading the novel. The problem was that although they were obviously anxious to get a 'package' together, Kettledrum had still neither script nor money.

Peggy Ramsay, who had no faith in Judd Bernard and had never heard of Annette Olsen, advised me to forget Kettledrum and throw in my lot with Stuart Lyons so that the movie could be set in England, *The Long Hot Summer*'s rightful home.

Kettledrum were not impressed. Legally they now had no claim on the book, but they were furious at what they saw as my perfidy and were 'shocked and disappointed' to receive my letter of rejection just when they were on the 'brink of success'. *Sauve qui peut.* I shall never know how things might have turned out in Hollywood. In those days, a year during which nothing concrete had happened seemed to me a very long time. I was quite unaware of the fact that some movies, such as *The French Lieutenant's Woman*, were 14 years in the making, that others took many years and multiple writers to complete, or that such seminal scripts as *Gandhi* had been turned down by every major studio before being rescued by Goldcrest, a production company itself ultimately to collapse.

There is no shortage of enthusiasm in the movie business. Stuart Lyons was as enthusiastic about *The Long Hot Summer* as Kettledrum – who would surely never speak to me again –

had been. He also had money, in the person of his backer, Charles Choularton, a Manchester businessman and chairman of Amalgamated Film Enterprises Ltd, keen to try his hand at producing movies. Stuart Lyons and Charles Choularton had very firm ideas about how they saw *The Long Hot Summer* (movie producers can usually articulate what they *don't* want, rarely what they do want) and were keen for me to write my own script. Driving to Pinewood Studios for meetings, lunching in the executive dining-room with the stars, must have gone to my head. Although I had no idea that only 20 per cent of a movie script is dialogue (during which it's time to buy the popcorn), that you don't *say* but *show*, that characters never *talk* to each other, and that there must always be a 'back story', I blithely assured them of my capabilities in that direction.

'Every sentence beginning "we think you've written a wonderful screenplay" ends with a request for extensive rewrites: the quantity of rewrites rises in direct proportion to the sense of wonder engendered by your work.'*

According to Billy Wilder, screenwriting it as much a craft as an art. 'You can come down from the mountain with a poem or novel, but not with a screenplay. There must be technique, there must be architecture.' The first draft of my *Long Hot Summer* screenplay ran to 3 hours 35 minutes (by which time it would be playing to an empty house); I set scenes in busy thoroughfares where my leading lady had to step off the bus among the passing crowds. I did not realise that at that point the passing crowds would cease to pass as they stopped to gawp at both camera and star; that you would have to clear the street of traffic, station

* Alan Plater

film crews on the tops of nearby buildings, hire thousands of pounds' worth of extras to people the thoroughfare – all for a three-minute 'take'.

Charles and Stuart were extremely patient. Although my initial efforts were frightful, they did not laugh once. The three of us stuck with it and, after a few months, not only had the First Draft been delivered according to my contract, but the Final Draft of *The Long Hot Summer* had been accepted, and I had been handsomely paid.

The Long Hot Summer referred to the summer of 1976, when for months a drought-ridden England basked in unprecedented temperatures more suited to the Mediterranean. Unfortunately the title not only conjured up racial tensions in the minds of an American audience, but had already been used in 1958 for a successful movie, based on a William Faulkner story, starring Paul Newman and Joanne Woodward.

I was not bothered. I had only to think up another title and, having completed the script to the satisfaction of the producers, it would be no time at all before I would be watching Lorna Brown come to life on the big screen.

How wrong can you get? There were meetings to discuss possible directors: Alvin Rakoff? And stars: Jacqueline Bissett? Alan Bates? Then, nothing. In the movie business, time, I learned, is not of the essence.

A bolt from the blue set the wheels once more in frenetic motion. Amalgamated Film Enterprises suddenly announced that they had 'sold my script on' to Bill Self, Head of CBS Features. Bill wanted the movie set in New York and Connecticut (instead of London and the Home Counties). I was to come, immediately, to the USA, to work on the script.

The difference between working over here and over there, is

that while in the UK both the writer and his work are under-valued, in the US his position in the pecking order is no higher, but his work is regarded more seriously and is subjected to stringent critical processes in an effort to improve it: what is seen by American producers as an early draft is often regarded by their British counterparts as the final product. When it gets to direction, a British director will show someone putting on his coat, leaving his house, opening the garage, getting into his car, putting on his seat-belt, driving off, stopping his car, undoing his seat-belt and walking up the drive of someone else's house. In an American film the actor would simply pick up his car keys and the next shot would be of him ringing a doorbell. While the British invest roughly 1 to 2 per cent of a film's budget on script development, which may require as much as 17 rewrites (*Four Weddings and a Funeral*) as well as a handful of scriptwriters (*Chaplin*), the American average is around 6 per cent. The producers do not regard this sum as extravagant. It is an investment that will be earned many times over.

My new contract, this time with CBS and supervised by agent Peggy Ramsay and lawyer Claude Fielding of Bartletts, de Reya in Piccadilly, stated that not only must I be lodged, for as long as it took, in a first class hotel (all expenses taken care of), but that my ticket to New York was to be first class. I was to taste the seductive life of Tinseltown, to join the illustrious ranks of such screenwriters as Aldous Huxley, William Goldman and Scott Fitzgerald, the proverbial 'schmucks with Underwoods'. It promised to be much more fun than bashing out my solitary 1,000 words a day.

CHAPTER THIRTEEN

Keep Biting the Bullet

—————⟫◆⟪—————

'You can make a perfectly decent living writing for films that never get made.'

Frederic Raphael

It is little wonder that Freud's *Studies in Hysteria*, and the first movie, both made their appearance in the same year. Film scripts are properties pushed around the system by more or less interested parties until either they get made or are banished to join the great dead script pile in the sky; and even studios producing Oscar-winning movies, such as *Forrest Gump* – which took $657 million dollars at the box office and paid the star and director $20 million each of the gross takings – reportedly 'lost money' on the project so that poor Winston Groom, the author who created Forrest Gump, had to fight (together with his lawyer) for his $1 million share of the net profits.

Fortunately I was ignorant of all this when, as the first snows of winter were falling, I arrived in New York. My hotel, with its hermetically sealed windows, overlooked the trees of Central Park. Prudently I consigned my valuables to the care of the safe-deposit clerk at the front desk (why did he want to know my *mother*'s maiden name?), where I had expected to find a reception committee but was given a message to say that my LA contacts had been delayed.

They arrived next morning on the 'red-eye' and, at the ubiquitous breakfast meeting, waxed rhapsodic over the merits of *The Long Hot Summer* for which Bill Self had electrifying plans. He handed me over to the story editor, who would work on the script with me and would be at my disposal for as long as I wanted, to facilitate my research.

The words 'Hollywood' and 'movie' were an open sesame. The Mount Sinai Hospital, which was to be the scene for the American equivalent of the London hospital where Lorna Brown is operated on for her fatal illness, laid on a public relations person who took me on a tour of the building – from operating 'rooms' to kitchens – whose time and patience were unlimited, and for whom no seemingly irrelevant question was too trivial. My anaesthetist became an 'anesthesiologist', patients' notes 'check charts', and the ward sister, 'senior clinical nurse'. I sat in the waiting area – 'Smoking prohibited. Visitors subjected to $500 fine, imprisonment for 6 months or both' – beneath the flickering wallpaper of the 24-hour TV, and eavesdropped on conversations concerning varicose veins ('The largest the surgeon had ever seen') and the latest salt-free diet ('Stay away from bacon and sausage, it'll kill you!').

I trudged from the Klingenstein Pavilion with its blue awning, on 5th Avenue, through Admitting, Maternity, and Ambulatory Surgery to doctors' suites; from the 'holding area' to the EKG

171

Department; from unit clerks to residents, making notes as I went. My guide could not have been more patient, and when we parted she assured me that she was not only looking forward to seeing the movie of *The Long Hot Summer*, but if there was anything else I needed to know – anything at all – I was not to hesitate to call.

Money was no object. Cabs were at my disposal 24 hours a day and I was given *carte blanche* to fill my suitcase with books (for research purposes!) from book stores which stayed open until midnight. I took the Conrail – Mount Vernon, Pelham, New Rochelle, Larchmont, Mamaroneck, Harrison, Rye, Portchester 'show the full face of your ticket please' – to Greenwich (Connecticut), where the story was to be set, and on instruction rented a Hertz car – to travel a few hundred yards – on arrival. The story editor was tough, but helpful and committed. We had script meetings in her suite, interrupted by the arrival of room service with jelly omelettes the size of miniature submarines, and lengthy calls from LA, during the course of which I heard the chill phrase 'Let the writer walk!' which confirmed my suspicions that screenwriters are dispensable and the first to be jettisoned from the film-making process.

I could have stayed in New York for six months, a year. It was all the same to CBS who picked up the tab. Unfortunately, after three weeks of dedicated research, pleasantly interspersed with a visit to Dial Press (the American publisher of *Aristide*), department stores, museums, and art galleries, my family grew restive and I returned – first class – to the real world.

The script went well. My 'squat' in Regent's Park became a 'loft' on Thomas rented by Lorna Brown's guitar-playing lover (ex school in New Mexico and Wellesely and adorned with chainsaw and tomahawk tattoos); Lorna Brown's doctor's surgery became his 'office', and Harrods – her favourite stamping ground – was transmuted to Bloomingdales.

Still on my New York 'high', I worked like a dervish. When the screenplay was finished I took it to Steve Sice of Scripts Limited, an office incongruously situated amongst the wind-dried ducks of Gerrard Street, to have it professionally typed. CBS were thrilled. I had done a 'great job'. Casting suggestions and production dates were bandied to and fro across the Atlantic. When 'heads rolled' at the studios and Bill Self was promoted into another division, his successor did not wish to support a project which belonged to the previous regime. Like Harold Pinter, William Boyd, Philip Roth, and countless other schmucks with Underwoods, I was out on my ear.

I know now of course that this is the name of the game. That until the cameras start to roll on the first day of shooting – and sometimes not even then – nothing is certain. That if the grass grows tall in the publishing world it reaches ominous heights in the cut-throat world of movies.

What goes up must come down. All that I was left with from those intoxicating days was the black-and-white ashtray, memento of lunch at One Fifth (its interior a facsimile of the luxury yacht *Caronia*) which sits on my desk, a shelf full of books (including one on *SoHo Lofts*), and a healthy bank balance.

My brief flirtation with the fleshpots of Hollywood was followed by an unexpected rejection by Hutchinson of my new novel *Proofs of Affection*, the inability to find a home for my second children's book *Prudence and the Red Roc Mystery* and the abortive search for an new agent.

I had no quarrel to pick with Deborah Owen but simply felt

173

that, as far as my career was concerned, I needed a breath of fresh air. Since by this time one Jeffrey Archer (then a backbencher) had joined Debbie's agency, I doubt if she was too bothered at losing me as a client. Over an amicable lunch at Manzi's we came to the parting of the ways.

Although Miss Weiner (who had now become 'Joyce' and stayed with us, heaving her bulk up the stairs to our attic guest room whenever she came to London) was no longer my agent, she was still my *éminence grise* as far as writing was concerned. Never, until her dying day (literally), losing faith in my work, she endorsed my break with Deborah Owen Ltd and pointed me in the direction of other agents. None of them was interested. I know now that the only significant people in the literary world are the writer and the bookseller. To be with neither agent nor publisher, when I hit bottom, seemed however to be the ultimate disgrace.

Although I had been brought up in a Jewish milieu, *Proofs of Affection*, my twelfth novel, was the first of my books to be set in my own backyard. Having made up my mind to confront my spiritual concerns, I knew that they must be expressed through a personal prism.

The title *Proofs of Affection* was taken from the diaries of Virginia Woolf. Speaking of her Jewish mother-in-law, Leonard's mother, she says: 'She was a woman capable of heroism but usually perceived as timorous and sentimental, continually demanding proofs of affection from her children and, I think, receiving them...'

The novel spans 12 months from one Jewish New Year (*Rosh Hashana*) to the next, I set out to examine the dynamics of contemporary Jewish family life, and in so doing to rebut the 'negative stereotype' of the Jew in literature perpetuated by such

English authors as Chaucer, Marlowe, Shakespeare and Dickens. Like Sartre's 'authentic Jew', Kitty Shelton is shaped by a Jewish past whose burdens she bears and which cannot be ignored. By their very nature, it is the triumphs and tragedies of this past that makes her image neither better nor worse than that of other women – as Scott or Lawrence would have us believe – and demonstrates that there are, among Jews, differences in culture, education, manners and customs, exactly as there are among other peoples.

Joyce Weiner was the first outsider to read the manuscript. She read it in a sitting and when she put it down there were tears in her eyes. It was good. It was very good.

Proofs of Affection hit the publishers' desks at the same time as the full force of the recession, which made them 'think twice before taking anything on'. Much to the embarrassment of Tony Whittome who 'liked the book very much ... thought it very moving ... and would have been proud to publish it', Hutchinson invoked the 'extraordinary times' and turned it down. The letter from Sidgwick & Jackson, to whom I submitted it next, was one for the rave rejection file:

'I'm afraid that we will have to say no to your book after all. *Everyone here without exception liked it* (my italics) and there is no doubt that in a more encouraging climate we would have jumped at it ... we feel that we will, for the time being, publish only 'blockbusters' *à la* Judith Krantz's *Princess Daisy* ... we are sure that some other publisher will snap you up...'

Their faith was misplaced. Although *Proofs of Affection* did the rounds of publishers who commented on the 'sad fact that the merit of the novel has to be outweighed by selling considerations', not one of them 'snapped me up'. Unsuccessful in my search for a publisher for *Proofs of Affection*, I turned my attentions to replacing Debbie Owen, and finding someone to represent me. I did not realise that in 'a difficult market' it was as hard to find an agent willing to take you on, as it was to find a publisher for your books.

Deborah Rogers, of Deborah Rogers Ltd, felt that because of the 'rather troubled times in publishing' she would not 'make the best agent' for my work. Carol Smith, of The Carol Smith Literary Agency, said 'it hasn't been easy to make a decision' but 'I don't honestly feel I am sufficiently on your wavelength to be a particularly effective agent for you'. Patricia Kavanagh, of A. D. Peters & Co Ltd wrote: 'I don't think things have ever been worse in publishing than they are now, and the kind of book that is being hardest hit is precisely the sort of novel that *Proofs of Affection* is: serious, thoughtful, neither a blockbuster nor a "category".'

I was clearly into the old 'between two stools' situation, and at my lowest ebb, when a feature about, and by, literary agents in a Sunday colour supplement led me to Elaine Greene who wrote:

'The function of the agency at its most basic, is the management of the business side of an author's work. It becomes much more than that when you have to decide which publisher the author will get on best with, and get a fair deal from. There is business acumen involved – and psychology.'

Elaine Greene attributed the longevity of her small literary agency to her impressive string of writers amongst whom was Phyllis James (now Baroness James). I liked both Elaine and her self-confessed *alter ego*, Ilsa Yardley, when I met them, sitting at a pavement table, for lunch at Uppers in Islington.

Of all the agents to whom I had sent the by now dog-eared manuscript of *Proofs of Affection*, Elaine Greene and Ilsa

Yardley had, each of them independently, gone overboard about the book. After all my reverses, by the time we were on to the coffee, 'Elaine Greene Ltd' had restored my faith in myself. Ilsa Yardley not only liked *Proofs of Affection* but found a willing buyer for it in that maverick of the publishing world, Livia Gollancz.

Livia Gollancz, a French horn player *manqué* was a law unto herself. From her Dickensian office in Henrietta Street, she set her unique stamp upon the publishing house foisted upon her by her father (Victor Gollancz), and if you had the misfortune to land her as your editor, she was capable of driving you to despair. She was as original in her appearance as she was in her 'no-nonsense' approach to publishing, and once you had breached the fearsome exterior which covered her reserve, she was kindness itself.

There were no leisured lunches at the Savoy or cavortings at the Caprice with Livia. You called for her at 5 minutes to 1, when she would appear with capacious shopping bag, her rosy cheeks (legacy of her horn-blowing days) obviating the need for make-up, buttoning her man's overcoat, and before you could say 'knife' she was striding off in the direction of Joe Allen's. Struggling to keep up, you would be regaled not with the latest goings-on in the publishing world, but with an up-to-date resumé of her Highgate allotment. Over lunch, at her usual table with its red-and-white checked cloth, Livia would have ordered her customary vegetarian dish, and be half way through it, before you had finished looking at the blackboard. The sprint back to Henrietta Street – no time for coffee – would be interrupted by a call at the fruit stall at which Livia, unselfconsciously, her unruly grey hair escaping from its customary bun, would fill her bag with oranges.

Livia liked *Proofs of Affection*. She rang me at home at midnight to tell me that she had been unable to put it down. I liked Livia. Until it came to editing when we would be locked in battle like a couple of stags at bay. Because of the time factor, Livia always won. Her method was unique. Having tied up the contract, she would keep your manuscript for several months during which there would be no word from her. A sudden telephone call, invariably at an inconvenient moment, to tell you that *the printer was waiting*, would send you scurrying in the direction of Henrietta Street where she waited augustly, pencil at the ready to make 'fussy little changes and pipsqueak variations on my copy'.*

Sitting by her side it was hard, with tilted head, to *see* the manuscript, let alone *read* the words which by now you had almost forgotten. I felt for poor Flaubert.

'Be brave, close your eyes during the operation, and have confidence ... You are doubtless cursing me with all your might at this very moment, but you may be sure that in all this I have only your own interest at heart.'

Livia, despite her musical background, had no ear for cadence, was oblivious to the fact that a good prose sentence should be like a line of poetry or that any author worth his salt has already done the cutting and slashing himself. 'You can't have three "saids" on one page,' she would state, crossing out and inserting words as she spoke. 'Let's put "exclaimed" here, "remarked" here, and "interjected" here!' It was almost as bad as 'ejaculated'. 'No, Livia,' I cried, looking for my guns so that I could stick to them, and the eraser, so that I could rub out her pencil marks. 'What about this paragraph?' A great sweep this time of

* S. J. Perelman

the pencil. 'Is it *really* necessary?' 'I need to think about it...'
'No *time*.' A touch of blackmail now. 'You do want me to keep
to the publishing date...?'

We would work all day. No coffee. The machine was broken
and no one had time to go out. 'You don't want lunch do you?
We have to get this to the printer.' Livia must have had a tank
like a camel, she didn't even get up to go to the lavatory. By the
time we reached the final pages it was dark outside. The
building was deserted. Everyone had gone home. I was exhausted
whilst Livia, spurred on by her efforts, was exuberant. 'You
don't need this ... and this ... and this...' she cried scoring
pages from corner to corner. 'It holds up the action...' 'It didn't
hold *you* up,' I objected weakly, 'You woke me up to tell me
that you couldn't put *Proofs of Affection* down.' 'I'm talking
about *readers*!'

The sideways-on words were making strange patterns in my
head whilst Livia was fresh as a daisy. It was useless to argue. I
was too tired.

The publishing was painless. I was pleased with the finished
product. We had a party to celebrate. Livia arrived on her
bicycle and tied it to the railings of St Katharine's Precinct.
Proofs of Affection, which had been so difficult to get off the
ground, ran to three hardback editions. It was bought by Futura
to whose notice it was brought not by Gollancz, who had had
difficulties in finding a paperback publisher, but paradoxically
by Judy Piatkus, an unknown fan of my work, and a publisher
in her own right.

I need not have worried about *Proofs of Affection* having
only minority interest. In a full page review in the *Spectator*,
Harriet Waugh called it 'an educative as well as enjoyable
novel'; *The Times* found it 'sensitive and marvellously satisfy-

ing'; the *Evening Standard* 'a classic of its kind'; and it reached number five on the 'bestsellers' list. I was extensively interviewed and the reviews were good, but it was my first fan mail to arrive in any quantity – from Jewish and non-Jewish readers alike – which vindicated my decision to explore my roots. The letters – 'I just had to write and thank you', 'in appreciation and enjoyment', 'human and satisfying', 'moving', 'unputdownable' – confirmed that my 'Jewish' novel, about which I had been so ambivalent, had 'transformed lives' as far away as Australia and New Zealand, and had 'entertained', and 'enlightened' those to whom the idiosyncrasies of Judaism had been a closed book. With its emphasis on the family and the schism of the 'generation gap', *Proofs of Affection* was testimony to the fact that if the core quality of a novel is human it will have universal appeal.

Proofs of Affection was my first novel (apart from the juvenile *Aristide*) to find a publisher in the USA. Through Ilsa Yardley it was brought to the attention of Harvey Ginsberg, fiction editor of William Morrow & Company, Inc. Publishers, of New York. I met Harvey, who told me how enthusiastic he felt about the manuscript over the statutory publishing lunch (Italian this time), and this meeting was followed by an extensive and amusing transatlantic correspondence.

I had to 'translate' *Proofs of Affection* so that it might be readily understood not only by the sophisticates in New York, but by those illusory readers 'in the backwoods of Alabama'. My paranoia over the desecration of my text was mitigated only recently when I learned that A. S. Byatt, a Booker Prize winner – supposedly a protected species – could not find an American publisher for her novel until it was not only 'translated', but 'beefed up', 'sexed up', and heavily edited. It was as useless to argue with Harvey Ginsberg about his paternalistic view, as it was to take issue with a publisher over anything. They *always* knew best.

Harvey did not know what a rockery was. Or the meaning of 'merry-go-round'. What was a 'duvet'? Was it a 'Yiddish' word! Recondite passages and obscure references gave rise to pages of comment and numbered queries inviting my considered reply. It was a far cry from the impatient and last-minute pencil of Livia Gollancz.

Proofs of Affection, in a new, American jacket, was eventually published 'quietly' by Morrow. In accordance with the precept that the 'circus doesn't creep into town', it sold its preordained number of copies and, although it attracted fan mail from such disparate places as Van Nuys, California, and Memphis, Tennessee, and was made the Jewish Book Club's joint main selection (together with a new novel by Simon Wiesenthal), it not surprisingly died the death.

Back home, on the strengths of *Proofs of Affection*, new horizons had opened up. I was in demand, at literary lunches and at book fairs, to sign copies of my new book, and was snowed under with invitations to 'speak' about it.

CHAPTER FOURTEEN

Can You Hear Me at the Back?

'To be altogether true to his spiritual life an artist must remain alone and not be prodigal of himself even to disciples.'

Marcel Proust

Years of actually getting up in front of an audience have taught me three lessons: you don't die; there's no right way to speak; it's always worth it.

Good writers are naturally dull creatures who rarely trust their own voices and, having said all they have to say in their books, they seldom make good speakers. Like ballet dancers they have chosen a profession in which they are able to communicate without speech, and there is no reason whatever to believe that a writer is capable of talking about his art simply because he is a practitioner of it.

Nabokov said: 'I think like a genius, write like an accomplished author, and talk like a child'; Montaigne complained of a slow mind and an incredible lack of memory; Emerson had a tied tongue and was wanting in command of imagery to match his thoughts; J. B. Priestley always found it easier to write about things than to say them and Philip Larkin had an inbuilt antipathy to speaking engagements: 'I don't want to go around,' he said 'pretending to be me.'

Unlike in the nineteenth century, when Charles Dickens's readings from his work drew enormous crowds, the public performances of writers – unless they also happen to be the contemporary reading man's crumpet, live in an old shoe factory, publicise their spectacular drug habits, have multi-syllabled names (preferably including the *particule*), come on strong to literary editors, have been sexually abused, circumvented the world in a balloon, married their agents, reinvented themselves as eccentrics, spent their advances on silicone implants, been prima donnas of the catwalk, sportswomen, film stars or serial-killers – no longer cause a stir.

The artist's only possible camaraderie, according to Flaubert, can be with other artists: for Proust the writer is not another citizen, a social creature with social duties: he is a solitary explorer, a pure egotist and the lecture an instrument of the bourgeoisie: 'Authentic art has no use for proclamations, it accomplishes its work in silence.'

Asking a writer to lecture is like asking a knife to turn a screw. In his lecture given in Vienna to celebrate Freud's eightieth birthday in 1936, Thomas Mann warned his audience: 'An author, my friends, is a man essentially not bent upon science, upon knowing, distinguishing, and analysing; he stands for simple creation, for doing and making, and thus may be the object of useful cognition, without, by his very nature, having any competence in it as subject.'

183

THE WRITING GAME

'Invited to lecture the writer is flattered. He feels invited up, after years of playing on the floor with paper dolls and pretend castles, into grown-up activity for which one wears a suit, and receives money or at the very least an airplane ticket.'*

He furthermore receives society's permission, by the terms of his contract, to immobilise an audience of hundreds (dozens at any rate) of fellow human beings, at which point he can only conclude that he must be an interesting and worthy person.

Invitations to go out into the world and speak, to groups, at seminars, as guest of honour at literary lunches usually come well ahead when you know you will have finished the work in hand and the pages in your diary are blank. Six months, nine months, a year, before the actual date, the telephone will ring and you hear the dreaded words: 'You don't know me but I'm the secretary/organiser/cultural *attaché*...' In the split second before they name their group, chapter, organisation, you know exactly what will follow and that once again, against your better judgement – lacking valid excuses, and with one eye on the main chance of selling a few signed copies of your books – you are going to accept the invitation. The thought processes are as follows. Somebody out there has read my work; somebody out there likes my work; somebody out there wants to meet me; the day will never come. It does. By which time you are fully committed to a new project, have a parcel of books to review, have been invited to Paris/ Stockholm/Milan, or are wanly recovering from flu and look like the dog's dinner. Playing for time by asking the caller to put his request in writing only evades, but does not resolve the issue.

* John Updike

Can You Hear Me at the Back?

I am now a seasoned commuter on the literary circuit, but age and experience have not diminished the mixed feelings with which I regard my name as speaker, on stiff card or coloured paper, beneath that of the organisation I am to confront. I always write down in advance what I am going to say. Being a poor conversationalist – writers speak inside and to themselves more than to anyone else – and possessed of a highly developed *esprit d'escalier*, I not only need time to refine my thoughts, develop a theme or follow an argument, but find that the printed text, the certainty that you have something to fall back on should your tongue dry up, your brain atrophy, diminishes anxiety. I am not alone in this. Sir Isaiah Berlin, a renowned and accomplished orator, confessed to extreme panic before, after, and during a lecture, for which he always wrote out at least 40 pages in advance.

The morning before Charles Dickens was due to speak 'he would take a long walk and in the course of that journey he would decide what topics he was going to raise. He would put those in order, and in his imagination construct a cartwheel of which he was the hub and the various topics the spokes emanating from him to the circumference: 'during the progress of the speech' he said, 'he would deal with each spoke separately, elaborating as he went round the wheel; and when all the spokes dropped out one by one, and nothing but the tyre and space remained, he would know that he had accomplished his task, and that his speech was at an end.'*

Preparing and giving a lecture and observing the courtesies with which it is surrounded, takes up a great deal of time. Actually getting to one's feet before an audience is the least

* Peter Ackroyd

185

stressful part of the manoeuvre. It is the preamble which unsettles, leads you to take a solemn oath that you will never again let yourself in for such a traumatic experience.

To start with, unless the venue happens to be in central London, it is often extremely difficult to find. You follow your carefully planned route to the public library at Sevenoaks, or Friends' Hall at Surbiton, only to find that new roads, flyovers, and one-way systems, have made a nonsense of your out-of-date map. As you track, backtrack, U-turn, and enquire your way in the dark from the blank faces of passers-by – if you are lucky enough to find any passers-by – who are 'just visiting' or newly arrived in the country, you wonder if, in the freezing fog, the driving rain, anyone is going to be foolish enough to venture out.

Like Henrik Ibsen, who always arrived too early at the station in case he missed the train, I am intolerant of unpunctuality and over-anxious about time. Worried about being late, I am invariably early and skulk in the car, sometimes for as long as 30 minutes, near to, but not outside, the lecture hall. Watching your audience drift in for their evening's entertainment and realising with horror that you are it, you hide your face, watching theirs in the lamplight for signs of enthusiasm. If no one appears, if the doors of the hall remain stubbornly shut, and you contemplate an empty street, you wonder if you have got the right night, the right date. A sudden blaze of light, a last minute flurry of arrivals, reassures.

It is hard to decide exactly at which moment to make your entrance. Too early will embarrass the organisers who are busy organising and will not know what to do with you. Too late will find them consulting their watches in a paroxysm of anxiety that you are not going to turn up. You pick up bag and briefcase and stagger in beneath a load of your books like a commercial traveller. You should not have to. The publisher, in the shape of the publicity department, pleased with your efforts at filling their coffers, *should* have supplied copies in advance. *They rarely do.* No matter how much notice you give them of your lecture they are liable to forget, have not ordered the books in time from Lewes or Littlehampton or wherever the warehouse happens to be, or have delivered them to the wrong place. Sometimes your way is barred. Officious dignitaries ask if you have a ticket and hold out their hands for your money as you try to sneak past. If you are lucky the chairperson will be looking out for you and will recognise you from the photograph on your latest novel. A sigh of relief goes round the committee. They attempt to lead you into the hall but after your stressful journey you are in urgent need of the Ladies' Room. From the cubicle you eavesdrop on the conversation of two members of the public who apparently have come only to get away from home or for the tea and biscuits and have no idea of the name of the speaker.

Seated on the platform, you cast a practised eye over the audience, noting the empty seats and wondering if Margaret Drabble or Muriel Spark would have filled the hall. The eager beavers in the front row meet your eye and you force a sickly smile.

If only they would let you get on with it. Get it over. But no. Your heart sinks as you realise that once again you will be relegated to the end of a litany concerning a forthcoming cello recital and a performance at the Royal National Theatre ('...a few tickets still remaining and we should be back in Crouch End/Cricklewood by 11.30...'). An announcement is made concerning a proposed visit to eastern Europe (Bohemian

Castles and Evening River Cruise). As members' minds are put at rest about days and dates and the availability of single rooms and wheelchair access, you wonder, hopefully, whether you have been forgotten.

'And now we come to the main event of this evening...' You have worked hard on your opening remarks, to get your audience on your side, in the right mood. Your carefully selected words are interrupted by a voice from the doors demanding to know if anyone is the owner of a Ford Cortina, registration number ... which is causing an obstruction in the carpark. You start again, only marginally unnerved. 'Can you speak up? We can't hear you at the back.' A microphone is provided. It whistles and distorts. The hand-held variety, with its trailing cord, provokes the irreverent thought that you should be breaking into song, and presents problems with holding your notes and juggling texts. You try again, keeping an eye on the back row to see if they are receiving you, on two women who seem to be exchanging recipes, on those who are not the slightest bit interested in 'Publishing' or 'Proust', or whatever you have come to speak about, but have settled down in the warmth of the library, until it is time for the refreshments. You soldier on, listening to the unfamiliar sound of your own voice and wondering whether you can hold the listeners' attention for the allotted time. As you warm to your theme you remark that an elderly gentleman in the middle reaches has dropped off, and that the recipe exchangers are busy scribbling. A glance at the clock and your diminishing pile of A4, with its double spacing, indicates that the ordeal is almost over. You carry your audience with you into the home stretch, coming in, neck and neck, with the teacups.

Can You Hear Me at the Back?

The applause rouses the sleeper. You sit down with the sensation of having been released from a particularly unpleasant session at the dentist's, pour water into a glass from the carafe in front of you. 'Are there any questions?' Silly question. What an audience wants to know from a writer is how he writes. 'Do you use a typewriter?' 'Do you write every day or only when you get the inspiration?' 'Where do you get your ideas?' You can deal with the catechism standing on your head and hope that it does not sound as if you are doing so. You recognise the filibuster who has got to his feet to tell you, at great length, about his experiences in World War Two – in case you would like to write a book about them – and deal tactfully with him. By the time the vote of thanks (accompanied, if you are not getting paid, by a shrinking African violet or some chocolates left over from Christmas) is made, you have already picked half a dozen raffle tickets out of the hat, and heard that various members of whatever-society-it-happens-to-be are celebrating birthdays (applause), and one has entered hospital for an operation (tuts), and another, unfortunately, suffered a bereavement (uncomfortable silence), and your audience is half way to the tea trolley and it is as if you have never existed.

You whisper in the chairperson's good ear. He grabs the mike: 'If anyone would care to buy a book which is priced at ...' mentions a modest sum. 'Our speaker will be happy to sign it.' The audience surrounds the table. 'How can my daughter become a writer?' 'She can't,' you say. 'But you became a writer.' 'I didn't have to ask.'

They riffle through the pile of books you have brought; can only manage Large Print, prefer one of your literary rivals, borrow their reading matter from the library. The pile diminishes.

189

Slightly. You drink your stewed tea and scoop the remaining paperbacks into the plastic carrier whence they came.

Heading for home you wonder if you can find the way. You no longer care. The ordeal is over and you won't think about the next speaking invitation you were foolish enough, vain enough, to accept. Not until the day dawns. Which it will.

Marginally worse than the lecture is the guest of honour slot at the literary lunch. Having sat through the three courses (plus coffee) of a meal which, no matter how excellent, you are too tense to enjoy, by the time it actually comes for you to carry out your gladiatorial role, you are both hoarse and consumed. After an hour of turning your head from one side to the other at the top table to answer the questions 'have you always written?', 'where do you find the time?', 'where do you get your ideas?' – which you are going to reply to later in your address – your throat is sore from shouting to make yourself heard above the buzz of conversation, and you are exhausted. You would love to escape and powder your nose before your ordeal, but you would have to fight your way through the hall and it is not *comme il faut*. Struggling to make yourself heard above the clink of the coffee cups, the *sotto voce* requests for sugar, you get to your feet and make a signal attempt to top the pudding.

Being asked to lecture flatters the writer. It lures him from his ivory tower, reassuring him of his existence, but at the same time it deprives him of his inalienable right to the healing silences of the self.

Most writers have to choose between being eaten up by themselves or consumed by other people, between their desire for love and companionship and their need to be alone and autonomous. Virginia Woolf recognised that the artist's urge

190

for solitude and anonymity has to be set against the desire for 'fame, society, money, gossip, parties, and involvements'. While she didn't want not to see people, she found continually being seen a pressure: she liked it when people came to visit, but loved it when it was time for them to go. Venturing into society, she tried not to allow herself to be 'drowned by it' and was keenly aware of the 'vacancy & silence somewhere in the machine', which underlay all her social activity of 'seeing people'.

Kafka hated everything that did not relate to literature: 'Conversations bore me, to visit people bores me, the sorrows and joys of my relatives bore me to my soul.' In order to maintain contact with his inner world, the writer needs to be alone and must seal his windows 'lest the air of the world seep in'.

According to Proust, 'To be altogether true to his spiritual life an artist must remain alone and not be prodigal of himself even to disciples.' Philip Larkin saw life 'more as an affair of solitude diversified by company than as an affair of company diversified by solitude.'

The writer knows that he should 'live all he can', and that 'it is a mistake not to'.* '...in him [the writer] ... two persons coexist; the one who lives and the one who watches the other live, the one who suffers and the one who observes this suffering in order to use it.'†

When the writer *is* persuaded to carry out his social duties, he will very likely be disappointing to meet. '...those who put pen to paper do so because they rarely trust their own voices, and

---

* Henry James
† Mario Vargas Llosa

indeed, in society, have very little to say. They are, as I now know, the least entertaining of guests.'*

In attempting to bridge the gap between his inner and outer self, the writer hides behind a mask which conceals his true identity and enables him to observe at the same time as he participates in events. This false persona makes other people uncomfortable and they turn away from him, thus reinforcing his role as outsider. Because the writer needs – and prefers – to be alone does not mean however that he is lonely. He does not have to *live* by himself – he too needs to be loved – and his solitude is even more rewarding if he knows that there is a loving partner awaiting his return. The ability to be alone is a valuable resource:

'No man will ever unfold the capacities of his own intellect, who does not at least checker his life with solitude.'†

Solitude enables the writer to get in touch with his/her deepest feelings and encourages the growth of the imagination. Social intercourse is fatiguing to the creative personality – which craves seclusion as others crave sleep – and sensory overload is inimical to productive thought. The need to be alone, to bridge the gap between inner and outer, differs from the capacity to be alone which is a mark of emotional maturity. By detaching him/herself for long periods at a time from other human beings, from the unacceptable noise levels of contemporary life, and maintaining contact with his/her inner world, the writer's mind is liberated and he/she creates a psychic-space around him/her which enables him/her to think. Solitude is therapeutic, and the writer's life is enriched not so much by personal relationships as by his/her work.

* Anita Brookner
† De Quincey

Can You Hear Me at the Back?

While according to his biographer, Jeremy Lewis, Cyril Connolly was 'both sickened by and central to the time-wasting, incestuous, back-biting swirl of the literary merry-go-round', Ernest Hemingway considered that 'writers who hang out with other writers are no bloody good' and Pushkin's Charsky '...avoided the society of his literary brothers, preferring men of the world, even the most simple minded, to their company. His conversation was extremely commonplace and never touched on literature.'

Disgruntled outsiders often claim that the literary world is dominated by small coteries of fashionable authors – the 'North London Mob', the 'Primrose Hill Bunch', and the erstwhile 'Camden Casa Nostra' – who eat, drink and play together, praise each other's books, give each other prizes and denigrate everyone else. Until I moved from my dreaming suburb to the fleshpots of Camden Town, I had no idea that, *pace* Pushkin who '...avoided the company of his brother men of letters, preferring to them people of society even the most empty', there is another world which beckons the metropolitan writer and which highlights the conflict between his need to confirm his identity and his desire to be alone.

On the last Wednesday of every month a group of local writers met for lunch at Koritsas, a Greek restaurant, a few convenient yards from the Camden Town tube station, in Kentish Town Road. The idea was the brainchild of local writer Hunter Davies and it was broadcast by word of mouth. The food was so indifferent, the sanitary facilities so unmentionable, and the restaurant so unpopular with the local population, that no previous notice was required of attendance, and the good-natured proprietors obligingly set the tables, to accommodate 3 or 33, at the very last moment. The arrangements

were haphazard. The 'luncheon' did not even have a name. At
12.45 pm, on the last Wednesday of every month 'a mob of
one-man bands ... playing all simultaneously and mostly
unheard'* laid down their pens and furtively crept from their
lairs in Hampstead or Highgate (a few from Blackheath and
Barnes) to brave the company of their peers. The writer's
sensation of feeling permanently ill at ease, is not ameliorated
by the presence of others similarly afflicted. Until the first
few bottles of retsina had been emptied, the atmosphere on
either side of the long table was awkward, the conversation
mundane. Penelope Lively, Shirley Conran, Margaret Drabble,
Beryl Bainbridge, Peter Vansittart, Marghanita Lasky, Bernice
Rubens, Salman Rushdie, Fay Weldon, Debbie Moggach and
many others, passed the small dishes of taramasalata, humous,
squid and tsatsiki, from one to the other and commented on
the weather or enquired politely what the other was 'working
on'.

One's position at the table, which in the early days extended
from one end of the restaurant to the other, was critical to one's
enjoyment of the afternoon. At one point one would be min-
gling at the bar, eyeing the company to see who was worth
talking to, and the next, as at some invisible signal, hustling to
lay claim on chairs placed strategically near the action – in terms
of the most outrageous and lively of the company – and as far
away as possible from the acknowledged bores. By some
invisible manoeuvrings, the founder members of Hunter Davies's
brainchild, the better-known writers, appropriated what became
the recognisable 'top' of the table, while more humble or less
pushy wordsmiths, banished to Outer Mongolia, flapped their

* Gloria Steinem

ears to catch the words of wisdom which fell from the mouths of the great and the good.

'Every word she writes is a lie, including "and" and "the"' was Mary McCarthy's opinion of Lilian Hellman. Prone to envy, perhaps because they work alone in a field where success is elusive and unpredictable, when writers get together, they sometimes have a tendency to slag each other off.

'We were a dreadful set of harpies; Middle-aged writers of mild distinction are singularly unpleasant to my taste. They remind me of those bald-necked vultures at the zoo, with their drooping blood-shot eyes, who are always on the lookout for a lump of raw meat.'*

While not as bad as poets with 'their petty ambitions and their cut-throat behaviour',† those familiar with both writers and people in show business say that on the whole the former are meaner, pettier, nastier, more narcissistic and more competitive, while the latter are more generous both with money and goodwill.

The Camden Town lunches were my initiation into the world of writers (if not of literature), and as each 'last Wednesday' approached, curiosity got the better of me and I looked forward – despite the sometimes less agreeable aspects of the luncheons – to leaving my desk and seeing who would be there. As I gradually became accepted as a 'paid-up' member (although we did not have to pay), as part of the furniture, while I did not alter my opinion of writers as a group I made many new acquaintances and friendships which have endured.

When Koritsas was sold, the 'luncheon' moved to Hampstead.

* Virginia Woolf
† Muriel Spark

THE WRITING GAME

First to Fagin's Kitchen, which eventually closed, then to a Lebanese restaurant from which one of our more outspoken members had us excommunicated, and later to the Everyman where the food – a preponderance of the fashionable 'potato skins' – did not appeal and to which not many people came. Later, the residue of Hunter's inspiration was to return to Koritsas (under new management), but by this time most of the original members, including myself, were too busy writing and pounding the literary circuit to spare the time to attend. Although a nucleus of two or three original members were still for a time to be found on every last Wednesday at the now renamed restaurant which opened under new management, the 'luncheon' gradually fell into desuetude and was later supplanted by monthly get-togethers at a Dickensian pub in Soho. The centrally located and hideously expensive Groucho Club – frequented by the 'café society' of publishers and publicists as well as the better-heeled writers – together with Auberon Waugh's Academy Club (now defunct) in Beak Street provided a more sophisticated option, while The Asylum in Rathbone Place, opened by writer and entrepreneur Michael Estorick, mopped up the surplus.

CHAPTER FIFTEEN

Getting the Balance Right

—=⟫•◆•⟪=—

'One must die to life to be more of an artist'

Rilke

A literary agent is one who understands the complexities of publishers' contracts with their reprint rights, serialisations, schedules of territories and scales of royalties, and is happy to employ a degree of assertiveness which his client himself would be embarrassed to use on his publisher. The occupation itself is little over a 100 years old and was brought into being by the arrival of mass literacy, the mechanisation of book production, and the publishing explosion of the second half of the nineteenth century.

Among current agents, no longer the slow-going amateurs of British publishing, Ed Victor with his multiple homes, his Rolls-Royce Silver Cloud and his high profile clients (Will Self, Iris Murdoch, Douglas Adams and Jack Higgins) is easily the most flamboyant. There is no longer any such thing as 'publisher loyalty' any more than there is agent loyalty. It's a case of dog eat dog and whoever promises the biggest advance gets the writer. Ed Victor's technique is to offer a publisher a manuscript – or possibly just a chapter – with a firm price-tag and a couple of days to consider it. At the end of this time the publisher is obliged to say yes or no to the book on which there is little room for negotiation.

All this however was yet to come. Even had it not been I was then, and remain now, incapable of writing the formulaic 'commercial' fiction sold by the likes of Ed Victor or Andrew Wylie.

When I switched to Ilsa Yardley, a lamb to Joyce Weiner's lion, I put my trust and my literary *oeuvre* in the hands of an agent of the old school. Unlike the American Debbie Owen, Ilsa and I were not only the same age, and on the same wavelength, but we were not divided by a common language. The fact that she was always available to her clients to whom she gave freely of her expertise, her time, and unlimited patience, made her worth her weight in gold.

The author/agent relationship has been compared, not unreasonably, with marriage, albeit a rather lopsided one. The agent is the first outsider to clap eyes on a new piece of work and her reaction both in terms of speed and quality of appraisal is of the utmost importance. Playwright Neil Simon (only partly in jest), reveals how he delivered a script to his agent and was outraged to find that she hadn't called by the time he returned to his flat: 'My God, the woman had twenty minutes to read the play, what else did she have to do?'

You must of course have confidence in your agent's critical ability and, if the relationship is to succeed, you should be willing to be guided by it. If you find yourself pulling in opposite directions you should find another agent more in tune with your particular style of writing. An agent must have faith in your work and in you as a writer. With these givens she will spare no pains to bring your manuscript to the notice of a specific person at an appropriate house – matching author to publisher – and will promote your career in general. A good agent will have her ear to the ground. She will be known to, and on good terms with, a variety of editors, although she will not spend so long lunching with them as to have neither time nor inclination for her desk; she will be aware of who is looking for what in terms of *genre*, who is firmly established (her star in the ascendant), and who is about to move 'house'. Authors of a respected agent with clout will be given priority, as well as serious consideration, by a publisher. Any manuscript rubber-stamped by her will automatically be deemed to have passed the first hurdle.

Ilsa Yardley, a director of Elaine Greene Ltd, was well known and highly regarded in the literary world, but it was on the personal level that she stood out as the ideal author's agent. The very nature of the work dictates that the author is temperamental. By this I do not mean that she is necessarily unstable, but that writing represents a curious phenomenon. An actor will strut and fret 'his hour upon the stage' and when the curtain comes down at the end of the evening he will step forward to acknowledge the applause which completes the creative process. Not so the writer. Wearily she writes *finis* on the last of her 300 hundred odd pages to be confronted with a deafening silence. There is no audience to applaud his sustained performance, no 'A' for effort, nobody either knows or cares. It will be a year or more, nine months if he is lucky, before anyone, other than his publisher, is even aware that he has written a book. Except for his agent. A good agent will not only give an immediate and considered opinion on the work, suggesting changes which may or may not be acted upon, but will sustain the spirits of the writer during the lengthy and often fraught period between penning the last word and publication. Besides being an extremely efficient agent, Ilsa Yardley was a copy editor par excellence and willing to undertake this onerous task in addition to her other duties. A manuscript can never be read too many times – it is in the nature of mistakes to creep in.

No matter how frequently Ilsa was telephoned in exasperation over the dilatoriness of an editor, the apparent apathy of a publicity department, the seeming lack of either communication or co-operation with the author by the publishing house, one was greeted with a sympathetic ear. Ilsa was never fazed and one had the impression, given by any agent worth her salt, that you were her only client.

During this time, unfortunately before I was able to dedicate one of my books to her which with her characteristic forthrightness she hinted that I should, Joyce Weiner died. I was the last of her friends to see her alive. Joyce and Margery had lived out their retirement in a cottage in Battle, Sussex. Theirs was not the archetypal cottage in its own picturesque grounds, but a converted artisan's dwelling in the centre of the historic town, the main thoroughfare of which passed within a few yards of its door. The old adage that 'it is not the place that makes the person but the person the place' was exemplified at 36 Lower Lake. The cottage was minute, the street door opening directly into the living room, but its ambience bespoke the whole world, with every available space – even above the front door – filled with books. There was of course no television set, no concessions to modernity other than the background heating the sisters had installed in deference to their age, and a welcoming fire burned perpetually in the tiny grate. Into these unassuming surroundings – one 'knocked-through' room, its tiny kitchen concealed by a cunning cupboard, extended by the narrowest of gardens in which Margery grew the old roses (on which she was a renowned expert and adviser to *Malmaison*) – poured a constant stream of celebrated visitors from the local Muggeridges (Malcolm and Kitty) and Longfords (Frank and Elizabeth), to anyone who was anyone in the literary world. Margery's cooking (second only to her gardening expertise) appeared miraculously from the confined space behind the cupboard door, and her excellent *daubes*, redolent of thyme, were interspersed in summer with *déjeuners sur l'herbe* in the Sussex countryside, visits to Battle Abbey, and jaunts to Bateman's, Rudyard Kipling's home.

Joyce had always suffered from high blood pressure and the stress and loneliness induced by Margery's death from a heart attack did nothing to improve this condition. When I heard that she was in hospital, conscious of the fact that she had not a single living relative (Margery had been the sum total of her family), I was prompted, despite the fact that it was a filthy and unforgiving winter's day, to put down my pen and take the train to Hastings to visit her. Outside the ward a young doctor warned me that Joyce Weiner was extremely ill. Although she admitted to severe pain in her chest and appeared to be breathless, I found her lying on her bed looking much the same as usual. Being Joyce, there was of course a book in her hand. It was the pre-publication copy of a new novel and, as she was at pains to point out, was dedicated to her by one of her ex-authors. It came to me that this comment was by way of reproach, and that I had never seen fit to do likewise. I made up my mind to repair the omission with my very next book. We spoke of this and that – Joyce was as punctilious in enquiring after one's family as she was after one's literary output – until she grew tired and suggested I have some lunch in the visitors' canteen. I did as she suggested. By the time I returned to the ward she was dead.

It was the end of an era. I do not think Joyce Weiner would have taken kindly to the sordid battles for review and shelf space of the more than 100,000 titles (including new editions and imported books) now published each year; with the cut and thrust of the new conglomerates; with the emphasis on marketing; with the fact that most authors receive a pittance in return for producing a finely crafted book and that only a handful can command fortunes because their names attract buyers; that a novel need no longer be *well* written (in the short term trash sells better than non-trash) only written by one of the literary Mafia who have dominated the publishing scene over the past 20 years, or by a young and trendy newcomer (preferably photogenic); that the newspapers ignore novels (unless by the above), W. H. Smith doesn't want them and the libraries can't afford them; and above all with the demise of the 'gentleman' in publishing. Of all the literati befriended by Joyce Weiner over the years, only a handful attended her funeral. Although I never did get round to dedicating a book to her, I think of her often and visit her grave with its headstone inscribed at her request with Browning's questionable assertion that 'The best is yet to be'. Joyce's memory is perpetuated by two hydrangea bushes in our garden, given to us with characteristic generosity as cuttings by Margery, and which we have christened 'Joyce and Marge'.

Although Ilsa Yardley was an excellent representative for

books, she believed that a good agent should stick to his last and did not handle television or film rights, a growth sector which demanded specialised knowledge.

The screenplay of *The Long Hot Summer* was still kicking around. Despite the best efforts of Stuart Lyons, who was confident that he would eventually find backers for the film, and his continued and cheery injunctions to 'keep biting the bullet', I was disappointed at the failure of this particular project to get off the ground. Uncertain if I had any future as a screenwriter, or if I should forget the whole episode, I gave *The Long Hot Summer* to a friend, Bruce (*Withnail and I*) Robinson, for his honest opinion and advice. Bruce, a highly paid scriptwriter, fresh from his acclaim for *The Killing Fields*, nobly agreed to read it. I say 'nobly' because reading other people's work is one of the more onerous tasks to befall a writer and one which he will generally do almost anything to avoid. The writer *cannot* offer a free reading and advisory service. There is scarcely enough capacity in his brain for his own projects, without the additional lumber of unpublished manuscripts written by tyros, or circulating screenplays unable to find a home. It took Bruce six months to read the script, a dilatoriness which I more than understood. He finally managed to get down to it on a flight to India, and his pronouncement was responsible for ultimately opening out my writing career and for setting it on its new trajectory.

Bruce was impressed and thought that on the basis of the script of *The Long Hot Summer*, I had a natural talent for writing for the screen. He pointed me in the right direction by introducing me, with the strongest recommendation, to his own film and TV agent, Linda Seifert.

Linda Seifert was tiny, young, attractive and giggly. Her offices, hung with movie posters, were white, pink, and feminine. It was hard to believe that from behind her immaculate executive desk strewn with giant scent bottles and with flowers in season Linda, an ex-barrister, engaged writers, producers and directors on both sides of the Atlantic, brought them together, and clinched multi million dollar deals.

A recommendation from Bruce Robinson was an open sesame to an agent whom it was as difficult to get to represent one as it was to get a movie made. Linda read the script of *The Long Hot Summer* and from that moment on we were in business. From having no agent at all, I now had two (three including Caroline Sheldon) and felt constrained to live up to their expectations.

At our very first meeting, at which Linda introduced me to her co-director, the beautiful and *soignée* Elizabeth Dench from Jamaica, who added as much to the décor as she did to the nuts and bolts of the business, Linda demanded that I return immediately and bring her every single book that I had written. I filled the car boot with my *oeuvre* and dutifully arrived in Brunswick Gardens. If I was surprised at Linda's request for all my books, I was even more surprised at the fact that this laid-back but dynamic lady actually *read* them. And read them she did. Having read, digested, and purported to like them, she set out to exploit them, and from that day to this her patience, determination and enthusiasm for my work, no matter how apparently time-expired, has not diminished. Of all the agents I know, Linda and Elizabeth are always accessible and not perpetually in a 'meeting'. To visit them and their enthusiastic staff, situated today in a tall narrow house in the heart of Soho, is to receive the shot in the arm of encouragement, the injection of faith, the charge of confidence necessary to do battle with the frustrations and vicissitudes of the movie world, compared with which those endemic to publishing are zilch.

'No writer can be a joiner. He must preserve his independence at all costs.'* The move to central London not only brought me to the Camden writers' lunches but to such institutions as PEN (Poets, Essayists, Novelists), of which I am now a Fellow and later served on the executive committee, the Society of Authors, where I also did my three-year stint on the management committee, the Writers' Guild, and the Royal Society of Literature which exists to sustain all that is best in English letters, and to encourage a catholic appreciation of literature.

International PEN (a federation of around 130 individual PEN centres in some 100 countries) is a worldwide association of writers. Its aim is to promote intellectual co-operation and understanding among writers that will both emphasise the central role of literature in the development of world culture, and defend it against the many threats to its survival. Wholly non-political, International PEN acts as a powerful voice in opposing political censorship and speaking out for writers who are harassed, imprisoned (and sometimes executed) by governments for the expression of their views. It fights for freedom of expression and opposes the tyranny and censorship of repressive regimes both of the extreme Right and the extreme Left. Founded in London in 1921 under the presidency of John Galsworthy, and with Joseph Conrad, George Bernard Shaw and H. G. Wells as founder members, centres were soon started in Europe with the active involvement of Anatole France, Paul Valéry, Thomas Mann, Benedetto Croce and Karel Capek. PEN members have included Nobel Prize winners. Writers such as

---

* J. B. Priestley

Alberto Moravia, Heinrich Böll, Arthur Miller and Mario Vargas Llosa are amongst its past presidents. The PEN charter affirms that literature knows no frontiers and that there should be unhampered transmission of thought between all nations. It pledges itself to oppose such evils of a free press as mendacious publication, deliberate falsehood and distortion of facts for political and personal ends. Its membership is open to all qualified writers, editors and translators who subscribe to these aims, without regard to nationality, colour, or creed. At the annual PEN Congress, representatives and delegates from each centre meet to hold cultural events and literary forums through which PEN seeks to further its ideals.

The desperately inadequate offices of English PEN are at 7 Dilke Street, Chelsea, and the members meet in the studio upstairs on Wednesday evenings. Besides a lively programme of talks and discussions on a wide variety of literary subjects, there are quarterly dinners at which the distinguished speakers have included Lord Weidenfeld, Lord and Lady Longford, Lady Antonia Fraser, Harold Pinter, Conor Cruise O'Brien, Lord Gowrie, William Cooper, Brenda Maddox, Frederick Forsyth and Melvyn Bragg. The proceedings were dominated in the early days (when PEN headquarters were at Glebe House) by David Carver and Angus Wilson, and over the years by Francis King, Antonia Fraser (trailing in her regal wake Harold Pinter and representing the formidable tribe of writing Longfords), Katharine Nott, Marjorie Watts, Harold Harris, Jasper Ridley and Lettice Cooper. When I became a PEN member this close-knit band was manipulated by the indefatigable PEN secretary Josephine Pullein-Thompson (herself a writer of children's books) later to become president. Respecter of neither rank nor title Josephine ruled her nursery of writers, no matter how eminent, with an iron and totalitarian hand.

Despite its annual International Writers' Day with its eminent guest lecturers – Anthony Burgess, Mario Vargos Llosa, George Steiner, Tom Stoppard, Saul Bellow, J. M. Coetzee, Doris Lessing – and awards (the J. R. Ackerly Prize, the Macmillan Silver Pen Award for Fiction, the Stern Silver Pen Award for Non-Fiction and the ST Dupont Gold Pen Award for Distinguished service to Literature), English PEN seems to some still to some to be a bastion of elitism, a closed shop of inbreeding from which the life-giving force of the new young writer with his iconoclastic and contemporary approach may well feel himself excluded. To her own discredit Josephine Pullein-Thompson tells the story of how every Wednesday night at Chelsea bus-stops young writers were to be found in tears. When asked what they were crying about they replied that they had just been to a PEN meeting and that nobody spoke to them. Under the present presidency of Lady Rachel Billington desperate moves are being made to try to change the situation.

'When we begin working, we are so poor and so busy that we have neither the time nor the means to defend ourselves against the commercial organisations which exploit us. When we become famous, we become famous suddenly, passing at one bound from the state in which we are too poor to fight our own battles, to a state in which our time is so valuable that it is not worth our while wasting any of it on lawsuits and bad debts. We all, eminent and obscure alike, need the Authors' Society,' stated George Bernard Shaw, 'we all owe it a share of our time, our means, our influence.'

The Society of Authors, championed over the years by such illustrious writers as Galsworthy, Hardy, Wells, Barrie and

Masefield, with Alfred Lord Tennyson as its first president, was founded in 1884 by Walter Besant to promote the interests of authors and to defend their rights. With its 6,000 strong membership it differs from PEN in that it is a limited company and has been certified as an independent trade union (not affiliated to the TUC). The society is non-elitist and goes out of its way to greet new members and make them feel at home. It has held some enjoyable weekend seminars, in which I have taken part, at the universities of York, Warwick, and Nottingham – on themes such as 'The Business of Writing' and 'From Pencil to Print' – at which 'names' and newcomers are made equally welcome.

The society, which has immediate access to solicitors, accountants and insurance consultants, campaigns for the benefit of the profession to improve terms and conditions and has recently been successful in establishing Minimum Terms Agreements with a growing number of publishers. It vets contracts, takes up complaints on behalf of authors, pursues legal actions for breach of contract (copyright infringement etc.), gives advice on manuscripts, assists authors in finding agents, chases unpaid royalties and at the moment is carrying out random checks of authors' royalty accounts. It publishes guidelines on matters of interest to the writer, from Permissions and Copyrights to Buying a Word Processor, Income Tax, VAT, and How to Sell Your Writing, as well as running a Retirement Benefit Scheme and Pension Fund. The society produces a quarterly journal *The Author* – an invaluable source of information – battles for tax concessions, supports the National Book Committee, the International Confederation of Societies of Authors and Composers, and the Congress of European Writers' Organisations. It hosts conferences, meetings and receptions and administers prizes –

the Somerset Maugham and Betty Trask awards for fiction and the Cholmondeley Awards for poetry – and nominates, through the Committee of Management, candidates for the Nobel Prize for Literature.

Above all the society has been instrumental in the introduction of the Public Lending Right Act (1979). Under this Act, payment is made from public funds to authors whose books are lent out from public libraries. Payment is made annually (in February) and the amount received is proportionate to the number of times (calculated on the basis of samples from 30 library authorities in the UK) that an author's books were borrowed during the previous year. Of total state funding of £4.9 million for the scheme, £4.25 million is distributed. At the time of writing the rate per loan is 2.07 pence, but this sum varies from year to year according to the number of titles registered and the funds available. Authors registered for PLR number 27,275, of whom nearly 10,000 received no PLR payments (because their earnings were calculated as under £5). Of the 17,512 who did receive payment, 93 hit the maximum threshold of £6,000 while those earning between £5 and £99 totalled 12,012. Thirty-nine authors received between £5,000 and £5,999, 231 received £2,500 – £4,999, 610 received £1,000 – £2,499, 787 received £500 – £999 while 3,740 authors netted between £100 and £499.

The tally lands on the author's desk each January. It represents a welcome shot in the arm for the struggling writer, a bonus (a percentage of which is not hived off by the agent) for those well established, and a sense of achievement, which publishers never seem to engender, for all.

According to the registrar of PLR, the scheme plays a 'vital role ... in sustaining authors' creativity'. Joanna Trollope, before she became a bestseller, remembers the importance of receiving her PLR cheque in the 'bleak month of February' and a great many writers' hearts are gladdened when the familiar annual printout arrives from Stockton-on-Tees. Despite the steady decrease in per capita library loans, they find that they have been rewarded for work well done (PLR is not a charity handout) and that a great many people have borrowed, if not necessarily read, their books.

The names of the seven (adult) novelists who record total loans of over a million are familiar: Agatha Christie, Catherine Cookson, Dick Francis, Jack Higgins, Ellis Peters, Ruth Rendell and Danielle Steel. In the categories only a little further down (loans over half a million and loans over 300,000) come many lesser known authors who write mainly for the library market and are often ignored by the book pages of the national press.

Romantic fiction is the favourite diet of British readers and the works of Barbara Cartland, Dorothy Eden, Victoria Holt, Jean Plaidy (Eleanor Alice Hibbert) and Margaret Pargeter are borrowed by more than 8,500,000 readers a year. The 'bestsellers' of Jeffrey Archer, James Herriot and Harold Robbins claim one-third of this figure, while books by 'serious authors' – such as William Golding – are taken from the shelves a mere 880,000 times. Dick Francis and Wilbur Smith are amongst the top ten most borrowed fiction authors, and P. D. James, Ted Allbeury, and Jilly Cooper amongst the 100 most borrowed adult authors.

While the PLR office is not able to disclose the amounts earned by individuals, it has been hinted that the 'star' performers do not dominate the library scene to the extent that their publicity suggests.

For many writers it is not the sum of money received which is important – although many authors have come to rely on this annual injection of cash – but the boost to his ego which the payment on the bottom line of the familiar green printout represents. Other than from his half-yearly royalty statements and, if he is lucky, the sight of his books in the bookshops, the writer is uncertain if there is in reality anyone 'out there' reading him. The irrefutable evidence that 100,000 or so people have actually borrowed his books (many of which may have been long out of print), gives a boost to his self-esteem out of all proportion to his actual share of the PLR cake.

When one author enquires of another his PLR figures, it is to test his own popularity as a writer against that of a rival, rather than to compare the financial gain which even at its zenith is hardly a king's ransom. With the continuing efforts of the registrar on our behalf, it may well be that at some date in the not too distant future, the financial rewards of PLR will be a reflection of the writer's true worth ('The chief glory of every people arises from its authors') and match the personal satisfaction he gets as a result of the scheme.

In addition to PEN and the Society of Authors, other professional organisations to which I now belong are The Writers' Guild of Great Britain (affiliated to the TUC), and BAFTA (the British Academy of Film and Television Arts).

While the Society of Authors supports the individual writer, the Writers' Guild (incorporating the Theatre Writers' Union) is a unique trade union for writers working in film, publishing, radio, television and theatre. With its emphasis on collective action the guild ensures that the writer will be represented and his voice heard on important legislative matters which are often susceptible to influence only by collective strength. For predominantly historical reasons, the Society of Authors (with its flat rate membership contribution) is a 'book-writer' orientated organisation, while the guild (which relies on a percentage of members' earnings) concentrates on screenwriters. In matters of policy, the two structures are very different.

One great benefit of belonging to the Society of Authors is automatic membership of the Authors' Licensing & Collecting Society. The ALCS is the British collecting society for all writers. It is a non-profit making company, set up in 1977, to ensure that hard-to-collect revenues due to authors are efficiently collected and speedily distributed. It chases the pots of money (£10 million annually) waiting for British writers in other European countries, such as Germany, where, under West German law, PLR must be paid to a foreign collecting society and not directly to authors. The additional income derived from this source is often very well worth having.

The longstanding question of whether both the Society of Authors *and* The Writers' Guild are still necessary, was confronted when talks took place to discuss the possible amalgamation of the two bodies. The guild, which took the initiative, had more to gain from the merger in terms of premises and assets, while the society saw it as an opportunity to welcome Writers' Guild members back into the fold. The talks soon broke down however and the idea of a single 'writers' union' which would provide members with stronger representation and better services was put on a back burner.

I was proposed for membership of BAFTA by screenwriter Bruce Robinson and seconded by the late David Deutsch, a renowned film maker whose father, Oscar, was the founder of the Odeon (OD) cinema chain. Under its president, H.R.H. the Princess Royal and council of management, which includes Lord Attenborough CBE, Lord Puttnam CBE, and Sir Sydney

Getting the Balance Right

Samuelson CBE, the Academy's principal aims are to promote and advance education and cultivate and improve public taste in the visual arts. It holds screenings, meetings, and special events (including masterclasses, seminars and panel discussions) at 195 Piccadilly, and hosts the Lloyds Bank BAFTA Performers Awards Ceremony at Grosvenor House (televised by the BBC) as well as fulfilling its charitable obligations. On the rank and file members such as myself, BAFTA bestows privileges such as use of the academy's club facilities, nominations and voting rights for the academy's annual BAFTA awards, and weekly screenings of films and TV programmes: approximately two screenings every weekday of a cross-section of international, recently released or prereleased films (accompanied by the latest Dolby sound) are held, often in the presence of producers, directors, writers and other members of the cast and crew. These movies are seen from the comfort of endowed armchairs, followed by a civilised Roux Brothers buffet supper over which views about the movies can be exchanged in congenial sur-roundings with fellow academicians.

By becoming a member of these societies I was at last able to enjoy the company of fellow authors and screenwriters on an *ad hoc* basis, and to compare notes with them on such seminal topics as publishers, agents, sales of books, and screenplays. When the Camden 'lunches' lapsed, I crossed the river as often as I could to the south London writers' lunches (Lee Langley, Wendy Perriam, Tim Heald, David Benedictus and William Cooper), held first in the Orange Tree pub at Richmond and later at the White Hart on the river.

Today I sit above the salt at the PEN quarterly dinners and campaign actively for a central London Writers' House, with lecture and resource rooms as well as restaurant facilities – of

213

particular interest to country members – for the purposes of which we have applied to the Arts Lottery Board for funds.

I am an active member of the Books to Prisoners Committee, unique to English PEN, which solicits and sends monthly parcels of books (providing encouragement and hope) to writers detained or persecuted for their opinions expressed in writing and without violence, in 25 countries, including Angola, China, Cuba, Ecuador, El Salvador, Kenya, Turkey, Syria, Tibet and Vietnam. Such work, supported by generous patrons such as Books Etc – who ensure that we have a regular supply of new books – has in many cases led to the liberation of imprisoned writers or at least an improvement in their conditions. While in many cases we are unaware whether or not our jiffy bags have actually reached the addressees, some are acknowledged by flimsy prison letters the contents of which not only vindicate our continued efforts but bring tears to our eyes.

As the pressure to join, serve and write articles for this, that and the other professional organisation grows and one's presence is requested at vigils (to show solidarity with imprisoned writers) lectures, meetings, dinners, outings, parties (Christmas, mid-Summer, farewell), prize-givings, receptions and fundraising events, the writer must take good care not to be too frequently sidetracked.

CHAPTER SIXTEEN

The Circus Doesn't Creep into Town

'Man is so made by nature as to require him to restrict his movements as far as his hands and feet will take him.'

Gandhi

An author's relationship with a publisher is, for reasons best known to themselves, always a delicate one. Despite the fierce dedication of most editors to their jobs (they are certainly not in it for the money) and the genuine motivation of art departments, sales and marketing teams with their firm commitment to the books they produce, one also has to cope with an inhouse pride.

My second book to be published by Gollancz was *A Loving Mistress* over which I not only again crossed swords with Livia but also with the Gollancz publicity machine. Livia liked my

215

new novel, which followed the successful *Proofs of Affection*, but she did not approve of *Odalisque*, an upmarket and carefully chosen title which, coupled with a full-colour reproduction of Ingres's *Odalisque Couchée* (naked and seductively disported on a *chaise longue*), intimated the theme of the book.

By the time of her twenty-fifth birthday in December 1800, Jane Austen had completed drafts of three full length novels: 'Elinor and Marianne' (subsequently *Sense and Sensibility*), 'First Impressions' (*Pride and Prejudice*) and 'Susan' (*Northanger Abbey*).

The title of a novel is the first part of the text and the power it has to attract and hold the reader's attention should not be underestimated. Choosing a title is an important part of the creative process and brings into focus what the novel is supposed to be about. While Charles Dickens jotted down some 14 possibilities – including *Stubborn Things*, *The Grindstone*, and *Mr Gradgrind's Facts* – to illustrate the social concerns dealt with in what ultimately became *Hard Times*, many novelists simply take the line of least resistance and turn either to the Bible, or to the works of Shakespeare, a seemingly bottomless resource which has yielded amongst countless other titles *Greenmantle*, *Cold Comfort Farm*, *The Name of the Rose*, *The Dogs of War*, *Under the Greenwood Tree*, *Summer's Lease*, *Remembrance of Things Past* and *Chronicles of Wasted Time*.

Arguing with a publisher about what your book should be called is to put yourself in a no-win situation. If you stick to your guns over the title and the book does not sell, it will be your fault; if you agree to change the title and the book does not sell, it will still be your fault – for writing a rotten book.

The Circus Doesn't Creep into Town

The objection to *Odalisque* was on the grounds that no book buyer, let alone the reading public, would know the meaning of 'Odalisque' (Gr. concubine or haetara, and by extension 'mistress'). Did it matter? How many readers know the meaning of *Iliad* or *Odyssey*? Yet sticking to these titles, even for English language translations, does not appear to have done Homer's epic any harm. An obscure but mellifluous title – the sound of which might in time become familiar – was, I felt, intriguing, especially when it was combined with the portrait of an unclothed temptress in the form of a wrap-round jacket. Livia stood her ground. So did I. In the end I gave in as I was to do later when I changed *Judgement of Paris* to *An Eligible Man* at the behest of London Weekend Television. Leaning over backwards to please everybody at Gollancz, I not only compromised my artistic integrity but ended up pleasing nobody.

Apart from the title and jacket illustration, Livia Gollancz had one other objection to the book in which the story was set out not in conventional chapters, but in a succession of short paragraphs, separated by line spaces, which meaningfully punctuated the narrative.

'People won't pay for white paper,' Livia objected, although this was by no means the first time this format had been used. She ordered me to elide my paragraphs into sizeable chunks of text, which would of course detract from the lyrical significance of the pauses. The battle, of commercial consideration over literary device, resulted in a draw. I went over the manuscript and obliged where possible but a compromise was reached and I managed, for the main part, to stick to the shape and order of my novel.

A Loving Mistress (1983) ran to two impressions, was

217

serialised on BBC Woman's Hour (on which I was also interviewed), published in Large Print, extracted in *Woman's Journal*,
and rights were sold to Italy. It was optioned for television by
Leon Clore (Miron Films), called in for consideration by MGM,
and according to PLR figures (16 years after publication) is still
being borrowed by more than 1,000 readers a year. That it was
only moderately successful in terms of hardback sales I put
down to the fact that the title – *A Loving Mistress* – promised
Mills & Boon but did not deliver it, and was responsible for yet
another novel falling between two stools.

'I know the value of publicity and am not opposed to it, but
for a man of letters modesty and an attitude towards readers
and fellow writers that suits literature is the best and most
effective publicity.' Chekhov notwithstanding, because of the
inexorable rise in title output and the burgeoning market for
information, books were now forced to contend not only with
each other but with tennis players and recalcitrant politicians
for newspaper coverage. However good a book may be, no
matter how numerous and enthusiastic its reviews, its chances
of commercial success will be slender unless it is vigorously
marketed. Although the book trade can never be as competitive
as the grocery trade – there is no copyright on baked beans –
publishers' sales forces had to turn to other retail strategies in
order to compete effectively and to see what merchandising
lessons could be learned.

Between the appearance of *Proofs of Affection* which owed
its success to reviews and word-of-mouth rather than any visible
publicity campaign on the part of the publishers, and the
submission of *A Loving Mistress*, I discovered that many successful authors, disenchanted with the publishers' efforts on
their behalf, promoted their own books. Ilsa Yardley intro-

The Circus Doesn't Creep into Town

duced me to the late Jeremy Hadfield, a publicity agent well known and respected in the book trade, who represented many authors and worked happily in conjunction with their publishers. Jeremy read my manuscript and thought that *A Loving Mistress* had immense PR potential, both for the quality of the writing and the topical subject matter. If I were to employ him, he was convinced that he could mount a successful national publicity campaign on my behalf. Agreeing with Truman Capote that 'A boy's gotta hustle his book' (which seemed only common sense), I was delighted with Jeremy's reaction to my novel and with his outline proposals for its promotion. I made the mistake of thinking that Gollancz would be equally pleased. To my surprise, Livia would have nothing to do with Hadfield Associates. Although Gollancz stood only to gain from the increased sales that the additional coverage of *A Loving Mistress* would undoubtedly bring, she refused to publish my book rather than co-operate. Ilsa and I were astounded at this dog-in-the-manger reaction. Livia had minimal plans and an equally minimal budget for publicising *A Loving Mistress* herself, yet refused to allow Hadfield Associates to do it for her at no extra expense. It was as if I had made some improper suggestion, and my relationship with Gollancz, and in particular with the PR department – who in the event did less than nothing to promote the book – became decidedly cool.

Having successfully fought her corner on the questions of title and publicity (or lack of it) for *A Loving Mistress*, Livia – for whom on a personal level I have nothing but respect – agreed to my suggestion of Ingres's *Odalisque Couchée* for the jacket, with the proviso that it was reproduced in black-and-white (rather than the evocative cerulean blue of the original), and reduced from its original in-your-face size to a miniature!

Despite the fact that a good book jacket immediately and accurately conveys the mood and content of a book, a large percentage of jacket designs are ill-conceived, and authors – who are often not consulted about them – are betrayed by the very people who, in their own interests at least, should be falling over themselves to make their work look irresistible. Using a sketchy and ill-defined turbaned figure climbing a rockface to sell a 'breathtaking story of love and passion' (Michael Ondaatje's *The English Patient*), or a fragment of a snapshot, a saint, and a painted plate to depict the 'secrets and lies' and 'guilty silences' promised by the blurb of Michèle Roberts's *Daughters of the House*, are hardly likely to catch a potential reader's eye.

The jacket design for Graham Greene's *Our Man in Havana* featured a sexy girl sitting on the edge of a desk. Greene announced that if the jacket went ahead he would change his publisher. In a recent letter to the *Independent on Sunday*, Muriel Spark begged, through their columns, to dissociate her 'name, mentality and intelligence' from that of her publishers. The bone of contention was the fact that the publishers, failing to respond to all requests and representations on the matter, was using 32-year-old quotes, now meaningless and unintelligible, on the jackets of her reissued books.

Covers, the all-important link between author and reader, which should appeal equally to either sex and to the whole spectrum of reading tastes, are, and always will be, the most discussed, the most fought about, and the most contentious topic in any publishing house. I have been luckier than many authors in respect of my jackets, many of which have been beautifully illustrated by artists such as Pierre Le Tan as well as by Adrian George (whose sketches of eminent literary figures appeared weekly in *The Times*). However, despite the fact that Simon & Schuster specifically requested my ideas for the jacket of *Golden Boy*, and I spent many hours tracking down suitable illustrations in picture libraries, marketing's unhappy choice was a man walking along a railway line despite the fact that my wealthy, eponymous protagonist *never ever* travelled by train! Their similarly inappropriate portrayal of my aristocratic heroine Clare de Cluzac (*Vintage*) wearing a shiny, green, puff-sleeved *long* evening dress (suitable only for a village hop) when the text dictated a sophisticated short black number at home in London nightspots, gave no clear picture of what to expect in quality and content from my two most recent novels.

The relevance of book jackets to sales is accepted, but the nature of them is often hotly debated by disgruntled authors who feel that the design of a book should be a supporting statement, an affidavit of his taste, and that it should not mislead the reader by misrepresenting his position. No author should lose sight of the fact that while it is his job to write, it is that of the publisher to publish. Because book jackets and blurbs (which I will come to later) however, are usually often the responsibility of people with impossibly heavy workloads, it is in the author's interest to monitor these matters as closely, and with as much tact, as he can.

Les plaisirs de la table commencent avec les yeux. As with the presentation of food, so it is with the writing of books. No one who has spent weeks planning, days shopping, and hours in the kitchen preparing a special meal, would be happy to see her creations inappropriately presented. She would take jolly good care to see that her painstakingly clarified *consommé* was not served in polystyrene cups nor her beautifully risen *soufflé* allowed to hang about until it subsided before it was brought to the table.

Flaubert – who purported to despise publicity – scorned those writers who put their photographs on their books, but anything which encourages the browser to pick up a title, to discover at a glance something about author and the content of his novel, is OK by me and it does not seem at all unreasonable for the one who has laboured to produce the book to expect the jacket to reflect accurately what he has written.

In 1985 Collins commissioned an enquiry to discover why the sales of Agatha Christie were declining. Erstwhile fans were unable to put their fingers on the reasons why they no longer read Miss Christie, but researchers discovered that there was amongst their responses one common denominator: the paperback jackets no longer conveyed 'the qualities of the author'. The illustrations were wholly unsuitable. They depicted blood and gore when what Agatha Christie's readers had come to expect from her was 'nice' murders. Christie said one thing, the jackets another. Collins redesigned them, with images more clearly linked to the text, and sales shot up.

If the buyer of a book shop or chain is not *instantly* impressed by a book jacket (he will rarely have time to read the blurb), his initial order, especially in the case of mid-list authors, may be small and the title will have little chance – short of winning a major prize – of picking up again.

'Blurb' is an eponym derived from Miss Belinda Blurb, who in 1906 appeared on the cover of a book by American humorist, Gellett Burger: Miss Blurb's picture bore no relation to the erotic contents of the book. In the early days the blurb was often written, sometimes at the last moment, by a junior member of staff who had only skimmed the text. She would ploddingly paraphrase the story (sometimes revealing far too much of the plot), fail to convey the magic, or core quality, of the writing, and frequently, and unforgivably, misspell, or mistake, the names of the characters. Now, however, blurbs are a key marketing tool and, since 52 per cent of novels are bought on impulse, what is written on the inside flap is of paramount importance. The author should be sent a proposed blurb, in good time, and if he is not permitted to redraft it, his suggestions for its improvement should be at least be given serious and top level consideration. The same criteria apply to the biographical details and the accompanying photograph which will generally correspond to the writer's image of himself. While Martin Amis lets us know that he got a First in English at Oxford, Julian Barnes doesn't even tell us that he went there – although, in a *volte face*, he legitimately reveals that he is the recipient of two of France's main literary prizes. Some authors disclose that they are married, occasionally together with the identity of their spouses; children are more likely to be acknowledged by women (Erica Jong goes so far as to name hers) than by men, and few authors over 25 mention their age unless, as is the wont of many female authors, they have subtracted at least 10 years.

The fragile partnership of author and publisher is often put to the test in the period between delivery of the manuscript and publication. The author, who often has intimate and specialised knowledge of the buyers his book might attract – be they beekeepers or biochemists – may be brimming over with ideas for its promotion. He may be consulted, but he is not always encouraged to play an active part in PR decisions.

THE WRITING GAME

No one will deny that, in commercial terms, the publisher knows his job and should be allowed to get on with it. There seems to be no reason, other than small-mindedness however, why an author who presents his suggestions in an orderly manner and at the proper moment, should not be invited at least to meet, if not to liaise with, design and sales staff, or why he should be regarded as a nuisance if he asks for a progress report on his book. If the publicity department has done its job, the author will be sent on a publicity tour, and interviewed, if not by national at least by local newspapers, in the week of publication of his book. He will travel from Southampton to Liverpool via Manchester and Stoke-on-Trent, to talk live on chat shows, answer listeners' down-the-line questions (clamped in massive and uncomfortable earphones) from the solitary confinement of claustrophobic studio cells, and be quizzed – between blasts of pop music – by disc jockeys who will no way have read his, if indeed any, book. The ignominy of all this – life on an Inter City train and if it's raining it must be Bolton – is compounded by the fact that despite his efforts, when wandering round the bookshops in Birmingham or Brighton to pass the time whilst waiting for his next assignment, there is every likelihood that he will not be able to find a single copy of his book.

This phenomenon has been experienced by writers across the board. Len Deighton is worth quoting on the subject: '...the London *Evening Standard*, which regularly serialised mainstream fiction, decided to buy the rights of *The Ipcress File*. When I told my publishers (Jonathan Cape) all this happy news I had the temerity to add "I hope you're printing enough copies so you don't run out of them while the serial is running." I was of course soon put in my place. I remember the publisher's stern reply as if it was yesterday. "You go on writing the books Mr

224

The Circus Doesn't Creep into Town

Deighton, and leave the publishing decisions to us." I did. The serial began on publication day: Monday. By Tuesday afternoon the few copies in central London bookshops had been sold. My book remained out of print for the whole serialisation and considerably after.'

This situation seems to come about because there is often no, or insufficient, communication between publishers' publicity and sales departments and I sometimes wonder if authors are not despatched on ineffectual jaunts, from Land's End to John O'Groats, simply to stop them ringing up the publisher to enquire about that most closely guarded secret of all, the 'sales figures'. Why these figures should be such a mystery is a mystery. It seems not unreasonable that the person who has written the book should be interested in how well, or badly, it is selling. True an author may be despondent if his novel is not doing as well as he anticipated, but he is not a child; he is fully aware of the difficulties faced by his publisher in selling books in an overcrowded and competitive market, and he should be taken into their confidence and not be treated like one.

The setting for *A Loving Mistress* is London (in particular the Rose Garden in Regent's Park) and Mauritius (*Ile Maurice*). For the former, in the period before and whilst the book was being written, I could be seen wandering round Queen Mary's Gardens with my notebook; *Ile Maurice* (for which I read Jaques Henri Bernadin de St Pierre's tragic story of *Paul et Virginie*), and the cyclone encountered by the lovers, were reconstructed from observations made in the course of my travels to the island in the Indian Ocean.

'How blissful to wake in a place where no one expects you'; during his 'passionate journeyings', Rainer Maria Rilke sought

225

to correct the 'accident of having been born in a particular place' and the countries, cities, towns and landscapes he moved through shaped his work.

Believing that experience derives more from what we feel than what we *see*, I travel primarily in order to travel, rather than to gather material for my books. Martin Cruz Smith's brilliantly successful *Gorky Park* was written without having visited Moscow, and some of our finest novels have been written with no more experience of life 'than could enter the house of a clergyman'.

None the less before 'the crowd has taken possession of places which were created by civilisation for the minority',* before Venice began to sink under the weight of its visitors (12 million a year crammed into the summer months), before one had to join an unseemly scrum in order to view the Sistine Chapel, and tourism threatened to ravage the modern world as the black plague did the medieval one, I followed the Nile in Egypt and big game in Africa, entered the Forbidden City, shed tears at the unexpected majesty of the Statue of Liberty, and wept before the Taj Mahal. I have risen at dawn to see the sun rise over the Grand Canyon, watched the 'calving' of ice in Alaska, followed in the footsteps of Mozart and of Byron, and pondered the enigma of King Solomon's mines. At the merest hint of a proposed journey I am up and away; before the idea of a foreign part has had time to coagulate in my head, I have packed my bag.

I travel not to go anywhere in particular, but simply to go, using ideas and incidents gleaned abroad in my novels but never making use of places in a straight account. I have no desire like

* José Ortega y Gasset

The Circus Doesn't Creep into Town

Flaubert – who was averse to movement and action – to travel stretched out on a divan, not stirring, watching landscapes, ruins, cities pass before him like 'the screen of a panorama mechanically unwinding', but I do agree with him that travel, like the humanities, should serve only to *enliven* one's writing style.

Just as being airborne – disagreeable as it might be at times (try China Airways or Aeroflot) – and the sybaritic lifestyle of an impersonal hotel generate ideas, travel confirms what a tiny place one occupies in the world and endorses the importance of personal observation for which the guidebook is a poor substitute. Before you can convey the 'essence' of India, you have, with your own eyes, to see dawn break over the Ganges, *hear*, with your own ears, the sound of the *dhobi wallahs* bashing the threadbare laundry on its banks. You have to clear your own path between goats being scrubbed and rugs being shaken, to bypass the sight of toenails being cut and ears being ceremoniously excavated as you weave your way between the sacred rumps of ambling cows, and bicycle rickshaws, and dodge the open sewers of the teeming city streets.

'...the eyes when I look into their pitiful homes are almost invariably steady, level and serene, the eyes of unconquered people uncrushed by their terrible circumstances, who know that what makes them human is inside them, and know also that if they become beasts it will be because what will make them beasts is inside them also.'*

As far as I am concerned, it is only through travel that the arts and the history of civilisation fall into place. Even though the

* Bernard Levin

much maligned package tour has today taken possession of artefacts and edifices created for José y Gasset's minority, I still feel the need to see them, if only because my geographical block – which reflects my total lack of sense of direction – matches my historical obstruction. When Lewis Carroll proposed 'the making of a map of England which would be the same size as England so that the user would always know where he was because he would be there' he must have had me in mind.

'Levin did not like talking and hearing about the beauty of nature. Words for him detracted from the beauty of what he saw.' One should always travel alone, or with a sympathetic and non-intrusive companion. Tolstoy's thoughts reflect my own: '"But look at the view," Sarolyenko told him when the horses had turned to the left and the Yellow River Valley opened out before them... "I can't see anything nice about it," Layevsky answered. "Always going into raptures about nature is to betray poverty of the imagination. Compared with what my imagination can offer me all those streams and cliffs are absolute rubbish, nothing else."'

While travel undoubtedly stimulates the writer's mind and, one hopes, has a beneficial effect on his prose, the lack of opportunity to travel is no excuse for 'not writing'. Jane Austen managed to produce perfectly adequate novels without leaving her parsonage.

In cities abroad, after visiting the obvious landmarks, I make for the museums, the parks and botanical gardens, the library and the local zoo which, despite the animals, is a place to study human nature. One of the perks of travel is the people one meets *en route* and who very often become lifelong friends. One strange encounter in France was with a charming English lady who modestly confessed to running a bookshop. Imagining her to be the owner of some browserie in a country town it came as a surprise when she confessed to being Christina Foyle! In Shanghai Peace Park I fell in with a professor of English in a wheelchair. An immediate friendship was struck and I corresponded with Kaikong and his family for many years afterwards.

Apart from fellow travellers, I collect 'snowdomes': those cheap plastic domes housing miniature Welsh castles, replicas of the Eiffel Tower or St Peter's Basilica in Rome, that erupt into snowy scenes when agitated and for most people are beneath contempt, but to my mind reflect the spirit of a place. One marked 'Made in China' portrays the Great Wall – topped with a strawberry! 'Smog in New York City' is filled with silver-grey pollution which obfuscates the sky when shaken. Snowdomes are probably descended, distantly, from the art of glass mosaics known as *millefiore* (thousand flowers), copied by the Venetians from the Egyptians at the time of the Renaissance. I was surprised to find recently that I was not alone in collecting this kitsch and that one enthusiast is a professor of Sanskrit at Calgary University. My other passion is bookmarks, and as years later I take books from my shelves, I am transported instantly by the gilt-tooled, fringed strips of leather in a variety of colours, denoting Boston and Beijing, Stonehenge and Singapore, to sights and cities I had all but forgotten.

Whilst travel, for this writer, is the icing on the cake of life, it also has its downside not least of which is travelling. I am no Amy Johnson, no Amelia Earhart, and have little faith in rods and pinions, human calculations and aeronautics. For me, every moment of untoward sound or movement of an aircraft, every jerk and jolt, spells disaster. I know the statistics. Airlines carry 100 million people a year; on average 7,000 of them are involved in accidents, with 80 per cent surviving (5,600) and 20 per cent dying (1,400); you have more chance of winning the lottery than being killed in an air crash; you are more at risk each time you cross the road. Were it not for the fact that flying is the only way to fly, given the choice I'd rather cross the road.

I would like to say that after so many years of filling suitcases I have reduced packing my bags to a fine art. I have not. I often wonder whether the fashion pundits who purport to travel round the world with one minimalist holdall containing a pair of jeans, a dozen white T-shirts and a Pashmina shawl, or the safari-suited journalist with torch, laptop, a spare set of underwear and a bottle of aspirin, are being equally economical with the truth.

Filling a suitcase entails choices and in the torment of making them I know that I am not alone. The advice to 'travel light' (like the mythical capsule wardrobe which fits snugly into a carry-on bag and covers any social situation) is not only deceptive – leaving one with insufficient changes in sweltering climates where even flimsy garments show a remarkable disinclination to dry – but leads one to being inadequately prepared and (clothes being an important area of self-expression) ergo psychologically miserable.

My travelling clothes – the ones in which I actually travel – are no problem. Years ago I discovered Rohan, lightweight travelling gear which will stand up to any climate from arctic wastes to Gobi desert. An added advantage is that their cunningly zipped pockets (some specially engineered to conceal passport and tickets) eliminate the need to carry a handbag.

That part is easy. It is filling the suitcase – already almost taken up with lotions and potions, current medication, sunscreens of various factors, books, notebooks, micro-recorder, cassettes, camera, calculator (I was never any good at converting zlotys into pounds), torch, films and umbrella – with vests and long-johns (the traveller's secret weapons), shorts and swimming gear, cover ups, comfortable shoes and 'a little something for the evenings', which necessitates choices as one closes one's eyes in a futile attempt to transport oneself to other climes.

The knowledge that these agonies of choice are due to negative childhood conditioning, to separation anxieties, to neonatal terrors, or that they represent a defence against the fear of flying, does not help. I work on the principle 'when in doubt pack it'. Whilst I will have prepared (three weeks in advance) for famine and sandstorm, siege and snow, have been known to take two almost identical sweaters or sundresses rather than choose between them and am inclined to travel as hung about as a bag-lady, the chances are that I will have forgotten to pack my toothbrush or some equally basic item.

CHAPTER SEVENTEEN

Glittering Prizes

'Fortune favours only the prepared mind.'

Louis Pasteur

Rose of Jericho was conceived, like the flash floods in the Sinai desert, in a single moment. After *Proofs of Affection*, I had no intention of continuing the story of the Shelton family, but it must have been on my emotional agenda whilst my conscious attention was occupied elsewhere. Lord Snow said that 'the test of a good book was whether you could remember its content a year later'. So many readers had written to say that they recalled every word of *Proofs of Affection* and that the characters were engraved on their minds, so many people had enquired – as if she were a real person – what happened to Kitty Shelton after her husband died, that the Rose of Jericho (*Anastatica Hiero-chuntica*), plucked from the dry stones of the Sinai desert and handed to me by our guide, proved to be the trigger which prompted me to write a sequel.

'The rose of Jericho is a sand-coloured, white-flowered plant, a few inches high, found in warm sunny locations. When mature and dead the small branches curve inwards forming a ball which in the wild is borne by the wind across the desert where its seeds are dispersed. These balls open and close again with moisture and dryness, even after many years...'

The analogy of the flower and Kitty Shelton was involuntary. It wasn't until I had finished the novel, that I realised that the characteristics of the eponymous rose mirrored those of the widowed Kitty, coerced by ex-concentration camp inmate, Maurice Morgenthau, once more into life.

Rose of Jericho wrote itself. Which is not to say that it was not premeditated. The two themes, bereavement and the Holocaust, both had to be researched.

Research is done on the iceberg theory: far more must be understood about a subject than is actually used in the novel or which shows above the surface. I made a study of loneliness and loss to get beneath the skin of the widowed Kitty Shelton, and – determined in the only way I knew not to be a bystander – read more than a 100 books about the Holocaust in order to perpetuate the memory of it through my protagonist, Maurice Morgenthau.

Discussing the difficulties of writing *Madame Bovary*, Flaubert describes the obligations of an author to his characters: 'Today ... as man and woman, both lover and mistress, I rode in a forest on an autumn afternoon under the yellow leaves, and *I* was also the horses, the leaves, the wind, the words my people uttered, even the red sun that made them almost close their love drowned eyes.'

To understand how Kitty Shelton *felt* after her husband's death, I had to *be* Kitty; to enter the mind of Maurice

THE WRITING GAME

Morgenthau, it was *I* – for the time that I was writing *Rose of Jericho* – who was the only member of an extended family to come out of the concentration camps alive.

The measure of my success is that *Rose of Jericho* is used by bereavement counsellors as a *vade mecum* for widows, and former victims of Nazi persecution insist that the author of the book must have shared their experiences to understand their innermost thoughts.

Rose of Jericho was published by Gollancz in hardback and, as a companion volume to *Proofs of Affection*, by Futura in paperback. It did not find a publisher in the United States but was distributed there by Gollancz (through David & Charles). It had excellent reviews in national and regional newspapers, and I felt that with this novel I had made the required breakthrough. It was an extremely productive time. My family was now grown up and launched on their various careers. The eldest was married – and divorced – and in the immortal words of Margaret Thatcher 'we are a grandmother'.

'They must go free/Like fishes in the sea/Or starlings in the skies/Whilst you remain/The shore where casually they come again.'*

Although the personal attention my daughters required seemed, even in adulthood, never to end – only to change – I was now able to devote more time and energy to writing. In addition to the novels and the screenplays, I was writing and publishing many short stories, and even composing songs (music and lyrics) which were made into 'demo' disks for my own amusement. It was at about this time, while Cambridge academics

* Kahlil Gibran

234

were busy distancing 'literary studies' from the act of reading for pleasure, that in addition to writing novels, I started to review them, an occupation which, as I was later to discover, has no bearing whatsoever on the craft of the practising novelist, although commenting upon Virginia Woolf's literary criticism in *Le Nouvel Observateur* (1982), Claude Roy observed that it was:

'... written with that understanding of the art which is the monopoly of those who can master that art themselves, since the only creative criticism is the one produced by creative writers.'

Although chewing over other people's work provided little stimulation for the novelist, I felt that the moment had come for me to look at novels from the other side of the fence. Judging a book is very much like judging a life except that there is no word of God in literary criticism and, contrary to received opinion, no such uniform entity as 'the critics'. There are only individuals reporting their independent responses to an artistic experience. Criticism in itself is not an art form, it neither innovates nor creates, and it is actually thought by some to destroy art and kill artistic values. 'Pay no attention to what the critics say: no statue has ever been put up to a critic'.* One critic will dismiss a novel as a 'work of unparalleled depravity', while in a different newspaper or journal another will praise it as 'a minor masterpiece'. Their pronouncements upon contemporary novels which are often given undue credibility and importance, often tell us a great deal more about the reviewer than about the work he is reviewing.

In his role as reviewer, Cyril Connolly 'whose own attempts

* Jean Sibelius

at reproduction seemed doomed to failure'* despised middle-brow novelists – 'what can you expect from slugs but a slug-track?' – and urged them to practise some sort of birth control. 'English fiction, he declared, was blighted by 'three colossal, almost irremediable flaws: thinness of material, poverty of style and lack of power.'

While established veteran authors with loyal readerships are condemned to critical silence, many novelists who regularly produce books which are not 'best' but steady sellers, find themselves mysteriously debarred from the exclusive 'top-novelists' club, not by virtue of the quality of their work but by the literary profile of the reviewer.

Mrs Woolf went through agonies every time she produced a new book and was desperately vulnerable to everything that reviewers said about it. In view of the fact that some of the comments were 'She doesn't write about anything', 'Her characters aren't real', and 'There isn't any story', this was understandable. Thomas Hardy never wrote another novel after *Jude the Obscure*, so upsetting did the critics find it and so upsetting did he find the critics. When *A Hundred Years of Solitude* (Marquez) was published, it got no good reviews at all, but after three or four years it became recognised as a classic.

According to Doris Lessing 'the critic secretly wants to kill the writer ... we all hate golden eggs. Bloody golden eggs again, you can hear the critics mutter as a good novelist produces yet another good novel; haven't we had enough omelettes this year?' Auberon Waugh, editor of *The Literary Review*, considers that 'Any discussion of art is almost always rubbish and is just intended to keep people in jobs in universities. If you've

* Jeremy Lewis

written something that comes out well you don't think "Ah art" you just think of it as a job well done.' This view is endorsed by Flaubert: 'It's a waste of time to read criticism. I pride myself on my ability to uphold the thesis that there hasn't been a single piece of good criticism since criticism was invented; that it serves no purpose except to annoy authors and blunt the sensibility of the public; and finally that critics write because they are unable to be artists, just as a man unfit to bear arms becomes a police spy ... Criticism occupies the lowest place in the literary hierarchy; as regards form, almost always; and as regards moral value, incontestably. It comes after rhyming games and acrostics, which at best require a certain inventiveness.'

Be that as it may, authors have often had cause to feel aggrieved at their coverage – or lack of it – by the critics. In the 1920s and 30s it was said that good reviews, by Arnold Bennett or Howard Spring, were worth a thousand copies in sales. Today in England, unlike in the USA where it is an academic discipline, serious criticism is largely directed to the literature of the past. Only nine per cent of the total of books reviewed are modern novels of which 75 per cent are by men. 'This is an important book ... because it deals with war. This is an insignificant book, because it deals with the feelings of women in a drawing room'.*

Book reviewing has been referred to (by those authors whose books have been overlooked) as a racket in which everybody knows everybody; literary editors are not forthcoming about which novels will get reviewed; and while editorial freedom allows scope for individual preferences, writers (in particular

* Virginia Woolf

the alumni of Professor Malcolm Bradbury's creative writing course) are notorious for taking in each other's washing.

That the world of literary criticism is elitist, male-dominated ('lady novelists' are lumped together, isolating them from the human race), and frequently reviews books by writers 'whose only talent is the galvanic virtuosity by which they are enabled to walk and talk years after their heads have been cut off'*, was demonstrated in a study of more than 5,000 book reviews which revealed extensive links between many authors and reviewers whose coteries exert a powerful influence on the publishing industry. The study produced a detailed analysis of the 100 most reviewed books and found that 1 in 3 of the authors of those books had also reviewed other writers on the top 100 list.

Genuine literature both entertains and instructs. It provides forms of psychological, philosophical, and moral enquiry and delineates through the imagination the experience of the times. Literary editors often look down their noses at 'entertainment', as if entertainment and engagement of the mind were two opposing forces. Despite the fact that Tolstoy maintained 'that if a piece of art could not be understood by the most lumpen peasant then it wasn't art', they appear to think (*pace* Mozart) that there is something basically substandard about 'tunes you can whistle'.

The critic's task is to set a novel in the context of social history, to analyse and not to judge, yet the bulk of literary attention is focused on books bought by a comparative few, while popular authors – Wilbur Smith, John le Carré, Robert Ludlum – are dismissed as 'word merchants' or (as if it were

---

* Cyril Connolly

something to be ashamed of) purveyors of the 'good read'. This accounts for the wide gulf between the books which get reviewed in the posher papers (the arts talking to themselves) and the books which the public actually reads.

Throughout my writing career I had wondered how one got to be a critic. Like so much else in life the answer was simple. You put your head round the door of the literary editor's office (cubby-hole) and ask. If you are an established author, he will usually be willing to try you out – at least once – and if you are successful he will be only too glad to add your name to his stable of reviewers.

Clive Sinclair, erstwhile literary editor of the *Jewish Chronicle*, gave me my first chance. Later I graduated to *The Sunday Times* and *The Times Literary Supplement*.

Philip Larkin used to ask four questions of a book: 'Could I read it? If I could read it, did I believe it? If I believed it, did I care about it? And if I cared about it, what was the quality of my caring and would it last?'

If one is to review literature one must first of all define it. It is not simply the 'product' of a man of letters, but a piece of work 'esteemed for beauty of form and emotional effect'. Although a book should have a well-constructed plot, in the grand order of things this is of minor significance. Sandra Cohen, literary reviewer of the *Jerusalem Post* says:

'I look for characters to come alive on the pages; people I can care about, whose tragedies touch me and whose triumphs make me rejoice ... I want settings to be described in such a way that I am there and can literally share the author's eyes ... see what he is seeing – ... there is no point in negative criticism, that is "appraising a book on the basis of what it has failed to accomplish, with the failings usually derived from the reviewer's

239

own notion of how he or she would have handled the subject".'

I realised that what I had undertaken so lightly was clearly a responsible and daunting task (Virginia Woolf wrote every sentence of her critiques 'as if it were going to be tried before three Chief Justices'), that criticism is a *métier* and that working writers do not necessarily make the best critics. Anyone can read a book and enjoy it, but only those who have mastered the skills of the 'literary critique' should be allowed to practise it.

The job of the critic is to set a novel in the context of social history, to appraise it but not to judge. The review should demonstrate, in the reviewer's *own words*, what the author has to say (nothing taken out of context and quoted from a work under review will ever sound any good) and decide whether he has done what he set out to do, and where he has failed, and finally to add any personal points that seem germane to the discussion of the book.

Since I had been given a responsibility in the sense of being the first reader of a book, one of my main obligations was to present clearly and interestingly the scope and theme of the work and let others know whether or not I thought it was worth reading. I was obliged to be critical, either positively or negatively, so that the reader would know that I had taken the work seriously.

According to Virginia Woolf, who was never induced to read fiction unless she had to make money by writing about it 'the only safe way of deciding whether a novel is good or bad, is simply to observe one's own sensations on reading the last page'. There are no guidelines for reviewing, and each reviewer has his own approach. The only imperative is that *he must read the book*. Although this would seem obvious, it is clear from many reviews that the overworked and underpaid reviewer has not fulfilled his obligations to the author but has flicked through the pages and picked up the theme from the summary on the jacket. This will not do, and no conscientious reviewer will contemplate it. The reader will expect to be told whether or not the book is well written, if the story unfolds at an acceptable pace, whether or not the characters have been well drawn. In most good novels it is not the author's description of his characters' appearance and surroundings which give the book its value, but their feelings and thoughts, and above all the relationship which they have, not with the author, but *with each other*.

My reviewing tools are a pencil, some used A4 envelopes, and a sofa to lie on. My method is idiosyncratic. I read straight through the novel, underlining in pencil any passage in which the author's intention is manifest, or which distils the essential flavour of the book. As I do this, I make a note of the page number on the inside of the back cover. When I have finished the book – and a book of several hundred pages can take a very long time to read – I go through the marked pages and using my notes as the warp and woof of my composition, try to weave them into a cohesive pattern which will, I hope, consist not merely of a value judgement – praising the work or blaming it and committing artistic homicide – but comprehending and explicating it. It is impossible, and undesirable, for a critic to be objective.

Although people more and more assume that the worth of a work of literature can be assessed by a panel of judges within months of its appearance, this is contrary to Johnson's opinion that 'no other test can be applied than length of duration and continuance of esteem'. Books are not written for critics, they are written for readers and no matter how lofty the intention of the work, there is no such thing as 'literary value', at least until time has spoken.

The reviewer should not begin his review by discussing the weather, the current political situation, or his own novels. He is being paid to talk about the book, not to justify his own existence. No matter how conscientiously he reviews the book, however, no matter how meticulously he whittles down his text to arrive at the allotted number of words, no matter how satisfied he may be with his efforts, the literary editor will have the final say. If he doesn't disagree with one's sentiments then he will quibble with one's prose. *In extremis* – no matter how carefully one has adhered to one's brief – he will use his autonomy to top or tail your review, sometimes rendering it incomprehensible and frequently drawing its teeth.

Reviewing has been called a full-time job for a half-time salary which can sometimes be augmented by a sprint to the Temple Bar bookshop. Here, if you are lucky, if you outrun the other reviewers, and if your review copies are no more than three months old, Thomas Gaston will reimburse you with 50 per cent of the jacket price.

One of the hazards of being a critic is being asked to review a book written by a friend. Struggle as one may to retain one's impartiality there is always, in the recesses of the mind, the thought that one might one day have to face the author. Most novel writers take this situation in their stride and realise that the reviewer, albeit known to him, is only doing his job. Only once have I been subjected to abuse, when I reviewed an extremely indifferent novel by an acquaintance. Not withstanding the fact that Aristophanes slagged off Euripides as an 'anthologist of clichés', a reviewer in *Le Figaro* dismissed

Glittering Prizes

Madame Bovary with 'Flaubert is not a writer', *The Times* judged *Jane Eyre* 'coarse bookseller's stuff' and the latest Dickens 'a twaddling manifestation of silliness almost from the first page to the last', I do not think it fair that any book on which an author has worked hard and which has taken a very long time to write, should be summarily dismissed and I fell over backwards to find some merit in the work. Despite my efforts, I received a vitriolic note from the author – considered amongst writers the worst of form – who has never forgiven me.

At Christmas time on the literary pages the review gives way to what the British call 'back-scratching', the Americans 'log-rolling' (an annual parlour game for literary insiders), F. R. Leavis 'flank-rubbing', and the literary mafia – who solemnly list each other's titles – 'Books of the Year'.

Novelist Stella Gibbons's cynical view of the exercise is summed up in the satirical dedication – 'to Anthony Pookworthy, Esq, ABS, LLR' – at the beginning of *Cold Comfort Farm*. The fictional Pookworthy was the thinly disguised novelist Hugh Walpole and the letters after his name stood for Associate Back Scratcher and Literary Log Roller.

In 1990 Ian McEwan's Christmas choice just happened to be his pal Craig Raine's 'distinguished, wilful collection of essays *Haydn and the Valve Trumpet*'; two years later Craig Raine loyally chose Ian McEwan's novel *Black Dogs*. Touching family loyalty was displayed by Michael Hofman in the *TLS* and James Buchan in the *Spectator*, who both included titles produced by their fathers. In the same paper Miroslav Holub, a Czech writer, reviewed the autobiography of fellow Czech writer – Otto Wichterle – which was not only unreadable, untranslated, and unavailable, but which was *not even published!*

Having proved that I could do it, I have to admit that I do not much like reviewing. It is time consuming, interrupts one's creative work, and the effort involved is out of all proportion to the remuneration one receives. Fortunately, unlike some writers, I do not have to rely upon the income from the publishers' jiffy bags which arrive on the doormat each week. All things considered, books should perhaps be categorised under the four simple headings devised by a class of schoolchildren: Boring; All right; Dead good; and Brilliant!

Paradoxically the biggest single influence on fiction buying today is not the review but literature's answer to Miss World: the Booker Prize, a marketing ploy dressed in the finery of a literary award. This increasingly hyped prize with its yearly jamboree, nursed by Martyn Goff, and televised live, may send the sales of humiliated novelists who fail to make the shortlist (and who have never had it so bad) into decline, and shoot undeserving winners on to the bestseller lists, while turning little-known authors such as Salman Rushdie (whose 1981 prizewinning *Midnight's Children* lay unread beside half the bedsides in the land) and Anita Brookner (*Hötel du Lac*) (who have never had it so good), into overnight sensations. This is not to say that these authors do not deserve their acclaim, although when the *Daily Mail* telephoned a selection of writers, critics, and publicists, and asked them what they thought of *Midnight's Children*, without exception they praised the novel. The *Mail* then asked them how the novel ended and equally, without exception, not one of them could say!

One of the reasons for the popularity of literary prizes such as the Booker and Whitbread, is that the 'experts' choose books for you that are 'worth reading this year', although by reducing the field to a manageable size and concentrating on books which appeal only to a small circle, which they then promote to a wider readership who rush out to buy them as if they were the best on offer, they do a grave disservice to the novel.

There is no harm in literary prizes other than the fact that they perpetuate the myth that excellence and prizewinning are synonymous. The Book Trust *Guide to Literary Prizes, Grants and Awards* lists, amongst others, prizes for first novels (the David Higham), prizes for authors under 35 (the Betty Trask), first novels by authors over 40 (the McKitterick), first novels by authors over 60 (the Sagittarius), prizes for second novels (the Encore), the David Cohen British Literature Prize (now in its 3rd year) of £30,000 for 'a lifetime's achievement', and the controversial Orange Prize for fiction by women. As awards are offered to books on just about everything – mountains, the sea, the Lake District, Greece, oriental rugs, environmental awareness, Christopher Marlowe and translations from the Swedish – and new prizes proliferate, it is almost a case of 'everybody will win and all shall have prizes'. Many of these prizes are presented at prestigious dinners. They provoke envy and vituperation amongst aspirant writers, as well as acute embarrassment on the part of the recipients who, frequently at a loss for words, recall Alice in Wonderland when she was presented with her own thimble by the dodo:

'Alice thought the whole thing very absurd, but they all looked so grave that she did not dare to laugh; and as she could not think of anything to say, she simply bowed and took the thimble, looking as solemn as she could.'*

The publicity engendered by these prizes often turns novelists, selling at most a few thousand hardback copies, into bestselling authors. But it must be understood that literature is not weight-

* Lewis Carroll

245

lifting and we are in the hands of mere opinion; that for the judges to get through all the year's entries they would each have to read a book a day for four months; that the winner is often the result of horse-trading, a compromise accepted by the judges after bitter in-fighting – the prize going to an inoffensive book by an inoffensive name; that hierarchy is what destroys people's personal values; that being ranked above or below is absurd and contrary to the literary idea; and that having to select the *best* from more than 100 books which differ dramatically in both style and content (a version of Christ's 40 days in the wilderness, versus a tale of obsession and loss set in an Indian pickle factory) is like attempting to compare Thomas Hardy with Eric Cantona or an omelette with last Tuesday.

In 1969 Jerzy Kosinsky's novel *Steps*, won the American National Book Award for fiction. Eight years later the same manuscript was sent, with no title and under a pseudonym, to 14 major publishers and 13 literary agents in the US (including Random House who originally published it). Of the 27 people to whom it was submitted, not one recognised that it had already been published and all 27 rejected it!

The declared purpose of literary awards is to reward worthy work, honour its authors, and enlarge the audience for high quality fiction by attracting to it a greater degree of public attention than the publishers of the books can bring themselves to seek. The Booker Prize, which has been accused of trying to find worthiness in books that are simply difficult or pompous (perhaps because the judges are academics or critics who are terrified to appear philistine in their choices), is the British equivalent of the French *Prix Goncourt* (dominated by the 'gang of three' Gallimard, Grasset and Le Seuil). It was first bestowed in 1969, since when it has received massive attention and established itself as our premier literary honour. While others have condemned the prize (sponsored by a food company as the Whitbread is sponsored by beer) for being turned into a media circus, Ian St James, a business entrepreneur who became a bestselling writer at the age of 40, has criticised it for being 'literary and precious and not reaching the real people who buy books on holidays'. He launched his own valuable (£28,000) prize with the aim of giving a dozen unpublished writers a year a chance to break into the big time. Within three weeks of his offer, Collins – which runs the Ian St James Awards – was reported to have run out of their print run of 500,000 entry forms.

My own first experience of awarding (rather than winning) prizes, was being sole judge of the short list for the Author's Club First Novel Award (1989), judging the Betty Trask Fiction Award (1991), and chairing the judging panel for the Jewish Quarterly Literary Prizes (1993) and the Macmillan Silver Pen Awards (1996 and 1997).

I awarded the Author's Club first novel prize, at their annual dinner, to *Holy Innocents*, by postmodernist Gilbert Adair now a respected contemporary cultural commentator who, I am happy to say, has gone from strength to strength. I am even happier that *Comforts of Madness* (by the then unknown Paul Sayer), which I spotted and praised whilst reviewing for *The Sunday Times*, went on to win the 1988 Whitbread Book of the Year Award.

While the Booker Prize can catapult an author overnight from respectable sales of a few thousand (if he's lucky) hardback copies to the bestseller lists (about which more later), the Nobel Prize for Literature (given to obscure Montenegran poets and Finnish fabulists) seems to carry with it the kiss of death. Marcel

THE WRITING GAME

Proust refused it and lived, while Ernest Hemingway accepted it and promptly blew his brains out. A sense of proportion about prizes may be restored by consideration of the fact that authors Laxness, Gjellerup, Sillanpaa, Echegaray, Pontoppidan, and Deledda (who they?) have all been honoured by the Nobel Literature Committee, while Joseph Conrad, Anatole France, Vladimir Nabokov, and Graham Greene have not; and that James Joyce and Franz Kafka never won a prize at all.

CHAPTER EIGHTEEN

One of the Hazards

⟫⬦⟪

'We don't want literature, my friend, we want a "bestseller".'
Anthony Burgess

Two people were to influence my life in the 1980s. Judy Piatkus and Miron Grindea.

The first time I heard the name Piatkus was when Alice Wood, fiction editor at Futura, told me that it was a complete stranger, Judy Piatkus, of Piatkus Books, rather than Gollancz, who had recommended *Proofs of Affection* to the paperback house. Later, through Norman Morris (of the Balfour Diamond Jubilee Trust), I was introduced to this extraordinary and independent publisher who unbeknownst to me had such great faith in my work.

Judy Piatkus started her successful and respected publishing company at home, with £1,750 and a partner, at the age of 24. After four years, with an investment of £25,000, she set up on her own in the West End where Piatkus Books was born.

THE WRITING GAME

When Gollancz unexpectedly turned down *A Second Wife* (sequel to *A Loving Mistress*) and my writing career seemed once more to be fragmented, it was Judy Piatkus who picked up the pieces. The rejection from Gollancz, after three successful books, came as a considerable shock. Whether through the fracas over Jeremy Hadfield Associates I had upset the Gollancz apple cart (in particular the publicity department) which now saw fit to give my new novel the thumbs down, I shall never know. It seemed a dastardly act.

Livia's letter, in which she broke the news to me, reflected, touchingly I thought, the good relationship I had had with her over the past five years.

'... I am also sorry, on a personal level, as I think that we had hit it off rather well, and the severance of our professional connection would be a personal loss to me – but that is one of the hazards of being a publisher.'

That *A Second Wife* was not worth publishing is given the lie by the fact that six years after its publication by Piatkus, PLR figures revealed that it had been borrowed by *17,520* readers and even today nearly 2,000 readers a year borrow the few remaining copies from the library. I firmly believe that my 'redundancy' from Gollancz was a question of politics rather than literary judgement.

Being left with an unpublished sequel on one's hands is no joke. By 1982 the tide was beginning to turn and the rot which was to engulf and consume publishers had set in. Enthusiastic as were many of their readers' reports on *A Second Wife*, nobody wanted, or could afford, to know. The previously 'editorially-led' book business, after so many years of being run by genuine 'bookmen' who valued their authors, knew their individual needs and respected their texts, was giving way to streamlined, market-orientated global corporations run by executives and accountants and more in keeping with the new cut and thrust ethics of the Thatcher years. The minnows were being swallowed by the monsters, slick new bookchains opening and library sales declining. Publishing was losing its personal touch as the men in suits realised that the market for books was not only bottomless but virtually untapped.

In 1985, British authors woke up to discover that the two respected publishing houses of Hamish Hamilton and Michael Joseph (owned by the Thomson Group) now existed only in name. In a £26 million takeover they had been absorbed, together with a basketful of lesser imprints, into the Penguin empire. The Octopus Group acquired William Heinemann (for £100 million); Reed International bought Paul Hamlyn (for £10 million); Random House (New York) – years later itself to be pounced upon by German based media giant Bertelsmann in a shock takeover – devoured Chatto and Windus, the Bodley Head, and Jonathan Cape (the 'holy trinity' of British publishing) for £17.5 million with Century Hutchinson (Random Century) as a chaser, while News International gobbled up William Collins (£293 million). HarperCollins (part of News Corporation) consumed, amongst other imprints, Grafton, Fontana, Flamingo and Thorsons, and Transworld (part of Bertelsmann), Bantam, Doubleday, Corgi and Black Swan.

These changes were an extension of a process which had been going on, more or less unnoticed, for some 25 years. Now the pace was accelerating. Small imaginative houses, finding it impossibly costly to run the whole operation of originating books and selling them at home and abroad, had gradually been absorbed into larger ones. The larger ones were now at the mercy of predators who could no longer afford to nurture a young writer in the hope that possibly his second or third book would make a profit, who were not interested in books – other than as commodities – and by imprudently decimating their lists cheerfully went about killing the geese that laid the golden eggs.

As the new professionalism, with its close attention to the bottom line, in which 'publishable' meant 'commercial', took over, the hazards of being a publisher – referred to by Livia Gollancz in her letter – were increasing. What exactly was going on?

If one man could be held responsible for making the individual publisher an anachronism, and helping publishing to lose its innocence, it was new broom Peter Mayer who transformed what had hitherto been a traditionalist, amateur 'profession for gentlemen' into a market-led business run by a new breed of entrepreneurs who lived by the sword and published for money rather than love.

Peter Mayer, born in London, raised in New York and educated at Columbia and Oxford, was the knight in shining armour who crossed the Atlantic in 1978 to rescue Penguin Books from the decline in which it had been since the death of its founder, Allen Lane. Mayer, who had worked his way up from messenger boy at the *New York Times* to setting up and running a small publishing company, Overlook Press, with his father, had also been an ad copywriter and a successful marketing man for cosmetics firm Avon. He was shocked by the fustiness of Penguin, which was producing books of a type which no one any longer wanted to read, and summarily removed 800 titles from the backlist and prised 100 people from their desks. He introduced the concept of the 'blockbuster' to England, and concentrated on 'lead titles' or 'bestsellers' which he promoted by aggressive marketing techniques hitherto un-heard of in the book trade. Books were auctioned, like cattle, to the highest bidder. Mayer's innovations, revolutionary as they appeared at the time, were small potatoes compared with what was to happen later.

Initially, English publishers protested at the cataclysm which had overturned their cosy if often financially precarious world. Once they had got over the shock however, many of them were quick to follow Mayer's lead and adopt the slogan of American editors: 'You have to write a big book, if not watch your ass'.

What effect did all these changes have on the poor author? Although even in the 1970s some bestselling authors and 'celebrity' writers had been given large advances, they were as nothing compared with the (then) telephone numbers (£625,000 to Michael Holroyd for his biography of George Bernard Shaw) now being bandied about. These previously unheard of sums marked the beginning of an era in which 'establishment' authors (William Boyd, Fay Weldon) commanded high prices, 'bestselling' authors Jeffrey Archer – one of his books is sold around the world every five minutes – and Ken Follett were in the £30 million league, and publishing houses, like football managers, tried to poach the outstanding players from each other.

All this meant that the average, well-reviewed novel with sales of a few thousand copies was of very little use to anyone. While an income of £10,000 a year might seem like a modest success for the author, it was peanuts to the booksellers and a drop in the ocean to a publisher who could only make a profit from authors selling not a few thousand, but a few hundred thousand copies.

For the mid-list or struggling writer the news was was not good and even Graham Greene, who believed that a close and enduring personal relationship with a publisher was essential to successful creative writing, twice changed houses in the face of a corporate takeover. As more and more money found its way into the pockets of fewer and fewer writers, new writers were finding it increasingly difficult to get their feet even on to the first rung of the publishing ladder.

An advance used to be money paid against the royalties a book was going to earn from the sales. Now publishers who had spent millions to buy a book, spent millions on promotion to earn back their investment. One anomaly of this situation, is that fundamental concepts have changed. Astronomical sums are now offered not only for romances, thrillers, horror, or science fiction – which dominate the blockbuster scene – by bestselling authors, but for books which do not even exist. As publishers trawl the shark-infested waters for memoirs of ex-prime ministers, ghosted autobiographies of fashion models and superstars, blockbusting sagas, and event-based novels of true-life murder and corruption, competition is fierce. News-papers (in their own interests) aid and abet publishers at the advance stage by offering serialisation against a guarantee of exclusivity.

This is all very well, but as the agent, Ed Victor, observed: 'Publishers try to create bestsellers by buying a brand name or spending a lot on promotion, but the book has to come alive or no amount of huffing and puffing can make it sell.' When push comes to shove, what all bestsellers have in common, whether high or low of brow, is the ability to make readers turn the page. The popularity of genre authors such as the Forsyths and the Sheldons, the Grishams, the Cornwells, the Steels and the

One of the Hazards

Cooksons, confirms the view that readers cannot be doing with the slim and perfectly formed literary gem which does not cut the mustard, and that as far as the bestseller is concerned, size is of the essence.

These days there seems to be an unhealthy obsession (amongst book *buyers* rather than book *readers*) with the bestseller list which drives the book business with a simple cycle: a book has only to hit the list for the giant chains to discount it heavily whereby selling more. The bestseller list originated 100 years ago when *The New York Times* first compiled a list of books 'in the order of demand'. The timing was no coincidence. In the 1890s the gap between highbrow and lowbrow books began to widen, and popular taste to be distinguished from aesthetic merit. Two factors were responsible: cheap printing, which made a mass market in fiction possible, and the increase in literacy which meant that reading was no longer an exclusive pastime and novels by Dickens and Trollope began to achieve bestseller status. Today's more populist bestsellers are dominated by a clique of about 50 authors, whose novels sell themselves by force of 'product recognition' and who offer a tried-and-tested formula for an enjoyable, if sometimes undemanding, read on which a loyal audience can rely.

This unreal state of affairs, the voracious expectations of the book trade that books can be sold like soap powder or dog food, and with no more intellectual involvement, is doomed in the long term to failure. Likewise is the cult of the 'celebrity author' willing to give his views on everything from animal welfare to adultery, which is now a major part of the publisher's marketing strategy. As author photographs (which have become an art form) and interviews with novelists appear with increasing

255

frequency in colour supplements and glossy magazines, publishers freely admit that a writer's age and appearance – synonymous with 'promotability' – can increase their enthusiasm for his book. An added promotional bonus is provided if the author is already well known (in politics or some other high-profile field) or has a newsworthy lifestyle. If his image is such that it can in addition tap into the 'yoof' market it could help to turn his novel from an average, into a mega seller.

PR firms, who may cast as many as 300 free copies of a book upon the waters, are fully aware of the importance of personalising an author and guaranteeing an appearance in national and regional newspapers as well as on radio and TV chat shows. Their object is to trigger a stampede to the bookshops and achieve the big breakthrough for which both author and publisher pray.

When Eric Segal went on the Barbara Walters show in the USA, he had sold only 2,500 copies of *Love Story*. Barbara Walters told him 'sit down and shut up and I'll do the talking'. Holding his book in front of the cameras she told her audience: 'This contains the most beautiful words about love I have ever read. Love means never having to say you're sorry.' The remainder of the print run was snapped up, *Love Story* was on the bestseller lists from that moment on, and the rest is history.

While some publishers assess the potential market value of the author before inviting bids for the book, others admit to withholding photographs of non-photogenic writers to whom advice concerning possible TV interviews or chat shows should be 'don't even think about it.'

All is not doom and gloom however. As the list of top-earning paperbacks shows, the assumption that 'bestseller' and 'quality' are mutually exclusive is misleading: Alan Bennett (194,309

copies of *Writing Home*), Stephen Hawking (618,000 copies of
A Brief History of Time), Jostein Gardner, a previously unknown Norwegian author, with his novel of philosophical
enquiry (*Sophie's World*, 161,080 copies), Vikram Seth (*A Suitable Boy*, over 32,000 copies), and Sebastian Faulks (175,000
paperback copies of *Birdsong*) are only outstripped by Jung
Chang's *Wild Swans*, an autobiographical story of three generations of her family set against twentieth-century Chinese history,
which sold a reputed four million copies worldwide, making it
the bestselling non-fiction paperback in living memory. This
good news is reinforced by the massive sales of classics such as
Middlemarch and *Pride and Prejudice*, and serious contemporary literary novels such as *Schindler's Ark*, which owe their
popularity to cross-fertilisation between books and TV and film.

For all the diaries of thirty-something journalists with their
deeply personal accounts of single motherhood or the perennial
hunt for the elusive male, the cutting-edge sagas of brutality and
savagery, the metres of gold-embossed and increasingly violent
crime, the outpourings of 'faction' by historians, horticul-
turalists, anarchists, gays, technophobes, artists, musicians, and
political activists with which we are bombarded, what most
readers want – and have always wanted – is the rare and
intelligent 'old-fashioned' novel which will confirm their own
prejudices, tell them something they did not previously know and
change the shape of the world for them.

Many such books have ways of selling themselves that defy
marketing strategy. They bypass the laws of publishing which
overlook and underestimate them, until the snowball of public
demand makes them into involuntary bestsellers. Perhaps the
most extraordinary British sleeper was *Watership Down*. Richard
Adams, a civil servant, had had his book turned down by

several London publishers. In 1972 it was issued in a tiny edition of 2,000 copies by one-man publisher Rex Collings. Within three years it had sold a million copies and continues to sell countless millions more. The two most commercially success-ful books of the 1980s which started out as 'slow burners' were *A Year in Provence* and *The Secret Diary of Adrian Mole Aged 13¾* by then unknown writers Peter Mayle and Sue Townsend. Both were catapulted into success by being serialised on radio after which they gathered their own momentum.

The buzz word here is 'word of mouth' which slowly but surely has turned novels such as Louis de Bernière's *Captain Corelli's Mandolin* into modern classics. First published in 1995 *Captain Corelli's Mandolin* is said to have sold more than 9,500 hardback copies and 200,000 copies in paperback and, despite neither book nor author having been put through the publicity machine, is still walking off the shelves. *The Alchemist*, another title which refused to lie down and die, sold a paltry 900 copies when first published. To author Paulo Coelho's delight it has now not only, according to his readers, had a profound influence upon their lives, but clocked up sales of two million copies in Brazil alone. Sir V. S. Naipaul – whose body of work (travel, fiction, history, politics, literary criticism, autobiog-raphy) is monumental – is arguably one of Britain's greatest living writers despite the fact that his first four novels, including *The House of Mr Biswas*, were largely ignored. Swimming against the swelling tide of media hype, Naipaul has remained unmoved by intellectual fashion and refused to participate in the promotional games which are considered imperative by so many aspiring writers.

While if you write well enough you may just still make it on to the bestseller lists (dismissed by author Don DeLillo as a form of 'cultural hysteria'), some publishing houses conveniently forget that they exist to sustain, nurture and sell *writers* without whom they would no longer be in business. As illusory profits fail to materialise, publishers who have sold their souls to big business might eventually find that those who have invested money in them have pulled the plug leaving them standing up in nothing but their (Emperor's) new clothes.

Judy Piatkus, like Duckworth, Peter Owen, Constable and John Murray, was one of the few successful small publishers to resist the overtures of the conglomerates and to remain independent. Although her company has expanded rapidly and now has a multimillion pound turnover, she prefers to remain in control of her operation and Piatkus Books is not up for grabs. As the gulf between the commercially successful authors and those of more discriminating appeal grows, Judy is not ashamed to admit to a love of *books* and says that she does not want to lose contact with them 'ever'.

I must be honest. Piatkus was not my first choice of publishing house for *A Second Wife*, which was followed by *To Live in Peace* (the final volume in the Anglo-Jewish trilogy) and ultimately by *An Eligible Man*. The Piatkus *forte* was nonfiction – 'how-to' and recipe books, gift books, women's interest, and health and beauty – and although it did have a strong and carefully selected fiction list, it was not, and did not pretend to be, an upmarket house.

My association with Piatkus was *force majeure*, but apart from the blow which was dealt to my pride over being published under a non-literary imprint, I have nothing but praise for the tight ship run by my new publisher. Judy carefully monitors the number of books she publishes each year, is extremely good on marketing, and is appalled at the lethargy of most publishers when it comes to publicity. As a result of this, one of the strengths of her company is promotion. To this end, Jana Somerlad (head of Publicity) pulled out all the stops for *A Second Wife* and arranged a comprehensive publicity tour. This was not all. I was consulted on the jacket (again by Adrian George), and in addition, and in good time, I was shown, and agreed the blurb. The usually fraught period between the signing of the contract and the publication of the novel was extremely harmonious. It still did not, however, encompass all the requirements of the Minimum Terms Agreement, which an author now has every right to expect.

Under the terms of the new agreement, to which many publishers have now signed their names while others cogitate, the copyright in an author's work shall only be invested in the publisher for a period of 20 (rather than 50 years); the publisher undertakes to publish a book no more than 12 months after the delivery of the typescript; the author *must* be consulted about copy editing, publication date, and all details of jacket and blurb, and furthermore is to be apprised of the size of the first and subsequent print runs, which are no longer to be the publisher's closely guarded secret. The agreement also enables the author to buy copies of his own work at 50 per cent of the jacket price (provided payment is made up front) and is entitled to expect at least 12 free copies. Accounts are to be made up at six monthly intervals and, perhaps most important of all 'any sum of £100 or more due to the author in respect of sub-licensed rights shall be paid to the author within one month of receipt, provided the advance has been earned.'

Although there is still a long way to go, the days when an author has to prise out of his publisher (if he is lucky) how well, or badly, his book is selling, and is the last person to be informed if a novel is to be reprinted or remaindered, seem at last to be numbered. Despite the fact that *A Second Wife* was painlessly published and its arrival greeted with a bouquet of flowers from Piatkus, it did not receive the critical coverage I had come to expect. I consoled myself with the fact that neither the works of Dante nor those of Chaucer were even printed, let alone published, and that it is the human spirit within a work that is responsible for its ultimate survival.

Foreign rights in *A Second Wife* were sold. To one country – South Korea. A year after publication, I received a letter from Lee, Min-ja, of the Sam-shin Gak Publishing Company in Seoul, enclosing 'the loyalties on you novel'!

The discomfort of being on a publishing list which included such titles as *Fast Cakes* and *More Fast Cakes*, was mitigated by the persistence with which I was courted at this time by arts crusader Miron Grindea, an eccentric *par excellence*, and editor of the international literary review *Adam*, which he founded in the 1930s.

Grindea was a charismatic and dashing, though now elderly Romanian. He had escaped persecution by the Nazis and, with his wife, Carola, a musician, arrived penniless in this country two days before the Second World War was declared. Publisher of such luminaries as Auden, Maurois, Koestler, Proust and Gide, who contributed to his journal, and friend of Benjamin Britten, Henry Moore, Christopher Fry and Stephen Spender, Miron had been on the panel of judges for the Wingate Award – now the Jewish Quarterly Award – for which *Proofs of Affection* had been submitted by Gollancz in 1982 (when it was also entered for the Booker Prize). Miron's vote for my book was outnumbered, but so impressed was he with my writing

261

that, with his inimitable dogged persistence, he set about tracking me down. Wearing a swashbuckling cloak and the red ribbon of the *Légion d'Honneur* in his lapel, he appeared on my doorstep one morning demanding a 'cup of *chai*' and we became friends at once. Having entered my life – which had I not taken evasive action he would have dominated with his unannounced appearances for 'cake' or 'quiche' in my kitchen – Miron, an intellectual capable of expressing his thoughts and opinions equally fluently in many languages, took a continuing and serious interest in my career. I spent many happy days in his Brighton flat which was filled with original works by Picasso and Cocteau (known personally to him), and in his books-and-music filled house in Emperor's Gate. The confidence shown in me by this literary guru, compensated for the blow to my pride caused by my summary rejection by Gollancz. Miron's faith was endorsed by the inclusion of a short story of mine, 'Moving', for publication in the prestigious *Adam*.

'Novels by serious writers of genius often eventually become best sellers, but most contemporary best sellers are written by second class writers whose psychological brew contains a touch of naïvety, a touch of sentimentality, the story telling gift and a mysterious sympathy with the daydreams of ordinary people.*

It was the economics of getting a novel on to the market which enforced the cultivation of 'mass market' books and in Britain, as in America, publishers fell over themselves to persuade promising authors to write blockbuster fiction, paying whatever it took to sign them up. Although not all of them fulfilled their promise and many of the six-figure advances paid

* Leonard Woolf

were never earned (leaving the publisher with massive losses), many publishers traded their literary acumen for 'a mess of hyped potage' and the age of the bestseller – in which sales figures were the criteria by which a book was judged – had arrived. This was nothing new. Tolstoy, writing in 1898, stated that: 'If a man is activated solely by mercenary considerations and has no true feeling to convey, his work will not be genuine, but at most a spurious work of art ... commercial inducements are certainly responsible for the immense flood of potboilers which swamp the market so that people may read, look, and listen for years for fresh things claiming to be artistic including a large number of 'best sellers', and may hardly encounter a simple genuine work of real value all that time.'

These sentiments were confirmed, in 1935, by Leonard Woolf: 'The publishers and booksellers between them are destroying the sale of books other than best-sellers.'

Would Thomas Hardy, whose first book sold 377 copies, would Trollope (who received £20.3s.9d for 4 novels), would Jane Austen (1,000 copies of *Sense and Sensibility*), have been given show cards and 'dump bins? Would they have found themselves on the bestseller lists, which are sometimes a self-fulfilling prophecy – known as 'ratcheting' – in which a publisher manages to get a title of his choice on to a bestseller list and thus persuades bookshops to buy it in bulk: once the bookseller has committed himself he will have no alternative but to display the book prominently – Hatchard's front table or the No. 1 space on the bestseller shelves of a large chain (bookbuyers, like record buyers, like being told what to buy) – and hey presto the title will be catapulted into the bestseller category.

While no one denies that bestseller lists are useful, many

express doubts about their trustworthiness. The most the lists can hope to do is to reflect what most customers are buying over the counter, in a limited market, in one particular week, and give an approximate indication of fast-selling titles.

Bestseller lists are compiled, in good faith, by organisations such as Bookwatch. The director of Bookwatch, Yorkshireman Peter Harland (an ex *Sunday Times* journalist), is the first to admit that because of difficulties in amassing data, EPOS (Electronic Point of Sale) notwithstanding, the lists are compiled from only a small sample of bookshops (excluding many airports, railway stations and supermarkets) and that a book which performs well in Land's End is not necessarily a bestseller in John O'Groats ('nobody in Scotland reads Fay Weldon'). Since over 80,000 new books are published each year in Britain alone, with half a million titles in print at any one time, the size of the database needed to fill in details such as category, title, author, publisher and price, of all of these on a yearly – let alone weekly – basis, would be impractical, and would need to be compiled on a national scale. Since no such system of classification exists, the key lies with persuading 'selected' booksellers, who own the necessary information, to part with it. BookScan, a new data-gathering service, now promises not only to revolutionise the book business but to change the face of the bestseller list by providing better sales data and enabling publishers to operate more efficiently.

You have only to talk to a bookseller in an unguarded moment to understand why the lists are unreliable. Having to answer telephone calls as to the sales of a title suggested by Bookwatch on a busy Friday afternoon is a chore, and one which is often delegated to a junior member of staff. Although booksellers using EPOS are unlikely to spend time tampering with their computers in the hope of getting rid of a few unsolds, the figures arrived at by this method reflect – according to some cynics – not those books which have sold well in the past week, but those on which the bookseller has over-ordered (like a restaurant's 'specials'), and which he wants desperately to shift.

In the week ending 16 August 1997, the *Bookseller*, the journal of the book trade, revealed outrageous discrepancies in bestseller lists compiled by BookTrack (data supplied by 1,500 retail outlets in the UK), and Bookwatch (printed in *The Sunday Times* and based on data from 628 shops). While BookTrack calculated that *The Last Governor* (Jonathan Dimbleby) sold 5,400 copies during the week, *The Sunday Times* figure was a modest 1,500! Two months later similar discrepancies were observed. According to the *Observer*, *The Nation's Favourite Love Poems* shifted 4,943 copies in a single week; *The Sunday Times*, however, credited the same volume with only 1,483 sales; and while the *Bookseller* gave *Bridget Jones's Diary* a figure of 5,783 sales (as estimated by BookTrack), in the *The Sunday Times* (Bookwatch) it swelled to 11,611 and in the *Observer* a weekly sale of 20,434 copies calculated from data supplied by 658 bookshops. It is obviously a case of 'You pays your money and you takes your choice'. If the bestseller lists were accurate, no work of fiction would be on them at all. As any book retailer will tell you, his true bestsellers – year in year out – are the *Bible*, the *Concise Oxford Dictionary*, the *Prayer Book*, the *Highway Code* and the *Thoughts of Chairman Mao*.

By suggesting books for inclusion in the first place, the compilers of the bestseller lists – like the publishers of public opinion polls – can influence decisions. Their readily admitted mistakes cast doubt upon the validity of their results which have been known to list not only books withdrawn before publication, but to include – for three consecutive weeks – those which have been out of print for the entire period.

The indiscriminate ranking of writers – the sales of a literary biography being classed above or below the latest diet craze – is about as significant as comparing the Egg Marketing Board's figures of the weekly number of eggs sold, with the movement of medium density fibreboard. Conning the public into buying a book which has become part of a certain trend or movement, negates T. S. Eliot's justifications for reading.

One of the anomalies of bookselling is known as the 'W. H. Smith factor': a book turned down by W. H. Smith – now cutting its stocklist to exclude anything but the most commercial titles – stands almost no chance, short of winning a major prize, of ever making it into a bestseller list. Until recently, when finding the new Wilbur Smith or Dick Francis has a higher commercial priority than cherishing a promising novelist, publishers have been prepared to take a loss on a first-time writer in whom they had faith. But, with one publisher reporting recently that its sales of first novels had declined from a scarcely glorious average of 1,200 copies to a derisory 564 in hardback, few can afford to continue with this happy tradition. With most novels today judged not on their literary potential but on commercial merit, few publishers are willing to take risks with new authors or new ideas, and even those novels which make the Booker shortlist will have little impact unless the writer is already well known.

As far as the big bookchains are concerned, all they do is consult the all-powerful WHS computer about previous sales by the author. If it shows that WHS ordered only 2,000 copies or worse still didn't take the book at all, no matter what the merits of that particular book they can afford to do nothing but follow suit. While the importance of aggressive book marketing has resulted in a situation where certain titles now sell far more copies than they ever did, the unfortunate majority, callously left to sink or swim, continue to plummet.

W. H. Smith, selling £7 million worth of books a year and responsible for 17 per cent of all sales, is Britain's largest bookseller and has sufficient clout to make a book into an instant bestseller. The 'thumbs down' from them can spell disaster for the publisher.

WHS's selection methods are idiosyncratic and have nothing whatever to do with literature. If a publisher plans to launch a book, say in December, he must toddle along to W. H. Smith in May. The competition is so fierce that if he doesn't have the cover, the marketing plan, the print run, the pricing, and everything at his fingertips by then, he might just as well not bother. At the W. H. Smith headquarters in Swindon, a 'jury' of five men and women considers 15,000 books a year and rates them on a scale from one to nine. The judgements are based on the appeal of the cover (an impressive marketing tool: customers look at a paperback jacket for one second before deciding whether or not to examine the book) the price, the number of pages, the amount of promotion by the publisher, and sales of the author's two previous books at WHS in the first 10 weeks after publication. The decision of the jury takes two minutes, and top rating will mean an immediate order of over 15,000 copies.

Using its electronic tills, WHS monitors the weekly sales of 250 titles. Its records show average sales for the 'top ten' of up to 4,000 copies a week, with the lead title selling up to 10,000. There are no second chances. The hazards of modern publishing are spine-chillingly demonstrated, as errors of judgement are smartly returned to the mammoth WHS warehouse at Swindon (where today it is rumoured that all is not well and that WHS is losing the plot) where they are tipped onto a moving conveyor belt in the 'book abattoir' and unceremoniously pulped.

CHAPTER NINETEEN

Reading for Pleasure

━━━▶◆◀━━━

'Reading maketh a full man; conference a ready man and writing an exact man.'

Francis Bacon

'There is only one way to read, which is to browse in libraries and bookshops, picking up books that attract you, reading only those, dropping them when they bore you, skipping the parts that drag – and never, never reading anything because you feel you ought, or because it is part of a trend or movement. Remember that the book which bores you when you are 20 or 30 will open doors for you when you are 40 or 50 and vice versa.'*

Reading opens doors to knowledge and experience of the widest kind. It manifests itself not as chaste references garnered painlessly from some website, but rather in mood and atmosphere, in specific allusions or small caches of detail which

---

* Doris Lessing

infiltrate one's writing. Mrs Trollope's advice to her sons was to read and read before ever they considered setting pen to paper themselves. While I can't think of any deprivation worse than being no longer able to read, my own reading habits have little to do with bestseller lists. The modern mind is overloaded with information and the justification for reading books (rather than newspapers or magazines or trawling the Internet) is to refresh and exercise our creative powers and stretch our sensibilities and understanding as the mere amassing of data never can.

'Read for pleasure ... never force yourself to read a book – it is a wasted effort ... if you don't feel that it has a direct bearing on your own personal interests, worries, problems, put it away.'*

While D. H. Lawrence advocated the closure of schools and the encouragement of illiteracy which would save the great mass of humanity from 'those tissues of leprosy' books *and* newspapers, most people need books not merely for the story but for companionship of the teller of the story (who has a greater knowledge of the world than they) and, more importantly, to affirm that they are not alone. Reading novels is a deep and life-enhancing pleasure which requires no political or moral justification. 'All normal people require both classics and trash'.†

Even the writer needs his quota of 'pulp' if only to develop the necessary criteria to write books that are 'good'. The true reader, hungry for anything and everything that brings the human predicament into the sharpest possible focus, is one who squirrels away a wide variety of books all year as they come to

* Arthur Koestler
† Bernard Shaw

his attention, and takes them with him on holiday whenever he goes. Those who rely on the gilt-embossed titles on display in stations or airports, read for relaxation and entertainment – distractions both valid and well catered for – rather than to understand the living culture of literature or to have their critical faculties exercised.

'Through fiction the reader can satisfy his curiosity about such enterprises as fighting or falling in love without having to submit himself to the dangers attendant upon them.'*

One great advantage of books is that, unlike other branches of the leisure industry they are always at hand and you don't have to leave home or put on a track suit or leotard in order to enjoy them. While I am a voracious reader I am not only embarrassingly forgetful of most new things I read, but when asked to name my favourite books, or which books have influenced me most, I am at a loss for an answer. The greatest artists are not commensurable. You cannot say that Bach is greater than Mozart, Mozart is greater than Beethoven. Different authors fulfil different moods, different needs, at different times and it is impossible to give a truthful reply.

One critic, challenged to name *his* three best books, replied *Anna Karenin*, *Anna Karenin* and *Anna Karenin*. I know what he means. *Anna Karenin* is the one novel which most authors would like to have written, and the one which on the grounds of characterisation, imaginative insight and evocations of contemporary Russian life, they all aspire to write. The conception of Tolstoy's great novel is said to have taken place at the moment when he picked up a story of Pushkin's, which his children had left lying around the house.

* Victor Nell

'*The guests arrived at the country house...* the story began. "That is the way to begin," observed Tolstoy. "Pushkin plunges his readers right into the middle of the action. Others would describe the guests, the rooms, but Pushkin at once gets down to business."'

That evening in his study Tolstoy wrote the first pages of *Anna Karenin* – acclaimed the world's greatest novel – the subject matter of which, the suicide of his neighbour's mistress, had been haunting him. *Anna Karenin* is both a love story and an indictment – of contemporary society, of hypocrisy, of liberalism, of religion, of a world which perverted all genuine feeling and crushed the ardour of the mind. It is an example of an author's ability to transmute his life into a work of fiction. Kitty's love for Levin and her reaction to the death of her brother-in-law, echo Tolstoy's own sentiments, while the birth of Kitty's baby reflects the tenderness he felt when his own first child was born. Tolstoy endows Levin with *his* physical strength, *his* love of the soil, *his* characteristic mood changes, *his* impulse to carry his ideas to extremes, *his* ability to 'destroy and recreate worlds'. Levin's convictions and views are those of his creator, whilst Karenin, Anna's husband, is his antithesis. Tolstoy, ahead of his time, has a psychoanalytical approach to his characters and he is less concerned with what they do than with the reasons for their actions.

Anna Karenin did not appear in novel form until 1878, one year after it was completed. First published in monthly parts in a magazine, the final instalment was rejected on the grounds that the views it expressed did not coincide with the editor's own!

The public library was set up in the mid-nineteenth century as a charitable effort to bring the possibility of self-education to the masses with the idea that if some miner or lathe turner wished to read Jane Austen or Immanuel Kant, he should be free to do so. 'The true literary education ... consists in reading and understanding and also memorizing literature, with the result that our experience, finding words to hand with which to measure it, acquires the fullness of a living culture.* The situation today is that public libraries, with their draconian cuts, are lending fewer and fewer books and are increasingly buying sound recordings and videotapes to satisfy the changing tastes of borrowers.

Q. D. Leavis observes: 'The training of the reader who spends his leisure in cinemas, looking through magazines and newspapers, listening to jazz music, does not merely fail to help him, it prevents him from normal development ... partly by providing him with a set of habits inimical to mental effort ... the practice that died only with the last generation of reading aloud in the family circle was the best possible insurance of good reading habits ... mere trash ... will not stand this test. We have no practice in making the effort necessary to master a work that presents some surface difficulty or offers no immediate repayment.'

One of the criteria of a 'good book' is that it changes the world for the reader. Into this category, in addition to *Anna Karenin*, come *War and Peace*, *Middlemarch*, *Ulysses* and *Madame Bovary*. On my shelves are the works of Thoreau and Nabokov, Kafka and Koestler, Huxley and Hemingway, Fitzgerald and Faulkner. I turn to Gide, Flaubert, and Queen Victoria for letters; Horace and Browning (Elizabeth Barrett) for poetry; Shakespeare, Molière, and de Musset for drama; and

* George Steiner

Bacon, Montaigne, de Rochefoucauld, and Emerson, for browsing and for illumination. I have not yet managed to find the time
to complete my reading of *Remembrance of Things Past*, which
is why I have not included Proust on my list, but I am humbled
and gob-smacked with what I have read so far.

Like Virginia Woolf I do not read many contemporary novels
unless I am on holiday or am paid to do so. There is not sufficient
time, and for the writer, as for the professional musician who has
hundreds of scores by heart, the constant study of 'masterworks'
is more rewarding than contemporary accounts of 'things that
never happened to people you don't know'.

The present popularity of literary biography is widely agreed
to have been caused by the failure of present-day writers to
provide gripping narratives about realistic people. The demand
for biography, by erstwhile novel readers unable to cope with
the fashionable schools of modernism (epistemological uncertainty) and postmodernism (ontological uncertainty), may well
be contributing to the downward spiral of fiction. With certain
exceptions, Hermione Lee on *Virginia Woolf*, Peter Ackroyd
on *Dickens*, Ellman on *Wilde*, I read little biography or 'books
about books', preferring to go to the primary texts and to
sort things out for myself. As far as fiction is concerned, I
enjoy Graham Greene, Anthony Burgess, Isaac Bashevis Singer,
Aharon Appelfeld, Saul Bellow, John Updike, Philip Roth
and Gabriel Garcia Marquez. I sometimes read books written by my friends – to see what they are up to – but the
danger here is that, like scientists who make the same discovery
at identical moments, they might be saying in print the very
thing I am about to say myself, and it could put me off my
stride.

'He was not a man, he was a continent; he contained whole

crowds of great men, entire landscapes.'* William Shakespeare
excels all other writers in cognitive acuity, linguistic energy and
power of invention, and his genius ensures that while we are
reading we become Iago *as well as* Othello, Hamlet *as well as*
Claudius, both Lear *and* his daughters. Writers make a vain
attempt to imitate Shakespeare's grasp of the human psyche and
there is nothing that one cannot learn from him.

'Shakespeare's unique ability, was to convey a thought,
original or familiar, profound or casual, in words that have
rooted themselves in the innermost consciousness of millions,
because *his thoughts correspond to what is already, unex-
pressed to be found there.*'†

This last, the ability to strike chords, to reach the human
heart, to find echoes in the soul of his readers, is the aspiration
of every novelist.

'In the old days you spoke of a person as being ill bred or well
bred, or cultivated. People read Henry James and Tolstoy and
talked about them at dinner. Now you just talk about what you
read in the papers.'‡

Although the reading of newspapers has been compared with
cardplaying, smoking, drinking, and idle conversation, as a
writer – like Schopenhauer – I find them a treasure trove of
human idiosyncrasy and quirks and for once find myself at odds
with Flaubert:

What would I learn from these wonderful newspapers
you so want me to take each morning with my bread

* Flaubert
† Bernard Levin
‡ Brooke Astor

and butter and cup of coffee? Why should I care what they say? I have very little curiosity about the news, politics bore me to death and the literary articles stink. To me it's all stupid making and irritating ... yes, newspapers disgust me profoundly – I mean the ephemeral, things of the moments, what is important today and won't be tomorrow. This is not insensitivity. It is simply that I sympathise as much, perhaps even more, with the past misfortunes of those who are dead and no longer thought of – all the cries they uttered, now unheard. I feel no more pity for the lot of the modern working classes than for that of the ancient slaves who turned the millstones – I am no more modern than I am ancient, no more French than Chinese; and the idea of *la patrie*, the fatherland – that is, the obligation to live on a bit of earth coloured red or blue on a map, and to detest the other bits coloured green or black – has always seemed to me narrow, restricted, and ferociously stupid. I am the brother in God of everything that lives, from the giraffe and the crocodile to man, and the fellow citizen of everyone, inhabiting the great furnished mansion called the universe...

T. S. Eliot maintained that the effect of daily or Sunday newspapers was to affirm their readers as a 'complacent, prejudiced and unthinking mass'. There is a more serious indictment. If there is an accident in your street, the report of it the following morning in the newspapers will have little in common with what you witnessed from your window. Injuries will be exaggerated, numbers miscalculated, names misspelt, events misjudged, and the scene generally misrepresented. Reading about it, you may be excused for thinking the one you see in print to have been quite another incident. Newspapers purport to inform, but they are not to be trusted, the only truths in them are the births, deaths and marriages, the rest is distortion, there is no other way to get the facts to fill the page.

'The idea that one can read books without having passed any exams is quite foreign to most young people.'* Surveys suggest a serious decline in the standards of literacy amongst teenagers, many of whom cannot even identify a main verb. Lack of formal grammar leads to woolly thinking, and children reared on TV are impatient, lacking the habit of concentration necessary for 'book learning'. A large majority of those who have passed through the primary and secondary school system can 'read' but not read and are unlikely to be found in a quiet corner, curled up with a book. Magazines such as *Viz*, *Zit*, *Brain Damage*, *Gutter*, and *Blob* are the preferred 'reading' of two in three male 18 to 35 year olds, a state of affairs which speaks for itself.

The statistics are not encouraging. In the United States it has been estimated that the vocabulary and grammatical comprehension possessed by a considerable majority of American adults has stabilised around the age level of 12 or 15, while in the UK many adolescents are unable to fill in the simplest forms, or to express themselves on any but the most basic level. One in four has difficulty in reading and writing, one in three cannot spell, and almost half of them have rarely, if ever, read a book.†

Reading is a form of thinking, and writing the expression of

* Doris Lessing
† George Steiner

thought. Sitting a child in front of a TV screen from an early age maintains him in a state of passive receptivity. Having a visual image imposed upon him, instead of having to use his imagination and interpret what he sees, encourages the same instant gratification that is to be found in alcohol or drugs. Finding himself unable to distinguish between the real and the unreal, the same adolescent may later roam the streets looking for the 'quick fix' of booze, drugs or old ladies to mug.

The difference between reading and watching television is fundamental. When we read a book we enter into a relationship with the author – what Henry Green called an intimacy between strangers – but when we watch television we all receive identical images. The television screen gives us the *illusion* of freedom but in fact allows us neither focus nor perspective.

If I see television as subscribing to a sub-literary culture, requiring few skills and developing none, why did I start to write for it?

I was head hunted, in 1987, by Jo Willett of Euston Films, while I was in the midst of writing the final volume of my Anglo-Jewish trilogy *To Live in Peace*. A newcomer to the 'heartbreak house' of the media world, I naïvely thought that I would have to drop my novelist's pen immediately and put on another hat. Between the time of that first meeting and the signing of the contract for *Shrinks* – a proposed new series for Thames Television – I had spent a stifling summer researching in New York, read a dozen books on the Israel/Lebanon war (for background material for *To Live in Peace*), and completed my fifteenth novel.

Where did you learn to write for television? I did not. Apart from reading one or two books on the subject, which only confused with their anecdotal text, I learned, like Shakespeare and Shaw, whom, I suspect never read a book on playwriting, by doing. The fact that dialogue has always been my *forte*, that when I write I see the story unfold as on a screen before me, that my imagination is strongly visual, was a great help in bridging the gap between the medium of novel writing and that of writing for the small screen.

I was not untried. I had written the screenplay for *The Long Hot Summer* which Linda Seifert had sent to Euston Films (Thames Television). Naturally, 'at that moment in time', Euston were not looking for features. But it was this script that proved to be the calling card which every writer needs. Andrew Brown (producer of *Shrinks*) was impressed with my writing, and sent Jo Willett (his assistant) along to see whether or not I was interested in writing for the series.

Watching television is one thing, *writing* for it quite another. It was a challenge, I was flattered to be asked, I wanted to find out if I could do it, and above all, unlike the rewards for fiction, TV paid grown-up money. After my refusal to write for the *Knight Errant* series in my youth, I was determined not to blow my chance again.

Thoreau famously cautioned against inventions as merely 'improved means to an unimproved end', while Socrates warned that the very act of *writing* anything would have negative effects, because it would atrophy the memory. My resolution to try my hand at TV was reinforced by the fact that I had fallen for the new technology, the 'kaleidoscopes' foreseen by George Orwell (*Nineteen Eighty-Four*) as 'vast machines programmed to produce newspapers, magazines and even novels and plays'.

To Live in Peace was the last novel to be written on my

electronic typewriter. It took two years to implement my decision to become automated. While I was by no means alone in
taking the giant step, the argument surrounding the use of
computers aroused strong feelings and deep divisions amongst
fellow writers who, whilst reared in a more genteel era, found
themselves, whether they liked it or not, in the age of technology. Iris Murdoch, Barbara Cartland, Susan Hill, Margaret
Drabble, Ben Okri and Tom Sharpe (who found technology
positively debilitating) are still wedded to the visceral feel of
their pencils (good enough for Shakespeare), fountain pens or
typewriters (albeit self-correcting), which are immune to viruses,
while growing numbers of authors opt for word-processing
packages – which give one the illusion that one is thinking
directly on to the screen – from which, unlike Lot's wife, they
never look back.

My resistance to writing on a computer had at first been
fierce. I had no time to do the hardware research; I was too busy
to interrupt the work in progress; I did not want any unfamiliar
machinery to come between me and my writing; the jargon of
the salesmen, a race apart with their bits and their bytes, their
spreadsheets and their databases, was incomprehensible; the
only technology I had so far managed to master, apart from that
of the internal combustion engine and the self-cleaning instructions on my American cooker.

In 1985, at the Society of Authors' conference at Warwick
University, computers were discussed. The panel of experts did
not then consider them an essential tool for the fiction writer.
Thoroughly confused I enrolled for a Wordstar course at
Imperial College. The information that 'document mode files
are binary and not listable, and non-document files are text files
and listable' convinced me that I was not computer material.

Expressions such as *toggle autopaging* and *echo consoles* immobilised my thought processes, and that hash meant anything
other than corned beef or fried potatoes was an eye-opener.
I put the project on the back burner, and it wasn't until 1987
that I decided to go for it. Having prevaricated for so long, I
knew that I must act quickly. I eschewed the cash-and-carry
warehouses with their enticing discounts, for a human and
friendly supplier (A. K. Systems Ltd) who promised to 'hold my
hand', and came away with Zenith hardware and Wordperfect
4.2.

In the event I did not need all that much underpinning.
Work was scarcely interrupted. Within two days the dark
ages of typewriter pounding – which now seem as remote as
those of the quill pen – were forgotten, and I had moved into
the age of the microchip. My first discovery was that a word-
processing package is more akin to the pencil than is the
typewriter. You can change and scribble, experiment and erase.
Nothing is permanent unless you want it to be. More specifically the work progresses faster; the keyboard – with its
automatic wordwrap – is far less tiring to operate; you can
work simultaneously on several different projects without getting up from your chair.

Say you are in the midst of a novel, and an idea for a short
story comes into your head. By switching into your 'ideas' file,
you can jot down a few sentences, store them, and forget them
for as long as you like. There is no chance that they will be
mislaid, as of old, amongst a myriad scraps of paper. By the
same token, when lost for words, or tired of invention, you can
call up some lecture notes which you must edit for future use;
catch up with correspondence. There will be no copies to make,
nothing to file. Everything will be stored in the computer's

obedient memory for future and easy recall. The psychological benefits of a clean copy of your text at the end of each day – or as often as you wish – cannot be overestimated. Demands for your 'bio notes', your CV, your updated entry for the *Who's Who of Writers* or other reference book entries, invariably arrive at the most inopportune moments. Once this information has been entered on your hard disk, it takes only moments to amend it as necessary and throw the switch on the printer.

Word processing is as fascinating as it is rewarding. It does not, contrary to the beliefs of some authors, get in the way of making marks upon paper. It makes more and better marks. All beginnings are hard, and of course I made mistakes. I 'lost' pages of text; after one false move the printer spewed out paper *ad infinitum* while I frantically searched the manual for the 'cancel print' command. There were moments in which I was reduced to tears and would cheerfully have given the whole thing back. But there is no need to panic. The computer is on your side. If you request that it erase, it asks politely if you are certain you wish to do so; it will search through thousands of words and hundreds of pages in moments for a fact or figure you have mislaid, count in nanoseconds the number of words you have written (invaluable for commissioned articles and book reviews), and considerately keep back-up files of everything you do. It also has a sense of humour. If you request that it look for the word 'diary' it will stop at interme*diary* and subsi*diary et al.*, until you learn to play it at its own game.

There are Mrs Grundys around who confuse the medium with the message and are convinced that the more computer literate you are the more your prose is likely to suffer. I would refer them to William Faulkner: 'Nothing can injure a man's writing if he is a first class writer'.

Today I still use Wordperfect (5.1). While I understand and appreciate that with the help of the more state-of-the-art software, the entire Library of Congress can be downloaded on to one's kitchen table, the Theory of Relativity Theory summoned at the squeak of a mouse, the 29 volumes of *Britannica* scanned in a trice, and two-thirds of all surviving Greek literature (up to the time of Alexander) can – thanks to Yale University Press – be retrieved at a stroke, the sniffing-out and fetching accomplishments of its insatiable memory cannot select and combine, gloss and associate through the irreplaceable combination of practice and intuition available to the human brain. For the moment at least, I refuse to do battle with Windows 98 (its seductive e-mail promising an infinite number of like-minded penpals), its beguiling Internet, and its catch-all websites which are superfluous to my needs.

I still have no idea *how* the computer works, but realise that as well as being immensely practical, it incorporates the 'Pac-Man Factor' and is liable to become addictive. Any day without its fix before the VDU produces severe withdrawal symptoms. Pencil wallahs contemplating the change over should be warned.

CHAPTER TWENTY

Writing for the Small Screen

———⫷◈⫸———

'Work is much more fun than fun.'
Noël Coward

For television writing in which the producer has no idea what he wants until he sees it written down, umpteen drafts on different coloured paper – was the fourteenth draft the pink or the blue? – are the order of the day and a word processor is essential. As scripts gain momentum by being written at the same pace as which the finished product is viewed, speed is of the essence.

Despite the fact that I had hitherto been ambivalent about what TV had to offer, I managed to persuade myself that I had something to contribute to the medium. The aim of the creative artist is to reach people. Most authors are lucky if they can sell a few *thousand* copies of their books, 10 *million* viewers, if the writer is lucky, can watch one episode of her screenplay in a single evening.

Every year Gabriel Garcia Marquez holds a TV workshop in

Cuba. His aim is to get 'soaps' made by established *writers* rather than by hacks 'whose criteria are those of soap vendors'. Television is an opportunity for the mass dissemination of one's ideas and in the right hands TV serials and series can be the visual equivalents of the works of Shakespeare, Dickens or Dostoevsky.

Writing for TV, meant forgoing the solitary freedoms of fiction and being a member (albeit the lowliest and most expendable member) of a team working on the pilot for *Shrinks*, an ongoing drama whose aim was 'to explode the myths about psychiatry and demystify the area'. The series was to be set in and around the fictional Maximillian Institute (the Max), a London psychiatric group practice located in some never-never land between Harley Street and the NHS. While in New York the shrink was regarded as a status symbol, in this country it still took courage for patients to seek psychiatric help and people were reluctant to admit that they needed professional assistance in coping with their lives. The original idea on which *Shrinks* was based, was for stories to be carried on from week to week, and while the series was primarily designed to be entertaining, it was at the same time hoping to encourage people to talk about, and share, their emotional experiences more freely.

The original encounter, on 22 June 1987, with head hunter Jo Willett who was looking for writers for the Euston Films/ Thames Television production of *Shrinks* was followed up, *six months* later by a visit from the script editor. Four weeks after I received the storyline from her, I had my first meeting with the executives of Euston Films who had read and been suitably impressed with the screenplay of *The Long Hot Summer* and wanted me to write the 90-minute pilot for *Shrinks*.

285

THE WRITING GAME

'I don't want it good, I want it Tuesday!'* After messing me about for five months they of course wanted the script 'yesterday'.

The guidelines for *Shrinks* were disappointing. The 'back story' was unintelligent, the script editor seemed not to know her job, the names of the characters (arbitrarily decided upon without consultation with the writer) were inappropriate and the first episode was to include a road traffic accident with the victim ending up on a life-support machine – a dramatic cliché with all the appeal of a wet blanket.

I fight with the script editor and manage to get rid of the life-support machine. I am not allowed to change the names of the characters, and the action is unreal (I know about psychiatrists, I am married to one) but I have to stick with it. The producer wants the story structure *tomorrow* (he neither knows nor cares that I am looking after my three young grandsons while their parents are on holiday) and will send a messenger to collect it. I realise that the scenario I have been given which has to do with child custody, wife battering, impotence, and marital therapy – valid enough subjects – is riddled with mistakes. I wonder who dreamed the scenario up and why they hadn't brought the writer in at the beginning. I do my best. 'It's fine' – to be going on with. The producer has a brilliant idea. It is filtered down from on high through his mouthpiece the script editor. He wants a thread on Huntington's Chorea. I spend a morning at the Royal Society of Medicine to research this rare genetic disorder and bring home a number of books and papers on the subject. The producer wants the psychiatrist from Melbourne to follow 'Australian Rules' football. Australia House points me

* Jack Warner

286

in the direction of Flinders' Australian bookshop. I become an expert on Australian Rules. I pick the brains of marital therapists for the 'marital therapy' story. Start writing first draft of Act One. Work like the devil. Ring the script editor. Act One is ready. I'm quite pleased with it. The script editor sends a messenger for it. She'll call me tonight. I bite my nails. Hear nothing. Not the next day, nor the next. A week passes. Call Euston Films. The script editor is off sick. Get on with Act Two. Two weeks pass. The script editor calls. 'Act One is great. There's some good stuff there...' That's not what I'm hearing. I don't like the tone of her voice. Two weeks pass. The script editor calls. 'About Act One: we've had a meeting. Australian Rules. The producer has changed his mind.' Really. Anything else? 'Write a girlfriend for Daniel. And, by the way, don't worry too much about the marital therapy...' 'Wouldn't it be better if I came to these meetings?'

It's like tying my feet and expecting me to dance. Two months later – the script editor has been off sick twice and is now preoccupied with thoughts of Christmas – she is pleased with the way things are going. Deadline 19 December for completion of first draft. Break my neck and deliver on December 14. Expect a round of applause. The script editor is off sick. The producer is away. The script editor rings. She's still sick. She'll try to read the script soon but number one priority is Christmas shopping.

16 December: Euston Films' Christmas party at Heal's. The producer is 'looking forward to reading my script *after* Christmas'. So is the script editor. The telephonist on the Thames TV switchboard has read it. Thinks it's terrific! And isn't the new storyline wonderful? *New* storyline? That's news to me. If there is a new storyline nobody has bothered to tell me about it.

THE WRITING GAME

Consoled by TV writers Laurence Marks and Maurice Gran (*Shine on Harvey Moon*): it's very laid back in TV. No enthusiasm or encouragement. If they don't sling the script straight back at you, you know you've done a good job. The producer and the script editor say 'see you in the New Year'. No mention of the script. Spend an edgy Christmas in Brazil. 8 Jan: the script editor rings. The script's fine but the producer is being tough about this one. Cut Daniel's girlfriend. I cut Daniel's girlfriend. A three-hour meeting with the script editor on Friday afternoon. The producer apparently wants a lot of rewrites but she can't read His Majesty's notes. Oh yes, she remembers. Andrew wants a director's script 'with action'; the court case is 'spot on' but will I do a full narrative breakdown – about 20 pages! The producer's notes indicate that he wants me to include such sickmaking dialogue as: 'it was a *peerless* day!' Peerless! 'How about the marital therapy?' 'Don't worry about it.' The narrative breakdown (for the director) is time consuming. Also the court case. Linda Seifert (my TV agent), alarmed at the extra work I am doing, reads the producer the riot act on my behalf. No extra money forthcoming. The script editor leans on me for new (umpteenth) version. I deliver. 'It's coming along nicely but we'll have to rethink the court case...' I thought it was spot on. I ask why they keep moving the goalposts. The script editor is mystified. She's got a bug and is going off sick. 2 Feb: the script editor says court case 'really works'. 3 Feb: deliver final draft. 12 Feb: have heard nothing. Ring the script editor. She was about to ring me. The producer is in LA.

I give up and start work on the final chapters of my new novel *Judgement of Paris*. 17 Feb: 'The producer's not too happy about the Huntington's Chorea'. I'm not surprised. I am now a world expert on Huntington's Chorea. 'I can't do anything about it until the end of the month.' 29 Feb: I have thought of a way round the Huntington's Chorea problem; tell the script editor. The producer calls from LA. The script editor tells him 'Rosemary's had a brilliant idea.' The producer sends love. Go home and do *another* rewrite. 7 March: deliver. 14 March: call Euston. The producer is in New York. 17 March: call Euston. The script editor has a bug. 31 March: the producer is back but the script editor hasn't managed to speak to him. She's 'fuming' and will call next week. Linda Seifert rings. London Weekend Television is interested in *Judgement of Paris*! 9 April: the script editor says they'll *definitely* be discussing *Shrinks* next week. I no longer care. 21 April: I call the script editor. She *definitely* has a note on her desk to call me, but there is no news. The producer is away. 28 April: ring the script editor. No news. 11 May: the script editor calls. Everyone thinks my script is terrific and final draft payment is sanctioned. 'Is *Shrinks* definitely going to be made?' 'The producer is still *very enthusiastic*.' 9 June: still no news. 16 June: the chief executive, John Hambley, has taken my script on holiday. He'll be back in two weeks. The script editor sounds down in the dumps. Must be getting a bug. 8 July: call the script editor. She's been fired. Two hours to clear her desk! Nice knowing you. 5 Oct: Jo Willett sends copy of *Shrinks* pilot with my credit on it. Some *idiot* has written in the marital therapy thread. It is lewd and crude! 20 Oct: I storm the bastions of the executive floor. The producer, Jo Willett, and the chief executive are present. I blow my top. This is not my script. Some idiot has written in the marital therapy. Whoever it is has no ear for dialogue, knows nothing about script writing, and less about psychiatry. It's Whitehall farce. I don't know who wrote it... Embarrassed silence. Everyone looks at floor. The producer speaks: 'I did.' Wish said floor would swallow me. The producer recovers. 'About Episode Two...?' I tell him London Weekend Television wants me to write an adaptation of *Judgement of Paris*: 6 × one-hour episodes and I'd rather adapt my own work where at least I shall be in control.

Eighteen months after first being approached, I bow gratefully out of *Shrinks*. In an expensive write-off, the chief executive elected to junk the original series (with the exception of 'my' almost feature-length pilot) and start again. A new producer was brought in and the set was rebuilt in accordance with a more populist approach in which there was no time for introspection and no patient received – or even appeared to receive – the attention of the therapist to which he was entitled.

Three years later, as was my right, I diffidently agreed to share the credits for the pilot with two others writers, Kay Trainor and the late Stephen Lavell, both of whom were contributors to the junked series. As I had predicted, *Shrinks* was an unmitigated disaster which sank without trace as did the BBC's *Eldorado*, the satirical and expensive soap set in Spain, Yorkshire's *Castle Haven*, the seriously dull *Miracles Take Longer* (Thames), Granada's *The Practice*, set in a doctor's surgery, and countless other turkeys.

The review in the *Sunday Telegraph* summed up *Shrinks* nicely: '...there is some entertaining material, but the script is clearly a committee job'.

After the débâcle at Thames, my experience at London Weekend Television reaffirmed my faith in TV. I was delighted to have the opportunity to adapt my own novel *Judgement of Paris* for the small screen and even more delighted to make the acquaintance of the LWT script editor, Frances Heaseman. Frances was enthusiastic, intelligent, an experienced editor highly thought of at LWT, and most important of all, on the same wavelength as myself. Working with her was a pleasure and during the writing of the six one-hour episodes we didn't exchange one cross word.

The beginning was dodgy. Although LWT liked *Judgement of Paris* and wanted to adapt it, they hadn't considered me as a writer for the series. Names of established TV writers such as John Mortimer were bandied about. I told them that I didn't want anyone else playing around with my story, assured them of my capabilities, and asked to be given a chance. On the strength of my pleadings and having read the pilot for *Shrinks* (with a disclaimer from me for the marital therapy), LWT grudgingly commissioned me to write a synopsis of *Judgement of Paris* and the first episode.

Frances and I worked in close harmony. I made my way weekly to her office on the eleventh floor of the LWT building on the South Bank, and in between times we worked in my study at home over Marks & Spencer sandwiches. All went swimmingly and I learned various tricks of the trade from Frances which I hadn't picked up from the Euston script editor with her perpetual bugs. Frances was a good teacher. We hammered out the storyline together. If I argued and Frances went silent, I knew that I was wrong. Nothing got past her critical eye. If a word, a line, a scene, did not 'move the story forward' out it came, no matter how clever, witty or original it happened to be. 'Does it move the story forward?' The words became engraved on my brain.

Adapting a novel for film or television presents certain problems. Whilst the novel is produced in solitude, a script is arrived at by 'committee', and one can only hope that one's horse does not turn out to be camel. Although in the visual medium there are limitations – industrial, technical, and mechanical – which literature does not have, there are also possibilities such as the editing of images, which embellish it. For the reader, there is a creative margin in the novel which does not exist on film or TV, where you see what the person looks like, and there is no longer any possibility of filling things in for yourself.

'Look, I like your book because Ursula Iguaran is very much like my granny, because Amaranta is just like an aunt I have, because Colonel Buendia is just like the father of friend of mine.'*

Film doesn't allow for that. In film they have the face of Anthony Quinn, they have the face of Sophia Loren, they have the face of Robert Redford, and it's very unlikely that anyone's grandfather looks like Robert Redford!

People watch the television adaptation of a book they enjoyed and are often disappointed to find that they no longer recognise it. Fiction and television are different media and must be kept apart. As well as learning from Frances to 'move the story forward', I had to externalise what was internalised, to expand the lives of the subsidiary characters in the book. I also had to change the title. My story concerned a recently widowed judge who is amorously pursued by three women. The title, *Judgement of Paris*, referred to the Greek myth in which three goddesses compete for the golden apple to be given to the 'fairest' by Paris, the son of King Priam of Troy. The analogy – according to LWT who was paying the piper – was, in accordance with the general levelling down of the service, too literary for the 'lower denominations' who might think they were being offered a travelogue about Paris!

After consultation with Frances, and the elimination of

* Gabriel Garcia Marquez

various spurious suggestions, *An Eligible Man*, comprehensible to the lumpenproletariat was arrived at. It was not my title. I did not like it. I did not like anything about it. I was not Alan Ayckbourn or Tom Stoppard however, and the matter was taken out of my hands.

The novel of *An Eligible Man* was duly published and paperback rights sold, pre-publication, to Mandarin. Several months later – I was getting used to TV timescales – LWT pronounced themselves delighted with the synopsis and the pilot I had produced for the TV version. I was contracted to write five further episodes, the equivalent of two full-length feature films, a mammoth task.

During this time I attended the famous (or infamous) American Robert McKee's 'Story Structure Course' run by International Forum at the National Liberal Club. The three-day course was for 'screenwriters, directors, producers, novelists, playwrights, film/TV executives, literary agents and story analysts' and included a special section on Film and Television Series for the International Market. McKee's case was that 'despite fine writing of characterisation, dialogue and description, of huge amounts of money spent on production values and promotion, the overwhelming reason projects fail, either upon submission, in development, or at the box office, is a lack of craft in "story structure", what was once called "plot".'

I was one of the first English disciples to sit, pencil poised, at the feet of the craggy, beetle-browed, cowboy-booted master. Since then, Robert McKee and Dr Linda Seger, who crossed the Atlantic in his wake, have become a must for just about every TV and movie writer in the business.

DAY ONE laid out a sound working method for progressing from concept to step-outline to treatment to manuscript. DAY

TWO demonstrated how fine writers put these concepts to work, by studying the screenplay of *Casablanca* (which McKee failed to mention had at least four scriptwriters). DAY THREE took a scene by scene look at the use of dialogue, the handling of exposition, the defining of character. It examined how beats and units built each scene, how scenes created sequences, sequences constructed acts, and how acts structured the whole story. The justification for the whole course was Robert McKee himself. An entertaining, plausible, charismatic six-footer, he held his tightly packed audience of writers, directors (many of them well known and with several credits to their names), and producers, mesmerised for an entire weekend as he lammed into 'inciting incidents', 'Eisensteinian *montage*', 'the negation of the negation', 'set ups' and 'pay offs', 'turning points' and 'antagonists', until we were goggle-eyed with exhaustion while the maestro, pausing only for gulps of black coffee and to light a fresh cigarette in the course of an eight-hour day, remained as fresh as a daisy.

I learned that in the media world literary craft does not matter, 'the story is the star' ('Sweetheart I haven't time to read it, tell it to me in a sentence'). That all stories share the same elements. That the relationship of the 'story' to 'life' is a metaphor. That 'fact' is neutral and has no meaning. I learned about empathy and sympathy, that the better the novel the worse the movie, to throw out the *deus ex machina* of the contrived ending, and to eliminate the shit. I learned about 'triangles' and how to use them, about 'positives' and 'negatives', that monologue is dialogue, and about 'writing on the nose'. And at the end of the day I learned the bad news that out of 40,000 scripts a year registered in Hollywood, only *300* are made!

Writing for the Small Screen

I came home reeling, but when I sat down at my word processor to write episodes two to six of *An Eligible Man*, I wondered what I had learned. With my two reporter's notebooks of closely packed notes – with their diagrams depicting 'conscious' and 'unconscious', 'contradictory' and 'contrary' notions, and how to get from A to B – before me, I tried to apply theory to practice. After half an hour of studying the 'conventions' implicit in my story, of trying to isolate the 'controlling idea' behind *An Eligible Man*, I wrote: *Story Structure Robert McKee 1989* in marker pen on the covers of the notebooks and consigned them to the bottom shelf of my cupboard where I keep my travel 'logs' and old diaries.

In scriptwriting, as in novel writing, you learn to write by writing. The 'story structure' comes as naturally as breathing, and to imagine that you can produce a successful screenplay by reference to 'set ups' and 'pay offs' is like expecting Picasso to paint by numbers. The true writer does not need to be told on which page to place his 'turning points' – although if he looks for them afterwards he will find that they are there – he 'feels' it from the back of his neck to the tips of his toes, and he 'knows' because he knows. Writing, film or other, can be learned, but not taught, and when push comes to shove *there are no rules*. The scripts of *Gone with the Wind*, *Citizen Kane*, *Brief Encounter*, *Lawrence of Arabia*, *Doctor Zhivago*, were not subjected to analysis by a team of LA script doctors.

While I thoroughly enjoyed the stimulation provided by McKee and Seger, and do not deny that I picked up some extremely useful tips from them, the danger of these gurus lies in their ability to blind the novice with formulae and to inhibit the aspirant with jargon. For the journeyman writer they are no more than an entertaining – if costly – few days out.

THE WRITING GAME

Television, unlike the novel, is a voracious consumer of material. Frances Heaseman – in her unerring wisdom – had made me pack so much into Episode One of *An Eligible Man* (if you don't grab your audience in Episode One you lose them) that there seemed to be precious little of the story left to spread out over the remaining five hours. It had to be conjured up. In the novel the 'eligible man' had two daughters who make fleeting and subsidiary appearances and are important only in so far as they affect the protagonist. For the TV series I not only had to breathe life into them but to 'give them life'. Whilst I might have known what went on in their heads, the viewer had to be shown their external lives. They had to be given not only a *raison d'être*, but friends and lovers. I had to go with them to their work places, follow them back to their homes. I was lucky in that, as always, my characters were real to me and that I was invited in. I made mental visits to a penthouse apartment on the river, a house in Hackney. To get to grips with the eligible man himself, I had to research activities dismissed in a sentence in the novel. I talked to experts on field sports, took my tape recorder to a 'meet' – where I was given a glass of sherry and some suspicious looks – and followed the hunt. I attended polo matches and learned the rules of the game. I breached the newsroom of ITN where I was shown round by a friendly reporter and primed about the presentation of the news. Overwhelmed with material and awash with notes, I wrote and I wrote and I wrote. I have never worked so hard in my life, and never with such enjoyment. Although the goalposts were still frequently moved, Frances deciding that it would be better to have D, E and F, when I had given her the A, B and C she had asked for, the criticism was constructive and the analysis shrewd.

Writing for the Small Screen

Legend has it in the trade that once they've got their screenplay in their sticky hands they lose your telephone number. *An Eligible Man* was no exception to the rule. There were optimistic rumblings about casting – Frank Finlay, Edward Woodward – and I was personally visited by every 'resting' matinée idol in the business, in an attempt to nobble the jury. Ten years after the delivery of the script – rapturously received by the powers that be – the series still has not been made. The vagaries of the biannual 'flexipool' (in which the scripts of all the independent TV companies vied for slots), the recession with its consequent redundancies, the government's cynical handling of the franchise deal, the fact that the whole of ITV drama was controlled by two people (insulting to the network) who were now looking for 'action adventure', the admission that another *Brideshead Revisited* or *Jewel in the Crown* would never be made (like *Shrinks* not sufficiently attractive to mass audiences) and the Gulf War, were all blamed.

Like hundreds of other talented and hopeful TV and film writers, some of the most previously successful of whom had as many as five rejected dramas on their hands, I found myself languishing in the dreaded 'development hell'. London Weekend were hopeful of producing *An Eligible Man* 'at some date in the future'. Other punters were keen to make the series, but head of drama Nick Elliot, who moved from LWT to BBC and back to LWT with the scripts under his arm, would not allow me to buy them back.

Ten years later Jane Tranter resurrected *An Eligible Man* as a vehicle for Ian (*House of Cards*) Richardson but: 'I'm not certain that this kind of territory doesn't demand a slightly fresher ... treatment.' I'm not surprised!

297

CHAPTER TWENTY-ONE

A Day in the Life of...

<hr/>

'An artist needs time to do nothing but sit around and think and let ideas come to him.'

Gertrude Stein

Once I had thrown the first pebble into the seemingly impenetrable pool of writing for television, several ripples came my way. Through Linda Siefert – who now had the unmade *Eligible Man* scripts to add to my calling cards – I was offered all manner of work. The most interesting of these offers came from Norma (*When Harry Met Sally*) Heyman, the producer of a proposed major TV film for the European market on the life of Christina Onassis, based on the book *Christina* by Nigel Dempster.

I met Norma and the co-producer in her elegant Ovington Square house, the UK home of Nelson Entertainments. We had a long discussion, rife with refreshments and enthusiasm, at which I was handed Dempster's book and asked to write a synopsis and screen breakdown which would incorporate my

A Day in the Life of ...

ideas, and explain the way in which I would tackle the subject. The synopsis had to be in their hands, not exactly yesterday, but in *three* days. I was not to worry about the investigative angle. The 'business' side of Christina Onassis's affairs had been thoroughly researched by a Harvard postgraduate student, and the legal aspects of her story worked on by European libel lawyers over the past year. Were I to be engaged, all this expertise – plus hundreds of tapes already obtained from witnesses to Christina's life – would be at my disposal.

I devoted an entire weekend to reading the book and deciding on my treatment. The subject matter was not only delicate on a personal level and intricate on a business one, but the ill-fated Christina's story moved randomly across Europe, from the United States to England, and back again.

As I bashed out my ideas I guessed that were I to write the story it would take over my whole life, would be dictated at every level by the 'European involvement', and that 'at the end of the day' it would be the Onassis story and not mine. On the agreed morning I biked my copy to Ovington Square and waited for the dust to settle. My synopsis and scene breakdown were of course 'marvellous' (*I* thought they were pretty good). It was *just* what they wanted. It had to be discussed, of course, with the head of Nelson Enterprises in New York, and they would call me after the meeting. Having got what they wanted out of me, Nelson Entertainments naturally lost my telephone number. When they found it and called, it was to say that impressed as they had been with what I had done – three days' work 'on spec' – and would like to engage me in the future on another project, they had decided on a 'name' to write *Christina* and had engaged Kathleen Tynan. What has happened to the project I don't know. It certainly hasn't appeared on my screen.

The next bike from Ovington Square carried *Norah*, the life of Lady Docker. The story was as tacky as it was dull and I politely returned it on the next bike.

Despite the fact that I had now read William Goldman's invaluable *Adventures in the Screen Trade*, a scathing exposé of the American film industry, I decided, before getting back to 'real work', to have one more stab at writing a screenplay, this time a 'Europudding' for the burgeoning European market. Linda Seifert, her co-director Elizabeth Dench, and I, formed our own production company Triumvirate Films and set about hammering out a storyline and producing a script. With commercial considerations in mind, we set the action in Paris (France was financing all the best movies), and with eyes on Paul Newman and Meryl Streep, made the protagonists American. It was my first experience at writing 'cold'. The storyline was concocted behind closed doors by the three of us, and after many enjoyable meetings and much hard writing, we had our script.

Linda and Elizabeth were pleased with the result. I had my reservations about it and felt that although it was competent enough, it was somehow written from the 'outside' and was lacking in the character, inner life, social relevance, ambiguity, difficulties and doubts of a novel. With *Paris Summer* as our working title, Linda sent the script to such accomplished directors as Karel Reisz and John Schlesinger, as well as to actors Meryl Streep and Paul Newman. It was enthusiastically received in various quarters, and we had several helpful suggestions (many of them contradictory) but no one was willing to put their money where their mouths were. Our script had, I thought, died the death, until a call from Peter Kendal – independent and BBC producer – announced that he had read

A Day in the Life of...

Paris Summer, thought it was wonderful, and was determined to make it, shooting to start next spring! Triumvirate Films crossed its fingers as Peter completed the movie he was now shooting, and turned his attention to *Paris Summer*.

As far as Hollywood is concerned 'a good script is a script to which Robert Redford will commit himself. A bad script is a script which Redford has turned down. A script that "needs work" is a script about which Redford has yet to make up his mind.'

Most Hollywood producers don't have time to read scripts. If you can't tell it to them in the proverbial sentence, or grab them in the first few pages, they pass. If your script gets to be the bedtime reading of the producer's wife, or girlfriend, you stand a better chance. It's a crazy business, and while *Paris Summer* was going the rounds I consoled myself with the fact that a successful film such as *Tootsie* (Dustin Hoffman, directed by Sydney Pollack), a major hit of 1982, took seven years, and ten writers before it got off the ground.

Paris Summer had been fun to write but unpaid and time consuming. I decided to leave the make-believe world of TV and movies, and get back to work.

Certain changes had now taken place in my personal life. My four daughters had all left home to make their way in the world and found their own dynasties, and we had bought a *résidence secondaire* in Provence. Despite extensive travels, my love for France had remained steadfast over the years, so when we fell upon the peaceful vineyard village of Plan de la Tour in the Maures countryside, we decided to buy a small stake in it. Our second home was, as always, bought on a whim. We were driving through the Var and arriving at Plan de la Tour at dusk, noticed some building activity on the outskirts of the village. We decided to spend the night at the Ponte Romano, a nearby hotel. Having a home in the Midi was something we had often discussed but had rejected (the air fares were too expensive) when the girls were still at home. Over dinner at the hotel we speculated idly about the 'infilling' which was taking place in the village. While we were doing so, to our utter amazement, we heard 'our tune' – *Near You* – the one to which we had danced at our wedding and which I had thought defunct, coming from the restaurant tape. We looked at each other, raised our glasses, and henceforth became *Plan de la Touriennes*.

Of course, in theory, what we would have liked was a Provençal *mas* in its own vineyard. We were not prepared however to cope with leaking roofs, crumbling fabric, frozen winter pipes and the habitual predators of isolated and un-occupied properties in the area in pursuit of our dream. We settled for an *appartement*, the top of a two-storey Provençal villa, with its 40-foot *terrasse* and view of the church and the surrounding hills. The *appartement* (2 bedrooms, 2 bathrooms and a vast *séjour* sociably encompassing the kitchen) took two years to materialise from a hole in the ground. How we man-aged to orchestrate the architecture of the exterior, and the design of the interior from a distance of 800 miles (praise be to the fax machine), I don't know. But to open the blue-green shutters in the mornings on to a silence long forgotten, on to a light – inspiration of Frédéric Mistral and of Cézanne – so intense, is to gladden the heart and vindicate everything.

While it is true that what starts out as a holiday home quickly becomes just another home (albeit one in which wasps nest in the eaves and June bugs cling limpet-like to the lintels), where life carries on much as normal, it is at a significantly different pace. Plan de la Tour is our lifeline. While in England we are uncomfortably aware of the increasing pressures of urban life where one is constantly distracted from what is real and important by people you don't know and events you can't influence, neither of us is yet ready to throw the whole crazy package – not to mention the solace of our nearby grandchildren – overboard.

Leaving the sensory overload of London, even for a long weekend, the essential civilities of French village life – the mandatory hand-shaking, the required kissing – brings one in touch again with the human dimensions of existence. Walking down the hill, *panier* on arm, to the shops, salutations are exchanged with passers-by. Here is Madame X in her pinafore and slippers; here is Monsieur Y, a prosperous vineyard owner who looks like nothing so much as a Provençal *clochard*. His ancient dog is at his ancient heels as he makes his flat-capped way to the sacrosanct 'men only' bench in the square. Leaning on his stick, he exchanges gossip with the retired black-clad shepherd and other *vieillards* (not as old as their gnarled looks imply) until the clock strikes twelve, and two minutes later twelve again, and one by sleepy one the shutters close and a tangible silence engulfs the cobbled streets.

In the *alimentation*, whose customers one greets both on arriving and on taking one's leave, time is forgotten as one fingers a misshapen local tomato which will taste not of Sainsbury's but of the sun. 'How will you eat it, *Madame*?' '*En salade*? Olive oil, *basilic*, a little sugar, some black pepper, and you have a dish for a king.'

An entire morning may be expended extolling the virtues of one's tomato, another in the extended ritual of exchanging one's *pages blanches* and *pages jaunes* for the latest telephone books, yet another in the village square greeting one's neighbours as one celebrates around a cauldron the *fête de vins chauds.* On Sunday mornings, as the church bells echo through the valley, the local *caves* dispense liberal glasses of free wine (donations in the box), hunks of country bread, local cheese and sausage, and Madame from *Le Clocher* – where year in, year out, her dedicated and uncomplaining husband cooks succulent steaks and paper-thin pizzas on a long shovel over a wood fire – has been up all night cooking: hams and pigs' trotters and chickens and a vast paella and tinfoil dishes of *crème caramel* to be taken home for the ritual Sunday lunch. There are monthly films, with heckling kids and ancient soundtracks in the *salle polyvalente*, dances where the butcher's wife waltzes with the baker to the echoes of early Frank Sinatra and the strains of *Comme l'Habitude*; stately cotillions in Provençal dress to the beat of a local band in the crowded *place*; talent contests, and judo displays, with the children included in everything, and the village dare-devils astride their evil-looking motorbikes looking on.

Thursday is market day when the local farmers bring their homemade jam and wooden bowls of multifarious olives and bug-ridden lettuces, and traders their mattresses and Provençal tablecloths, and stallholders their lacy bras and knickers (*La Perla* at a fraction of the price) and branded silk-and-cashmere Paris sweaters (fallen off a lorry), their slithering fish and fragrant wheels of cheese. Here you will meet the local restaurateurs, buying the wherewithal for their unchanging *plats du jour*, the familiar villagers eyes sharp for a bargain, the English with their voices and their accents, escapees from some Alan Ayckbourn play.

The *appartement* is hard to heat in winter, but soon the almond blossoms and mimosa will bring the first signs of spring. In May we take our picnics to the thyme-scented hillsides, and in June, as the purple bougainvillaea trails sloth-fully down the apricot walls, we lie supine on our terrace. September is *vendange* and we watch with pride the dusty black grapes being picked in 'our' vineyards. In October the goats and sheep return from summer grazing and wild mushrooms are sprouted by the autumn rains. At Christmas time, gathered round our *cheminée*, surrounded by friends, we read, converse – there is no television – and roast sweet indigenous chestnuts on our pine-scented fire.

Tout passe, tout lasse, tout casse. Our village appears in a book entitled *Les Plus Beaux Villages de France*; there are four *boulangeries* from which to buy your morning baguette where there was once one; *l'épicerie* anomalously stocks *les cornflakes* and *le chutney* and, other than on Thursday mornings, the market square now doubles as a car park to relieve the traffic congestion in the narrow streets.

All is not lost however. France still provides us with our *douceur de vivre*, while life in London, despite the fact that our daughters are no longer at home and we can spread ourselves out in St Katharine's Precinct – studies and studios – becomes increasingly frenetic.

A Day in the Life Of in the Sunday colour supplements never fails to intrigue me as I turn to the penultimate page curious to see how other people pass their days. While some are woken by their musical alarm clocks 'Hello baby ... this is the Big Bopper speaking', or open their eyes to 'mangrove poles and coconut leaves' on tropical islands (where they brush their teeth over the bushes), others wake up in a 'posh hotel' and 'blowtorch last night's make-up off', or rise at 4.15 am feed three schnauzers and a canary and are at their desks at 4.30 am. Most of them seem to have cats and housekeepers, eat either an 'elaborate breakfast' or sanctimonious slices of wholemeal bread spread with low calorie cream cheese, or bowls of muesli. They lunch, if indeed they 'bother at all' on sandwiches brought to them on a tray (by aforesaid housekeepers) and order takeaway curries ('can't cook a thing') before turning out the lights at 10.30 pm or going to bed in the small hours 'exhausted' and not sleeping very well – except those who are 'dead to the world the moment I touch the pillow'.

My own working day begins at 6.30 am when I get up. If I open my eyes any earlier I allow myself a few productive moments of reverie between sleeping and waking, during which long-standing problems present with instantaneous solutions, and ideas arrive unbidden. 'Only dull people are brilliant at breakfast'.* If I *have* to talk first thing in the morning – and over the years I have trained myself at least to be polite – it is with a modicum of words and a disengaged brain. 'There's a button off my shirt', and 'Remember to open the garden gate for the dustmen' have nothing whatever to do with my writing day.

I go straight upstairs, one floor, to my study. It could be winter or summer. I don't look. I switch on the computer and find my directory. The hard copy (paper) of the previous day's work will be waiting. I read through it and correct it on the screen. I glance at the note I have left myself concerning the next subject or sentence, and adjusting my chair – like a pernickety concert pianist – and putting my hands over the keyboard, switch into 'writing mode' and am away.

After a morning hour my back tends to get stiff. I go downstairs to pick up the newspapers and the post, glancing

* Oscar Wilde

only at the headlines and the more interesting of the letters, junk the junk mail and breakfast on coffee, oatcakes and a banana, both winter and summer. Breakfast coffee, in a large cup, is robust and black. I carry it up to my desk where I forget to drink it.

The next break is for a bath (in winter) in which the ideas come, or a summer shower in which they don't. Begrudging every minute of time wasted in necessary unnecessary activities, I pull on my writing clothes as I climb the stairs.

Sometimes the telephone will ring. The cleaning lady, on one of her 'days', cannot come. Her child (an asthmatic) is ill, she must take him to the doctor. Her handbag has been stolen in the market (with my door keys in it), she must go to the police. I don't know whether to be glad or sorry. If she doesn't turn up I have to find time to clear up the messes of the previous days, if she does I have to enter into dialectic about her indolent and abusive common-law husband (should she leave him?), look at the child's school report, or help with her tax return. I make a note on the desk diary to ring the locksmith to change the front-door locks. It is the first erosion of my day. There are others. It is one of the hazards of working at home.

As I open the door to British Gas who want to read the meter, or the Disabled (selling dusters), or a bewildered Dane looking for the pastor ('this is a private house, we are nothing to do with the church'), or take in a delivery of wine for next door, I console myself with the fact that at least I haven't had to wait for buses, sit on a paralysed M25, or play sardines on a commuter train.

If the postman doesn't ring, this time with a parcel (usually of books), for which he needs a signature, my next coffee break (in which I hang the washing whilst waiting for the water to boil) is

307

more for the exercise, four flights of stairs each way, than the caffeine. On my brief excursions to the kitchen I take care not to glance into other rooms, at empty glasses, at dead flowers, at unmade beds. First things first. Even the curtains in the sitting-room sometimes remain closed until lunch.

It seems like five minutes. I am getting tired. My mid-morning coffee is cold in the cup. It is one o'clock. There are 5/6/7 new pages on the screen. I stretch and wonder who has written them. Limp as a rag doll I enter the real world – I have forgotten to phone the locksmith – come back to earth.

After lunch of fresh fruit (apples, oranges and bananas, or apples, strawberries and peaches) according to season, it is a toss up as to whether or not I succumb to a Churchillian nap, waking refreshed after exactly 20 minutes of untroubled, *quasi* nighttime sleep.

Like a novel in progress, a household has to be *managed*. A little forethought precludes the necessity of peering into the fridge for ten minutes before dinner wondering what to eat. There are usually chores to be done. I walk to Camden Town with armsful of dry cleaning, bizarre lists of shopping (tooth-paste, marker pen, stamps, mushrooms, Balzac's *Lost Illusions*), shoes or artefacts to be repaired. If I am able to ignore the errands, and at weekends, I take my exercise in the park switching to automatic pilot and glancing to neither right nor left.

The afternoon stint in my study is devoted to correcting the morning's efforts and printing them out, making notes for the next day's work, research, speaking to agents, highlight-ing newspaper articles with coloured text markers and filing them away. As my working day draws to a close I may write a further few paragraphs but, like the artist who cleans his palette

A Day in the Life of ...

and puts away his paints, I make it a habit to clear my desk each evening. Arriving at a cluttered desk is like getting up in the morning to a sinkful of dirty dishes, and is no way to start the day. To this end I empty my wastepaper basket, return reference books to their rightful place on the shelves, and to the best of my ability restore order to the accumulated chaos.

Periodically, begrudging the writing time lost, I go to the hairdresser to have my hair cut or coloured. I don't mind growing old, I don't think about it until I confront the mirror; I don't much like *looking* old. Despising myself for my vanity, I sit for hours beneath porcupine spikes of silver paper, flicking through glossy magazines at a rate of knots. Occasionally I cook. Usually we go out, alone or with friends, to the Camden Brasserie where the food is unsauced and freshly cooked, to a PEN dinner, or a BAFTA screening. On Tuesdays and Thursdays, at the *Alliance Française*, I improve my French. We are in bed by 10.30, sometimes after a game of Scrabble (to the accompaniment of some good music) played in deadly earnest. It sounds dull. A writer's life has to be. The only valid hours are those spent in creation. The rest of the day has somehow to be filled.

Saturday, the Jewish Sabbath on which one *attempts* to abandon all manner of work and live as if one has nothing, still holds a special meaning of family communion. When you have a large family it can be more tiring than work. On Sundays, in addition to the daunting pile of newspapers begging, if not to be read at least to be glanced at, the decks must be cleared for the week ahead. There are letters to reply to, bills to be paid, mailing-list subscriptions to be renewed, insurance claims to be filled out, book-keeping to be done, invitations to be replied to, requests for stories ('can't you just write a short one for next week!) to be dealt with, talks to prepare, book reviews and articles to be written...

My 'day in the life of' is a tissue of truth. The one I have described is what my producer at Euston Films would have me describe as a 'peerless' one. It is not like that. I am sick. Of one of my chronic complaints, an infection, broken rib or other unforeseen catastrophe. A daughter is not well, and will I look after a grandchild for what is referred to as 'a little while' but turns out to be several precious hours; a second daughter is in domestic crisis which takes precedence over my writing; another most urgently needs to use my computer to type out her CV having left a critical job application to the eleventh hour; the fourth comes round bearing marital problems and any chance of my doing the school run? The local butcher is writing a book and wants me to read the manuscript. A friend has a 'brilliant' idea for a novel and is sure that when I hear it I will jump at the chance to 'collaborate' with her. An acquaintance sends a clutch of dog-eared, misspelt, illiterate, overwritten typed pages, from South Africa and is sure that I won't mind submitting his *chef d'oeuvre* to publishers on his behalf. There are urgent requests from TV companies for immediate outlines and synopses. My printer gets temperamental and jams paper in its maw necessitating a call to, and a visit from, the maintenance engineer. The waste-disposal is also jammed and owing to our idiosyncratic plumbing the dishwasher comes out in sympathy. They are digging the road up in the Precinct, and will I please shift my car? There is a delivery of granular salt (10 hefty bags necessitating a tip and all I can find is 20p) for the water softener, it coincides with a Jehovah's Witness at the open door. The window cleaner or the tree surgeon call on one of their biannual visits, they are unable to function without a compassionate ear and regular infusions of tea.

'Ordered Ideas' people, of which I am one – gathering ideas and forming theories, researching information and organising data in a logical way – are not only capable of working hard over long periods of time, but make heavy demands on themselves.

On looking back through my diary I see that in the course of a single year I have organised the flat in France (entailing three visits), written six episodes of *An Eligible Man* for TV, travelled to Norway, had a breast lump (benign) removed, demanding daily hospital attendances and draining of a subsequent haematoma, organised a daughter's wedding at the Groucho Club, held a publication party (for *An Eligible Man*) and a Ruby wedding party – like Nabokov's Vera I love arranging things 'be it a party with punch, a visa or a wedding' – reviewed five novels, prepared and given a talk to the Authors' Club (having read and assessed the six novels competing for the prize), spent three painful weeks in bed with a 'back' episode, written a screenplay, celebrated the Passover (20 for Seder night), supervised the work and suffered the upheaval of a third attempt by builders to rid our basement of damp (pickaxes and cement mixers), and had the outside of the house painted in accordance with the quadrennial requirements of the Crown (during the course of which the elderly painter put his head in my study window with the gratuitous information that 'Barbara Cartland does it lying down!').

'He is a splendid man and a great artist ... a man who doesn't let himself worry about anything ... not politics, nor socialism, nor Fournier nor Jesuits, nor the university. Instead he *rolls up his sleeves* like a good workman and is there to do his job from

311

morning till night, desiring to do it well and loving his art... I worry more about a line of verse than about any man... The love of Glycera or Lycorn will outlive future civilizations. Like a star Art watches undisturbed as the world spins round ... the Beautiful keeps its place in the firmament.'*

The greatest events in Flaubert's life may well have been 'a few thoughts, a few books, certain sunsets on the beach at Trouville' and he may well have 'lived differently from others'. For women writers it is not so easy, and one has to strike a balance between imaginative and everyday life. I have taken no account in the above of birthdays and anniversaries to be remembered and cards and presents to be bought, of visitors from abroad who arrive inopportunely and without warning and demand to be entertained, and of friends to be kept up with in person or by mail, of servicing one's teeth and one's car (can it really be time again for the hygienist, the MOT), and of necessary encounters with maintenance and repair men, with doctors and ophthalmologists. As far as the writer is concerned, it is so not so much a case of 'A Day in the Life Of', as of condensing one's life into a day.

* Gustave Flaubert

CHAPTER TWENTY-TWO

The Giaconda Smile

<hr/>

'Bell's palsy results from an inflammation of a major facial
nerve. It causes pain in the jaw and numbness and drooping
on one side of the face that gives patients a split-faced appearance – happy on one side, sad on the other. The manifestations of Ramsay Hunt syndrome are identical to Bell's palsy
but are more severe and carry a graver prognosis.'

Kedar K. Adour, MD

On 11 June 1993, a day that was to be etched on my memory,
two weeks after returning from a Writers' Exchange visit to
Hollywood, I awoke to find that the right side of my face was
paralysed and that I was unable to close my eye. Confirmed by
my GP as Bell's palsy – named for Sir Charles Bell, a Scottish
doctor who first described the condition in the early nineteenth
century – it later revealed itself in its more severe form, Ramsay
Hunt syndrome, a condition which permanently damaged the
facial nerves.

THE WRITING GAME

The primary goals of the Writers' Exchange to Hollywood, were to develop relationships with appropriate executives in the US industry; to gain a better understanding of the business and creative process when writing for the US market; to meet the creative personnel who have written and developed successfully for the international market; to introduce them to professionals from studios, networks, cable, production companies, agents, actors, lawyers, international sales agents, publishers, writers, story editors, writer/producers, guilds and trade associations; and, above all, to teach them how to 'pitch' or present the essence of a story so that it could be easily grasped ('if you can't enthuse me with an idea in a couple of sentences, how am I going to sell it to the American public?').

Although this latter seems fundamental, 'pitching' or selling a story or idea by describing it verbally, is virtually unknown in Europe, where we do not have a pitching culture, and in the UK diffident writers, usually low in self-esteem (it goes with the job), have to bow, scrape, and lick the boots of agents, editors and producers even to get their stuff read. If you wanted to sell your writing on the other side of the Atlantic it was a different story: you had to put everything on a plate and label the vegetables.

The convention was that you had one minute to make your initial pitch, reducing the essence of the work being presented down to the minimum. There was no need to tell the story, merely to indicate what sort of story it was, explain why it would appeal to audiences, and to which audiences you thought it would appeal. In other words, a 'high concept' was necessary. One good sentence would help to suggest to a potential investor, studio executive, director – or writer you wished to work with – everything they need to know about your project. A really good sentence, explaining your idea, while at the same time indicating the advertising potential, the title etc. was one which would avoid burying the listener beneath a mass of detail. Having done your homework, you should be able to give the answers *before* you were asked the questions, the most important of these being 'why would someone want to watch my programme?' This meant knowing everything you needed to know about the person or company you were pitching to, so that they had no doubt what was in it for them, and above all show them how they could make money out of you. A classic example of a good pitch line is that for Ridley Scott's *Alien*: 'Jaws on a spaceship', which immediately indicates to the dumbest executive how the film can be marketed and why the studio should buy it.

If your idea was for a feature or TV drama, the stories had to be about characters with which the audience (not only in New York and San Francisco but in a Kansas trailer park) could identify. This was not because the audiences wanted to experience the lives of your characters but because they wanted to gain insight into themselves. Their own emotions had to be invested in a character so that they could 'feel' what he was going through. In this vicarious experience lay the key to success.

Being able to present yourself well and your project succinctly, so that the buyer does not lose confidence in the person pitching, was nearly as important in Hollywood as having a good script. An indifferent script with a good pitch is more likely to get made than a good script with a bad pitch from a writer who has not only scuppered his project but has *let himself down*. For the purposes of packaging and pitching, he must learn not only how to talk but when to stop talking and when to change direction, how to inspire confidence, how to be the centre of attention (not easy for British writers), and how to go out on to the stage (remembering it is crowded with others) and be the star of the show.

The first surprise for our small group which included the head of drama for BBC Wales, a Scotsman, a Spaniard, and two South African writers, was the fact that in the USA the writer is a VIP and that when we got off the plane and presented our passports denoting us as writers, the eyes of the immigration officers lit up with respect.

The five-day tour, for the duration of which we appropriately stayed on Sunset Boulevard – the Sunset Plaza Hotel – included a mind-boggling *seven to ten* meetings a day, every day – starting with breakfast and finishing with 'drinks and hors d'oeuvres' (Citadel Pictures), and an open-air industry dinner at Orso's on W. Third St – at venues such as Home Box Office (Century Park East), Hearst Entertainment (South Sepulveda Boulevard), the Writers' Guild of Los Angeles ('if it flickers it's ours'), Twentieth Century-Fox and the Sundance Film Institute. Turner Broadcasting, in the person of the director of original programming, Betsy ('are you my breakfast?') Newman, fed us eggs easy-over and pancake stacks at some ungodly hour at the Peninsula Hotel, and we also got to visit established and hospitable writers such as the English Duncan Gibbons (later sadly to die in the fire on Topanga Canyon) and Jeffrey Lewis, in their homes.

In five days we saw more vice-presidents, more agents, more executive directors, more attorneys, more writer/producers, than most people would get to meet in a lifetime. Unlike in the UK where in shabby, messy offices one would be offered tea or coffee (how many sugars?) in polystyrene cups, we were served tea, coffee, and every other drink (diet or otherwise) known to man, in china cups and crystal glasses in elegant rooms, at polished board-room tables presided over by executives groomed – the women with impeccable highlights and manicured nails and the men squeaky clean at 8.30 in the morning – to within an inch of their lives.

After 24 hours in the unreal world of *Primetime* and *Lifetime*, of Pacific Palisades and Burbank, I found, to my surprise, that with new confidence, and in response to the fast-moving, hard-hitting milieu with its voracious appetite for programmes, I was up there pitching with the rest of them and managed to convince more than one VP (who regularly invested their leisure time to read up to five scripts a night) that they would be stupid not to read mine. I learned and I learned: that it was hard to get anything into development that didn't come from a major novel; that 'cerebral' movies cannot be made; that violence sells; that the 1/2 hour comedy is the bread-and-butter of the networks; that most successful pitches had big stars attached; that the flavour of the month was 'squalid white bitches who kill'; that some networks wanted only female-oriented movies (no Second World War, no Westerns, no love stories, no Indians, no issues, no rape, no disease of the week, no homosexuality, only white girls with guns or sexy duplicitous women married to rich older men); that what sells product best is what is familiar; that executives listen to 25,000 pitches a year; that TV programming is a 'wraparound' for advertisements; that the English have no money, the French are confused (if you feed a French film crew hotdogs or hamburgers they walk) and that America is the prime TV market therefore the issues must be American; that if it happened to you it was OK for TV, and above all that the *bottom line was money*.

THE WRITING GAME

I left several ideas for TV series and the script of my movie *Paris Summer* with agents and studio executives ('sounds like a treasure trove', 'keep in touch with your projects', 'feel free to put a script in the post') and on a Hollywood high returned to the UK and the unholy mess that was British television.

Two weeks later, having, I am sure, picked up the herpes virus on the plane, I came down to earth with a bump.

The appellation 'Bell's palsy', with its labial consonants, is an unfortunate one in respect of the fact that those smitten with the malady are, by virtue of the consequent paralysis, unable to pronounce the name of their affliction with anything like the clarity which would render it comprehensible. This aberration – compounded by the lopsided view of oneself reflected in the mirror, lack of tears in and an inability to close one eye, unilateral loss of taste, drooling, the difficulties of eating and impossibility of drinking with any semblance of dignity – seemed mildly funny in the initial stages. It left one completely unprepared for the reality of the situation which was that the next two and a half years would be no laughing matter.

Although my GP was familiar with the manifestations of Bell's palsy, a not uncommon condition of sudden onset, he was not too happy about the severe pain in my eye and before referring me to neurologist sent me to see a consultant ophthalmologist who although indubitably well qualified was decidedly lacking in sensitivity.

Cheerfully writing out a prescription for eyedrops after he had examined me, he shocked me – for the second time that day – by casually stating that while I could temporarily cover the offending eye with an eyepatch, in due course the eye might very well have to be *sewn up*.

The Giaconda Smile

Like so many minor operations, a tarrsorophy – to give the stitching together of the eyelids its technical name – may in the hierarchy of medical procedures represent no big deal to the surgeon. To the unprepared patient, or to me at any rate in my already somewhat stunned state, it came as a nasty surprise and I was unable to take in the ramifications. It had all happened so fast that I assumed he must be kidding.

The neurologist, a jovial fellow of Falstaffian proportions, tickled my eyes with cotton wool, asked to see my lopsided smile, made me touch the tip of my nose with my eyes closed, looked in my ear on the affected side and having made the diagnosis – surprise, surprise – of Bell's palsy, a debilitating facial paralysis for which although there was as yet no specific treatment, he prescribed a six-day course of steroids which were thought by some to be of some help. The condition, he assured me, would start to improve within two weeks. Three months should see a complete recovery. The fact that my right eye was now excruciatingly painful he put down to 'dryness' – I was unable to blink – and I got the impression he thought I was exaggerating the pain. After a strong dose of reassurance, he sent me on my way. He did not ask me to come back.

On the way home I called in at the chemist for an eyepatch but the upper eyelid was so far retracted that the concave shape of the patch, even combined with a gauze pad, did not do the trick. I was still unable to close it and wondered why I had not been better advised as to the mechanics of the thing. It was some time and a great deal of pain later that I concocted my own device from a British Airways eyemask, made of soft black material, which I cut in half and stitched and which lay flat and tight against my eye keeping it firmly closed.

Blissfully unaware that the full physical manifestations of my condition were yet to exhibit themselves, I regarded philosophically the minor misfortune which had befallen me. I consoled myself with the fact that it could after all have been an incapacitating stroke or cancer, managed to avoid the sight of my contorted face in the mirror, battled against the tiredness which now consumed me (which I put down to shock), and got on with my life.

Forty-six extremely large books – fiction and non-fiction – had just been delivered to my home. They were entries for the 1993 *Jewish Quarterly* Literary Prize for which I was chairing the judging panel. Politely averting their gaze from my bizarre appearance – lopsided face and black eyepatch – my fellow judges strained to decipher my slurred speech, devoid of 'p' and 'b' sounds, as I struggled to explain the rules and regulations. Reading 46 books monocularly was only one of the hazards. Driving was not only dangerous but a nightmare (difficult to glance in the right-hand wing mirror with the left eye without taking one's eyes off the road), and I am not at all sure that I was legally allowed to do so. It was as nothing compared to coping with the shock horror at my appearance on the faces of those who knew me (my cleaning lady burst into tears) and in the expressions of children in the street who laughed and ran away.

Like a pirate, with my black patch beneath which the eye like a hundred hot knives continued to bedevil me, I managed as best I could. It was a week later that a pain in the affected side of my face, as severe as any as I had ever had, woke me in the night. Neither paracetamol nor coproxamol made any impression on it. By mid-morning of the next day I was in agony. When the bluff neurologist, to whose consulting rooms I was

320

once again taken by a kind-hearted friend, declared breezily that my symptoms were *dental* rather than neurological and that the problem lay in the tempero-mandibular joint, warning bells rang in my head. The fact that I passed out from the pain in his consulting room seemed not to affect the diagnosis. All day I was shunted from dentist to oral hygiene centre and back again. I had local X-rays, whole mouth X-rays (in a revolving machine), and seven deep and painful injections which I was assured would relieve the pain but which did not do so in the least degree.

Two days, and many anti-inflammatory drugs later, the pain abated. Having assured me that neither this episode nor my latest symptom, a sore and ulcerated tongue, was 'anything to worry about', the neurologist suggested that a planned holiday in our French home would do me the world of good. I suspect he was glad to see the back of me.

The entire holiday was spent in total exhaustion, unable to eat, and being unsuccessfully treated by an extremely sympathetic French ophthalmologist who diagnosed an ulcerated cornea (which untreated could lead to blindness in the affected eye) and prescribed antibiotic drops, vitamin A ointment – a popular French nostrum – and 'steri-strips' with which to keep my eye closed. '*Il faut qu'il soit bien fermé.*' If her well-meaning advice had been as good as her subjunctive (the steri-strips did not do the trick), I would have been laughing all the way to the pharmacy. In pain, and exhausted, unable to sit up in the car and having to lie down on the back seat all the way across France because of my eye, we cut the 'holiday' short and I thankfully returned home to the comfort of my own bed.

I was not short of advice. Well-wishers extolled, with varying degrees of insistence, everything from 'visualisation' and reflexology, through 'healing hands' and the 'Facial-Flex' exerciser (first used at George Washington University for stroke rehabilitation), to cranial osteopathy, applied kinesiology (muscle weakness linked to an imbalance of energy within the body!), acupressure and acupuncture (unblocking energy pathways or meridians which have never been satisfactorily established), aikido, Alexander technique, anthroposophic medicine, aromatherapy, aston patterning, aura soma, autogenic training and ayurvedic medicine (and these are just the 'a's'), offered by self-appointed practitioners who were unable to get their diplomas sanctioned by academic bodies because academic bodies require academic proof.

It is one of the tenets of alternative medicine that the body is wired up in such a perverse way, that the best place to look for the source of illness – and to treat it – is almost anywhere but where you have the pain. A reflexologist believes that all the body's organs are connected, like some intricate telephone exchange, to the feet, and the iridologists that illness can be diagnosed by looking at the iris and consulting their diagrams (if you are prepared to wait while they find the right page), although I would just as soon trust a copy of *Home Doctor*. According to a report in the *Journal of the American Medical Association*, while a test group of iridologists who were shown 143 photographs of irises did no better than chance in divining illnesses, one of their number diagnosed kidney disease in 88 per cent of the patients who actually had kidney disease; the fact that he also diagnosed kidney disease in 88 per cent of patients who did not have the illness, sheds some doubt on this particular branch of alternative medicine which seems to have an answer for everything from appendicitis to piles.

The Giaconda Smile

It was Bernice Rubens, a fellow novelist, who suggested that I have a go at acupuncture which had apparently seen off the Bell's palsy of a friend.

My views on complementary medicine were coloured by the fact that although many people were willing to put their faith in one form or another of its unscientific treatments, its practitioners were governed by no professional body (making sure that they did the job properly and did not harm rather than help their patients); its 'cures' were anecdotal and unconfirmed by clinical trials; and that while it has been used to treat everything from depression and backache to allergies, skin problems, heart disease, addictions, low sexual vitality and the ageing process, it completely fell to pieces in the face of organic illness, and was impotent when confronted with damaged nerves or a broken rib. Alternative medicine may possibly help at certain levels, if only by virtue of the therapeutic effect on the patient of being touched and stroked (whether physically or mentally), or the personality and dedication of the therapist (who sometimes uses the number and importance of his clients, together with the distance they travel to see him, as a yardstick of success).

While orthodox medicine may not have all the answers, it does at least have some. If I say that I regard such cults as homoeopathy, with its simple-minded principles (as determined by guru Samuel Hahnemann at the end of the eighteenth century) with the utmost scepticism – its absurdly minute doses might affect the susceptible mind but are too infinitesimal to influence the body – you will know where I stand on alternative medicine: yet even I was seduced by the violent and threatening message aimed even at sufferers from terminal illness 'if you don't come to us you won't get better'.

323

THE WRITING GAME

Not having been offered relief for my symptoms from the orthodox school, I decided, against my better judgement, to take Bernice's well-meant advice and consulted a renowned Chinese doctor who stuck a few needles into my face to test for tolerance, before assuring me that he treated a great many Bell's palsies and that in *two weeks at the most* I would be completely cured.

One month later, having faithfully attended his clinic daily for a trial by extremely painful needles which I was in no state to endure, and having been prescribed an evil-looking mixture of what I was assured was herbs and roots, which I was instructed to soak and brew but which smelled so foul that it ended up down the sink, there was not *one iota* of improvement. One sadistic lady operator who delighted in revolving the needles to their maximum in my already painful face, said that in her local village she twirled them ten times as hard. When I apologised for not having the fortitude of a Chinese peasant, she looked at me pityingly. When I paid the good doctor and told him that I had done my very best to go along with his treatment but in the absence of any improvement felt disinclined to pursue it further, he said that the status quo was entirely my own fault – for failing to drink his tea. I refrained from asking him in what clinical trial it had been proven that facial nerve paralysis could be relieved by drinking tea, no matter how foul, but managed to hold my tongue as he pocketed the not insubstantial cheque.

With my eye still troubling me and the original ophthalmologist having nothing further to offer other than surgery, which I was unwilling to undergo, I consulted another, the son of a good friend. Almost casually he asked me if it was an attack of shingles which had brought on my condition which he conceded that for Bell's palsy was extremely severe. Had I, he enquired, had any spots or rash of any sort in the region of the ear?

Now. When I first went to see the neurologist I had had two painful and encrusted small spots in my ear on the affected side of my face. Not appreciating the connection, and not wishing to bother so eminent a neurologist with such trivia as a couple of spots – be they in the outer ear or elsewhere – I had not drawn his attention to them any more than I would have done to a minor cut on the finger. He had however looked down my ear with his auroscope and had failed to notice them. These, my excruciatingly painful eye, the lesions on my tongue, and the severe pain I had had in my face (which he had put down to a misplaced joint), were indicators that the virus which had assaulted my immune system was not that of Herpes Simplex (Bell's palsy), but Herpes Zoster (Ramsay Hunt) with its more severe paralysis, post-herpetic pain, higher incidence of complete denervation, increased risk of complications, and a significantly poorer prognosis. According to double-blind trials which had been carried out in the United States, patients who were given *early treatment with acyclovir, in addition to prednisone*, and for 21 days rather than 6, were likely to make a full recovery and less were left in an unsatisfactory state.

Once again I returned to the affable neurologist who, after shamelessly referring to his textbook of neurology, agreed that the ophthalmologist was absolutely right and that he, unfortunately, had 'made a mistake'.

His apologies, accompanied this time by rather embarrassed laughter, fell on extremely irate ears. I underwent an MRI scan, chest X-ray, and blood tests at his instigation – what if he had missed something else? – but did not return to his consulting room.

Acyclovir, an extremely expensive drug, was started. It was of course too late. The neurologist at the Royal National Hospital for Nervous Diseases, as thin as the other was fat, as serious as the other was flippant, said he was very sorry. He also apologised, not this time for his negligence but for the poor prognosis, confirmed by neurophysiological electrical tests (more needles in the face) which indicated that the nerve fibres themselves had been severely damaged.

The eye continued to be the worst problem. Sometimes I wept with pain and despair. A chance meeting on the stairs with an ophthalmologist from the Atkinson Morley Hospital, whose consulting rooms were in the same house as my husband's, not only turned out to be my salvation but avoided the tarrsorophy towards which, as the only option, I seemed to have been heading. The first thing Mr Ian Mackie did was to rip off my eyepatch and hurl it on the floor. 'You won't be needing this any more!'

I explained that although other opinions had prescribed various brands of sticky-tape with which to keep my eye closed, in addition to either bringing me out in a rash, or removing the skin from the surrounding area, or both, they failed abysmally to do the job for which they had been employed, due mainly to the 'crocodile' tears which paradoxically accompanied the dryness and which coursed constantly down my face.

By the time I left the consulting room my cornea had been diagnosed as once again severely ulcerated *due to heat and abrasion from my homemade eyepatch*, my eyelashes had been plucked out one by one (by turning inwards they had added to the abrasions), and my eye had been treated and comfortably closed with 'Blenderm', a surgical tape for which as the months went by I would be eternally grateful to the manufacturers.

Miraculously the ulcers healed. Although I still had to tape the eye shut as it did not as yet close spontaneously, the abrasions did not recur and I was able to maintain the eye in reasonable comfort by the judicious use of the tape and by the application of drops to keep it moist which I applied frequently and which I carried with me wherever I went.

During the course of my illness, commented on by so many and helped by so few, two other guardian angels were to appear. The first was Diana Farragher, senior physiotherapy teacher at the Withington Hospital, Manchester, and the second, Kedar K. Adour MD, director of research in the Department of Otolaryngology – Head and Neck surgery, at the Kaiser Permanente Medical Center in Oakland, California.

Diana Farragher had pioneered the use of 'Eutrophic Electrical Stimulation for Bell's Palsy' which according to exhaustive studies had a therapeutic effect not only on the drooping muscles of the face and eye, but on the gratuitous tears, the facial spasms which occurred as the disease progressed, as well as the contractures and synkinesis which later occurred. That her findings were disputed by some neurologists in whose opinion electrical stimulation varied from being counter-productive to recovery when administered in the first few months, to ineffective, did not deter me. Diana was not only an acknowledged expert on the small muscles of the face, but was the only professional I came across to offer much needed support in a little understood but distressing condition. Her consulting room in the Manchester suburb to which I regularly took the Inter-City train, was a rogues' gallery of photographs of patients, both men and women, young as well as old, whose hideous grimaces bore an uncanny resemblance to my own.

It was explained to me, with the help of diagrams, that the facial nerve comprised the nerves to all the muscles inserting into the skin of the face, and the nerves carrying the sensation of taste from the front two-thirds of the tongue to the brain; that it supplied the muscle that raised the eyebrow, the muscle that closed the eye, the muscle that wrinkled the nose, and the muscle that opened and closed the lips. For the first time I felt that somebody actually understood what I was going through, that somebody actually cared whether or not I got better, and possibly more importantly still, that I was not alone.

Diana's treatment – for which she showed me before and after pictures of many of her patients – was stimulation with electrodes placed at strategic points on the face combined with a programme of facial exercises. Whether 18 months' dedicated daily use of the tiny, portable machine with which she supplied me and to which I religiously attached myself for two hours each day, was actually instrumental in the degree of improvement I achieved – supported by three monthly photographs which caused us considerable amusement – I shall never know. Only that Diana's ongoing encouragement, support, and empathy were invaluable.

Since the onset of my illness I had read every paper on the condition that I could lay hands on. The name which recurred most frequently in the bibliographies in the medical journals was that of Doctor K. K. Adour.

After an initial phone call, Kedar Karim Adour rang me from San Francisco. This telephone consultation was followed by an exchange of helpful letters and hilarious faxes, and culminated in a much appreciated personal visit which cemented a bizarre friendship which continues until this day.

The Giaconda Smile

⟞⬥⟝

Kedar Adour, founder and president of the Sir Charles Bell Society which disseminated and exchanged information about the disease in a newsletter to 150 experts in the field in 26 countries through mail and e-mail, turned out to be not only to have been engaged on research into Bell's palsy for the past 30 years (in a paper published in 1989 in the Annals of Otology, Rhinology & Laryngology, he posits that Bell's palsy is responsible for the enigmatic expression on the face of the *Mona Lisa*), but a physician in the true sense of the word, a fellow-writer – with several plays to his credit, including *The Giaconda Smile* – and a good friend.

By the time our exchange of faxes began, almost a year after the onset of the illness, although my face had resumed some semblance of normality and my eye, thanks to Ian Mackie's ongoing care required taping up only at night, I was left with a persistent bad taste in the right side of the mouth from which there was never any relief. 'Disgeusia' – the best description I could come up with was that it was like putting your tongue on a live battery – resulted from the severity of the damage to the chorda tympani, the nerve from the middle ear to the tongue, and was my most distressing symptom. In the absence of any helpful advice on this side of the Atlantic from neurologists and ENT surgeons who had neither seen such a severe case of Ramsay Hunt before nor encountered the specific symptom, Professor Adour suggested that a simple neurectomy (severing the chorda tympani nerve) might relieve the condition in which case the successful outcome should be reported in the literature.

After liaising with Professor Adour (and joining the Sir Charles Bell Society mailing list), Mr Jonathan Hazell, an ENT surgeon, agreed to carry out the procedure with the proviso that

I should not be too disappointed if the simple operation did not do the trick.

Today, six years after the event, while there has, as predicted by the neurophysiological test, been some recovery, I am left – apart from a certain degree of self-consciousness – with permanent spastic paralysis of the muscles on the right-hand side of my face (treated every six weeks with injections of botulinum toxin to relieve the spasm and twitching and improve the appearance), an eyelid which closes incompletely (necessitating taping up at night, gustatory tears (which stream down my face embarrassingly as soon as I start to eat) as well as with the only slightly modified bad taste in my mouth from the mainly unsuccessful neurectomy.

Although the episode, in terms of shock and trauma, left much to be desired, I managed during its worst excesses to make a speech at the reception given by the *Jewish Quarterly* and to present the prizes; to be 'mother-of-the-bride' to my fourth daughter (disguising my face and eye beneath a Freddy Fox hat); establish relationships with a new publisher and, most therapeutically of all, to get on with my work.

I have never been either especially vain or particularly beautiful, I have however always taken a pride in my appearance and enjoyed the challenge of making the best of an indifferent job. Although time has now passed, I have still not completely come to terms with the ravages of the exceptionally and unluckily severe attack of Ramsay Hunt syndrome and cannot resist looking in the mirror each morning in the hope that I am miraculously cured. Apart from my occasional anger at the initial failure of diagnosis and appropriate treatment (which might or might not have limited the damage), it has left me permanently, if not at first glance, handicapped, with a drooping mouth and eyelid, unable to whistle (but then I never could), a lack of expression – leading those sitting on my right hand side to think me extremely disagreeable – and not so much a smile as a sneer.

In the grand order of things the visitation was neither mortal nor life-threatening and I could, of course, have been afflicted with something very much worse. If the episode has taught me anything it is the value of determination and persistence in reading the literature and in 'finding out for oneself', and that physicians, like the rest of us, not only come in all shapes and sizes but are, not to put too fine a point on it, fallible.

If everyone were to lay his troubles on the table there are few who would not pick up their own again. As far as Ramsay Hunt is concerned, all I can say is that I could have done without it!

CHAPTER TWENTY-THREE

The Play's the Thing

———⟫⬧⟪———

'...there is nothing so pleasurable for a man as to have produced a play that delights the town.'

Samuel Johnson

When, after much travail, you finally finish a novel and lay down your pen, there is no applause. If you get any response at all, it is likely to be 'what time's dinner?'

When, by the grace of God – and the generosity of the backers – you finally get a play staged and the curtain comes down on the last act, the reaction is immediate and falls on the ears like the gentle dew from heaven.

For one reason or another (the rise of TV drama, the popularity of programmes such as *EastEnders*, *Brookside*, *London's Burning* and *The Bill*, videos, the cinema, and the stinginess of the Arts Council have all been blamed), the retreat from live theatre has been remorseless, and the odds against an unsolicited script being produced are many hundreds to one. If you do get past first base, from finished script to opening night can often take as much as four years. That's if you are extremely lucky. It is a question of offering the right 'product' at the right time to the right people, and many successful and established playwrights – such as Peter Shaffer (*Five Finger Exercise* and *Equus*) and Nichols (*The National Health, A Day in the Life of Joe Egg*) – regularly have work turned down by theatres and not only amass accumulations of rejection letters but have a growing pile of playscripts languishing in drawers. When the situation is analysed this is hardly surprising. What is surprising is that stage plays see the light of day at all. Although the author receives a percentage of the gross box office, plays – except of the top-notch, long-running, popular musical variety (such as *Cats, Joseph*, and *Blood Brothers*) financed by impresarios who already have several long-running successes on their hands – RARELY MAKE MONEY FOR THE BACKERS and there are more turkeys than hits. Even if the West End theatre is full every night, five out of every six plays do not make a profit. It is a truism hard to explain, but the fact that investment is rarely realised has less to do with the quality of the production than with the capitalisation of the show, with 'knowns' such as actors' salaries and estimated weekly running costs, and 'unknowns' such as the concurrent scheduling of popular TV programmes, the unexpected onset of inclement weather (both of the hot and cold variety), the vagaries of the newspaper and transport industries, the pressing needs of parliamentary elections, the success of terrorist groups in driving away the tourists, and the scheduling of major sporting events which take precedence over the demands of the box office. One has, in addition, to take into account such imponderables as the ongoing health of the actors, the spleen of the reviewers, the tendency of theatres to reduce published seat prices not only for students, senior citizens, groups and matinée audiences, but for Uncle Tom Cobley and All, and the mischievous intervention of the tabloid newspapers.

'...Every writer of fiction, though he may not adopt the dramatic form, writes in effect for the stage.'*

In 1992, for no conscious reason and with no reference to the earlier version written 30 years earlier, I rewrote *Visitor from Seil*. By dint of working night and day, it took me one week and I was delighted both with the play – which in my innocence I imagined would be an instant success – and with the fact that I had produced the sort of piece I should like to see; one which not only had hidden depths but one in which people say and do things that made me laugh. I knew little about the theatre other than as an occasional theatregoer and nothing at all about its nuts and bolts. Having been foolhardy enough to open the Pandora's Box of playwriting, I learned the hard way.

Although I was now lucky enough to be represented by new-style, high-flying agent Sonia Land (ex-finance director of Collins) for my novels, and Linda Seifert (Seifert Dench Associates) for TV and film work, I knew personally no agents who dealt with stage plays. As a newcomer to the field, I was aware that most plays are produced through personal contact and was disinclined to start at the bottom of some theatrical heap. Linda Seifert, who had expended and continued to expend, so much energy on my behalf, was not keen to take on *Visitor from Seil*. She had little experience with stage plays and knew it was a thankless task. 'You can't even get producers to *read* plays,' she said. 'It'll take about four years.' I twisted her arm. Her estimate was exactly right.

* Charles Dickens

The Play's the Thing

Apart from my ignorance of the correct way to set out a stage script (first page, top right, header with draft number, name of play and author, second page, cast list, third page ACT 1 centred, fourth page SCENE ONE underlined; only use brackets for stage directions within dialogue and keep them in capitals etc. etc.), I made two major errors. My first was to have a cast of 10 characters. Only subsidised theatres such as the Royal National Theatre and the Royal Court, and then only rarely, can afford such excesses, and a cast of five or less means that the play will immediately fall into an acceptable budget. My second mistake was to make *Visitor from Seil* an ensemble piece with no role for a star with a reputation for putting bums on seats, and no virtuoso carrot to entice a name actor (and by extension theatre management). Carried away with content and construction, such practical considerations as actors' salaries and the number of props entailed (about which more later) had not entered my head. Neither, I must confess, did it bother the 50 or more theatres and producers to whom Linda submitted *Visitor from Seil*. My play either languished on the slush-pile of the 20 to 100 unsolicited scripts the theatres receive each week (script-reading is generally fitted in around an already overloaded work schedule and no one can read more than half a dozen scripts a week without some kind of brain damage), or came winging back with such nebulous comments as 'we have enjoyed reading the script, but I'm afraid I don't feel that it is right for our present programme' (Theatre Royal Plymouth). 'Unfortunately we have no slot in the foreseeable future, therefore we are unable to take matters further with this piece' (Thorndike Theatre Leatherhead). And '...I don't think the play is right for our theatre at the moment' (Bristol Old Vic).

There were more constructive comments: 'Rosemary needs to recognise that each time she goes to a blackout that represents the end of a scene. Once she knows her acts contain not two scenes but twenty she may be a little more economical with them' (Stephen Joseph Theatre Scarborough), as well as an encouraging letter from the London New Play Festival (Sadler's Wells):

'*Visitor from Seil* was highly recommended on the festival's shortlist. The readers thought it was engrossing, warm and effortlessly written with great integrity. The play has believable dialogue and rounded characters. We felt that the festival would not be able to do justice to the play and that it would suit a permanent set and better technical facilities.'

John Wallbank, of the Churchill Theatre Bromley (where the play was later to run successfully) wrote a sharp note 'I am afraid I found it very much a play written by a novelist – a lot of speeches were very long and there was a lot of symbolism which I didn't altogether unravel!' while the Nottingham Playhouse returned the script with the reader's comment that 'the play is extremely sophisticated and very clever in both its content and structure. The characters are finely drawn and deftly constructed. The humour is effective on an intellectual level as well as on the more basic "one-liner" level. All in all the marks of an experienced writer are apparent.'

As the *Visitor from Seil* rejection file thickened and flourished I returned to my day job and before the play was actually staged had produced two more novels, *Golden Boy* and *Vintage* as well as finishing a second play.

No matter how many people read and like a script, it won't be produced unless a director wants to direct it. Having a director who likes, and is tuned into, your work is often more useful than having a theatre. It's not until you put the two together that you have a production. In September 1993, almost a year after *Visitor from Seil* had been written, I had what was to prove my first theatrical breakthrough. Graham Watkins, artistic director of the Redgrave Theatre Farnham, wrote to Linda Seifert saying how highly he thought of *Visitor from Seil* and that he would like to talk to me with a view to putting it on. As far as I was concerned it was a *fait accompli*. Getting a play on was a doddle. Little, very little, about the theatre, did I know.

Although by this time I was struggling to cope with the disfigurement and physical difficulties left by Ramsay Hunt's disease, I made my way to Farnham. If Graham Watkins had remarked my contorted face, the crocodile tears which streamed down my cheeks from the affected eye all through lunch, he purported not to notice. I had explained the reason for my eyepatch and my generally bizarre appearance, and nothing more was said. We discussed the script of *Visitor from Seil* and it was hard to know which of us was the more enthusiastic. After Graham had pointed out gently that the play, as it stood, would run for almost three hours (an indulgence permitted only to Shakespeare and his ilk) I agreed to make some cuts. Such was my excitement at the prospect of actually having a play staged that at that particular point I would have agreed to the lead being played by Mickey Mouse.

Three weeks after our meeting, Graham Watkins left his job as artistic director. Not long after that the Redgrave Theatre itself went dark. As far as *Visitor from Seil* was concerned I was back in square one. Bloody, but unbowed, I called Graham at his home in Worcestershire. 'Why don't you come and have a cup of coffee when you're next in town,' I said, 'and we can have a chat.' As far as Graham was concerned, *Visitor from Seil* was a dead duck and it had not occurred to him to pursue the matter further.

Over coffee Graham agreed that, subject to mutually agreed cuts, he would take on the play, in which he still had every faith, on a freelance basis, and would try to find a producer for it. Dudley Russell, friend of Graham's and husband of poet Pam Ayres, was our first taker and towards the end of 1994 (two years after the play was written) Dudley confirmed that apart from its uncommercial title, he liked the play and that his company, Acorn Productions, was keen to produce it in the autumn of 1995 provided the required capital could be raised. After much discussion and many meetings between the three of us, *Visitor from Seil* became *Home Truths* and a pre-production budget was produced together with projections for potential profit and loss. We were on our way.

Or were we? Two years later no capital had been raised, no theatre found, and Dudley Russell, who had started out with such genuine enthusiasm, had apparently gone to ground.

Once I get my teeth into something I don't let go. Although Graham by now had other fish to fry, I refused to let my one real contact with the theatrical world slip away. It was early in 1996 before he came up with another producer, Richard Haddon, and once again we were in business.

Although this time things went more smoothly, they did not progress more speedily, and Richard's plans for staging the play in the autumn of 1996 soon proved unrealistic. March 1997 (four years after *Home Truths* was written) seemed the earliest date we could aim for.

The chicken-and-egg situation was a cliché I was to hear many many times during the next nail-biting year when my hopes that *Home Truths* would actually be put on went up and down like a yo-yo and I was hurled abruptly from the heights of unbelievable excitement to the depths of disappointment and despair which did little for my mental health. How could one attract 'angels' without the bait of a 'well-known' cast? How could one attract theatrical stars capable of putting bums on seats when there was as yet no money in the kitty to pay them? How could one get theatre managements to commit themselves to dates when one had neither? This is a common situation which leads even the most proven entrepreneur to play games. You tell the theatre management, keeping your fingers crossed behind your back, that you've actually signed up Faye Dunaway or Judi Dench, when all you have done is discuss the project with their respective agents. If the theatre bites, you tell Faye, or Judi, that this or that theatre has been secured and, one hopes, if they are not in LA or Alaska by this time, sign them up.

Despite the fact that it took months to track them down on film sets in the Australian bush and Canada – where the last thing they had time for was to read new scripts – a top-notch cast was eventually provisionally lined up for *Home Truths*. Christopher Cazenove (Ben Carrington of *Dynasty*), Edward Hardwicke (Anthony Hopkins's brother Warnie Lewis in *Shadowlands* and Dr Watson in *The Secret of Sherlock Holmes*), and Lynda Baron (well-known stage actor and star of the BBC's *Last of the Summer Wine*) were all enthusiastic about the play and agreed to attach their names to the project although to a man their agents refused to let them sign contracts until the eleventh hour. The reason for this fragile situation (the stars could pull out at any time) was that right up to the first day of rehearsals they needed to be unencumbered. Steven Spielberg just *might* call with a role which would net thousands of dollars for a few days' work rather than the equity pittance for 14 weeks of living out of suitcases in crummy provincial digs and appearing six nights a week (with matinées on Wednesdays and Saturdays). I never did understand why actors voluntarily undertook this arduous life and, particularly in these days of film and TV work, I still don't.

The minor parts were less difficult to cast. One of them, young Parisian Estelle Skornik (Nicole of the 'Nicole-Papa' TV Renault adverts) later to attract much unwanted media attention, was my personal inspiration which in the event boomeranged.

Theatres were finally contacted and the management of number one venues such as the Theatre Royal Nottingham, the Yvonne Arnaud Theatre Guildford, and the Churchill Theatre Bromley, agreed to take *Home Truths* on the understanding that we could guarantee the above 'names'. Like everything else in the theatre it was a dicey situation.

As far as the finance for the show was concerned, an optimistic Richard Haddon assured us that the money was the least worry and that when the time came it 'would be there'. In the event it was not there and Graham and I made lists of solvent friends, charitable trusts, and in Graham's case producers with whom he had previously worked, to whom prospectuses might be sent in an attempt to raise the £125,000 (in 100 units of £1,250) needed to get the show on the road.

You would think that an impressive document offering potential backers an opportunity to invest in 'the world première UK touring production of *Home Truths* by Rosemary Friedman, directed by Graham Watkins and produced by Richard Haddon' and with the above cast would have the punters clamouring at the doors. Or would you? Having made it clear to my friends and relations that it was not a begging bowl I was holding out, but offering them the chance of a gamble (the high-risk nature of which was clearly set out in the prospectus) with the added perks of free seats for *Home Truths* and an invitation to the first night party, they revealed their true colours.

Sir Cameron Mackintosh (*Jesus Christ Superstar* and *Les Misérables*), Paul Elliot (the king of Panto) and Stoll Moss Theatres all invested cautiously, securing a piece of the action just in case the play was a hit; Jamie Barber (artistic director of the Yvonne Arnaud Theatre Guildford) had sufficient faith in the play to come in with Richard Haddon as co-producer; a mega-rich acquaintance volunteered to put up almost 75 per cent of the money, which as far as he was concerned was a drop in the ocean. Our excitement at this generous gesture was matched by our disappointment when for political reasons, and for no fault of his own, he was obliged, at the very last moment, to pull out. When eight weeks before rehearsals were due to start, the major actors still had not committed themselves and were muttering ominously about film parts being offered to them in the spring, the theatres were vacillating, and the money had still not been raised, the situation began to look dire. On a trip to India I was unable to eat and lost almost a stone in weight. Whether the reason for this was that Indian food is not my favourite, or the fact that I had nightmares every night about the tenuous state of *Home Truths* – did I have a play about to be produced or did I not? – was unclear. The fact that when I came back from India in January I discovered that the producer had prematurely bought a Christmas tree and Tesco's entire remaindered stock of Christmas crackers (props needed for the production), did nothing to reassure me.

Because the production was still wobbly and the date of

rehearsals uncertain, Graham Watkins, who had his living to earn, had meanwhile undertaken a short directing job. When everything finally fell into place, actors signed up and theatres booked, the director himself was unavailable. Like the many other hurdles, this one was eventually overcome. Rehearsal rooms were booked in Kennington and although the Theatre Royal in Brighton, where the show was to have opened in March now had to pull out, miraculously, or so it seemed to me, we were finally under starters' orders.

In the pre-production stage, it helps if the writer is present at discussions about set, costumes, publicity, music etc. Not because one wants to control everything, but because one might be able to contribute an essential piece of information which is germane to the script.

The first rendezvous with the 10 strong technical team which Richard Haddon had assembled took place at my house. Meeting the production supervisor (responsible for every aspect of cast and production whilst on tour), the set designer, the costume, lighting, and sound designers as well as the assistant stage managers (actors in their own right who doubled as understudies) brought home the fact that not only did *Home Truths* look as if it was actually going to happen (barring the many theatrical hiccups which had on more than one occasion been known to occur) but that a monster, totally out of my control, had now been unleashed.

On the first day of rehearsals I was as apprehensive as a child going to a new school. Although I had already met two of the cast (Christopher Cazenove had been to my home to discuss his role and Estelle Skornik had also come over from Paris for the day), I was introduced by Graham to Lynda Baron, Biddy Hodson, Prim Cotton, Che Walker, Clive Marlow, Nichola

Bryant and Tony (*Me and My Girl*) Howes – a first-rate line-up and as skilled and charming a bunch of actors as one could hope to meet.

The 'read through' of the play with which the rehearsals kicked off, was my first magical experience of hearing voice given to words which hitherto had existed only in my head. Over lunch in the canteen, the cast of *Home Truths* mingled with the cast of Walt Disney's *Beauty and the Beast* (shortly to be staged at the Dominion Theatre) which – accompanied by cameras for a future TV documentary – was rehearsing in the same building.

On day two the serious business began. The assistant stage managers taped out an area on the floor identical to the proportions of the stage and the actors familiarised themselves with the position of the various doors and windows from a beautifully constructed scale model of the set over which I almost became a cropper.

I had already had a long meeting with the accomplished designer who wanted to know exactly how I saw the country cottage, where the action was to take place. When the first drawings were produced, he had positioned the inglenook fireplace on the opposite side to the one I had indicated in the script. While he swore that he had followed my instructions to the letter, I pointed to the stage directions. 'It says here quite clearly "fireplace L". "Exactly. That's where I've put it." "But you've put it on the *right*." ' After much to-ing and fro-ing I realised what I had done. 'Left' from the point of view of the audience, which was where I imagined myself when I wrote the play, was always referred to as 'right', ie, the right of the actors. Was my face red! The drawings had been done and although the set designer said they could easily be changed at this stage the director stood firm. I was to live with my mistakes. I was not prepared to. It would throw the entire action off course. I stood my ground. There was a confrontation, our first. Because he felt sorry for me the director climbed down, the fireplace was changed to stage right and all the other directions altered accordingly. It was a mistake I would never make again.

Having had the read through, the next two days were spent in 'blocking', working out the moves of the characters so that they ended up in the right place and did not trip over each other. Given the size of the cast, many of whom were on stage at the same time, the manoeuvres had to be repeated over and over. This arduous task having been completed and with three days of the three-week rehearsal period almost gone, the nitty gritty, or what was the most exciting part for me, began.

According to Lynda Baron, the period of rehearsals was the most enjoyable time of a show. Although very hard work for me, with long, intensive hours followed by rewrites to do at home each night, the three weeks I spent in Kennington (sustained by Dunkin' Donuts from the garage next door) were fascinating, utterly absorbing, and totally unlike anything I had hitherto experienced. Used to the solitary life of the writer, I found the camaraderie, and the fact that I was part of a polished and highly experienced team – who uncomplainingly and unpaid volunteered to rehearse overtime (in the pub) and on Saturdays – extraordinary.

Estelle Skornik – Stacy, from the mythical island of Seil (lies in reverse) – had minimal English. She showed considerable courage in coming to London, with which she was unfamiliar, and appearing on the English stage. We were however lucky enough to have as assistant stage manager in charge of the

The Play's the Thing

 ⟨decorative divider⟩

'book' (script) Scots' Natalie Quevert who was bilingual. It was a source of great amusement to the other actors when every suggestion made by the director was translated, virtually simultaneously into French.

Writers are not always welcome in rehearsal rooms and are known either for sitting silently with their noses in a book on the sidelines, or, like intruders from Mars, putting in their oars and arguing with the director at every available opportunity. Determined to be in at every minute of the metamorphosis of *Home Truths* from page to stage I tried to steer a path between the two and gradually my presence on a daily basis was not only accepted but actively encouraged. As the three weeks whizzed by, the thing that surprised me most was that the actors carried their scripts with them throughout the rehearsals and made little or no attempt to learn their lines. Dying to point out to Graham that time seemed to be running out (in case he was unaware of it), I managed to button my lips. I did not keep them buttoned at all times and it was hard to know when to intervene and when to leave things to the director who obviously enjoyed his role as God. The actors bowed to his supremacy, and even the most experienced of them put up a schoolboy hand before making a diffident suggestion either about interpretation or whether the writer confirmed their own sense of reality. The issue was often decided not on my own sense of a consistent reality, but on the basis of what the actors thought was real.

'In this connection I should love to ban the word "would" from rehearsals – as it appears in phrases like "Oh, he wouldn't say that, surely" or "But would he actually do it this way?" Writers don't generally commit a line or a gesture to paper unless it conforms to their sense of a consistent reality. But it can obviously clash with an actor's sense of reality... Whose "would" are we in?" ... In most rehearsal situations actors are in the majority, in some they have the whip hand. So the issue is often decided on the basis of what actors think is real.'*

While actors make their own notes on the text as they go along, they also rely upon the writer to appraise them which gives them the reassurance that are being watched over and cared for. While many of the director's views coincided with my own, several did not. Conscious of my newness to the game and Graham's omnipotence, I trod carefully, but more than once had my wrists slapped for 'playing director'.

As the three weeks drew to a close, the last of the money had been raised and the Theatre Royal Nottingham lined up for the first night on 1 April (not auspicious!), the actors were still 'on the book' and uncertain of their lines. Since the director seemed unfazed, there was nothing I could do. Once again it was partly my fault. I had included so much business and so many props (including a turkey, bottles of wine and a full set of table linen, cutlery and crockery for Christmas dinner) in the stage directions that hours of rehearsal had to be spent sorting out the problem of getting the paraphernalia on and off stage which, in view of the tight budget, had to be done by the actors themselves.

During this rehearsal period much else was going on. After the delicate question of top billing was resolved, a poster was produced which (unlike many of my book jackets) delighted me in every way. A paragraph of small print 'Please note *Home Truths* contains scenes involving nudity' (required by law) seemed not only over the top but to give entirely the wrong

* Steve Gooch

impression of a serious play in which for a few, firelit moments, Estelle Skornik – a free spirit – was required to remove her clothes. My reservations turned out to be justified.

As the first night drew near the actors were still 'on the book', the costumes had not been delivered, the set was behind schedule and stage management was still without many of the props (including a Christmas pudding and a dead rabbit). Sleep became a thing of the past. None of the problems were by any stretch of the imagination mine, but the precarious state of *Home Truths* confirmed the opinion of American critic George Jean Nathan that the opening night when weeks of hard work come to a climax and an audience is asked to witness, absorb, and hopefully appreciate the creative results, is the 'night before a play is ready to open'.

None the less the first night could not be postponed. The Friedman supporters, including my four daughters and their husbands, one granddaughter and many close friends, occupied an entire carriage on the train to Nottingham. My bedroom, in a hotel near the Theatre Royal, was filled with flowers and good luck cards and although I was a nervous wreck and unable to appreciate it to the full, it was a heady time. Seeing my name writ large outside the imposing columns of the various theatres (those which had not forgotten to display it) which were adorned with blue *Home Truths* posters was only one of the unaccustomed pleasures. They included sitting in the stalls for the 'technical' – a run through of the play with lights and music – and lurking in the foyer as the good burghers of Nottingham collected their tickets at the box office and shuffled into the auditorium to see *my* play.

Unsure whether I was to be mortified or delighted by having my inner self exposed to what was a gratifyingly large audience

including my nearest and dearest (not to mention most critical),
I took my seat at the back of the auditorium. As the lights went
up on what had been a controversial set, the sensations I
experienced were akin to those of childbirth and I clung to my
husband's hand as I relived the pains.

Of course they clapped. First night audiences are trained to
do so. But it was the fact that you could hear the proverbial pin
drop throughout the entire course of the action, that nobody
coughed or rustled sweet papers, nobody left after the interval,
that signified the fact that despite the usual hiccups – missed
cues, telephones refusing to ring and lights and music coming on
in the wrong place – the play had worked.

Drinks in the circle bar where, as in every venue we went to,
the theatre groupies were waiting (it was the first time I had
been asked to sign an autograph book), were followed by the
official party in the ballroom of the Quality George Hotel to
which the investors were invited. There was much kissing, of the
air and genuine variety, eyes were mopped and 'darlings' rever-
berated round the room. Unreal as it was, it was highly enjoyable, and as the cast relaxed on the dance floor and, hours after
midnight, got into their stride, I crept away to my bed and slept
for the first time in months until it was time for my breakfast
meeting with the director to discuss the costumes which, in the
event, had turned out to be dire.

The problems in getting the show on the road turned out to
be as nothing compared with those which occurred while the
show was on the road. In the normal course of events, the
costumes, after consultation with the cast – often they are taken
shopping by the costume designer – are ready for approval well
before the dress rehearsal. Because they did not materialise in
time (more kittens!), the day of the performance was the first

time the company had clapped eyes on them. A minor revolution took place. Many of the cast refused to have anything to do with what had been provided (my husband had to lend Christopher Cazenove his tie) and preferred to appear in their own clothes. Seeing the abysmal outfits which had been thought suitable I did not blame them. After a stand-up battle with the producer who was understandably reluctant to come up twice with money (although the choice of costume designer had been his), a new designer was engaged whose only misdemeanour was expecting two of the ladies in the cast to wear red, which provoked more demonstrations of the vainglory with which the theatre is hedged about.

The play moved round the country from Nottingham to Lincoln, Lincoln to Guildford, Guildford to Darlington and Darlington to Bromley, and as I lost my way in Kafkaesque backstage passageways – where I visited the cast before and after the performance – and took my seat in the auditoria, it became clear to me that *Home Truths* was in many respects no longer the play I had written.

Although my contract clearly stated that nothing I had not written or approved could be spoken on stage without my permission, lines were inserted (either by the director or the cast) in my absence, which made me cringe; two of the characters intended to be serious but with a dry sense of humour, would have been more at home in a Robertson Hare farce, and another, intended to be serious and respected hero of the Second World War was transmogrified into a daffy old man; critical lines, which I never managed to reinstate, were omitted on a nightly basis; I was asked to do rewrites, which I duly delivered, but somehow these were never incorporated.

These deficiencies, to which I constantly drew attention, were attributed to insufficient rehearsal time and the hectic pace of the tour. So too were the lamplight which mysteriously appeared in the *fireplace* when the lamp was switched on; the fact that in stage *left* windows it was dark while stage *right* was in broad daylight; that the *Marriage of Figaro* emanated from a radio not yet switched on, and snow – crucial to the action – refused to fall. Although my objections were declared valid by the director, he refused to pass them on to the cast who must now be 'left alone to get on with it'.

A playscript, like a musical score, is a blueprint for performance and is at the mercy of the director's (conductor's) interpretive vagaries. It was a frustrating experience and I could understand why it is that many established playwrights insist upon directing their own plays.

While each venue had its drawbacks (tacky dressing-rooms, poor acoustics, sloping stage) and advantages (pleasant digs, weeks spent by the sea) it was at Newcastle-upon-Tyne that the shit hit the fan.

Somebody had tipped off the *Sun* newspaper that Estelle Skornik appeared nude. Despite the programme proviso that photography and sound recording were strictly forbidden during the performance, a photographer from the tabloid sneaked into the front row of the stalls and at the crucial moment flashed his camera.

Notwithstanding the fact that Christopher Cazenove, on stage with Estelle at the time, gallantly stepped forward and urged the audience to 'stop that man' as he made a run for the exit ('Actor thwarts cameraman on Nicole's over-exposure' ran the headline in the *Daily Telegraph*), the following morning's *Sun* came up with a photograph of Estelle above the caption 'Nicole bares her bodywork in last night's play'.

The Play's the Thing

Contrary to received wisdom not all publicity is good publicity and other newspapers were not slow to make a killing from the *Sun* (I never did find out who tipped them off.) 'Men pack audience to see nude "Nicole",' announced the *Brighton Argus*; 'Renault Clio girl Nicole bared all before a packed Key Theatre' declared the Peterborough *Evening Telegraph*; '*Home Truths* and Estelle have already hit the newspaper headlines because one scene involves the actress taking her clothes off' *Hello!* magazine revealed in an interview with Estelle. Despite the fact that the two-page interview was sandwiched between one with Joan Collins and an article about Princess Diana, I was not too pleased. I was even less pleased when the reviews of *Home Truths* quickly became coloured by the barely concealed desires of young male critics on the provincial newspapers to enjoy a salacious evening at the theatre. When their expectations were thwarted, they dismissed as disappointing the rest of the play which they made no attempt to take seriously.

If you put your head in the stocks you must expect rotten tomatoes. While I was disappointed, but not too bothered by the turn of events, the reaction of some members of the cast was very different. One of them accused the director of lack of artistic integrity and intimated that unless the offending scene was removed, he would walk out of what was now threatening to become a 'freak show'. Since the brief and tasteful moment of nudity was crucial to the play and sensual rather than erotic, theatre management, the director, the producer and myself refused to remove the scene. The fracas blew over but the damage had been done and *Home Truths* never quite got back on an even keel.

How important are reviews? When Murray Burnett (with

351

Joan Alison) wrote *Everybody Comes to Rick's*, the play from which the seminal film *Casablanca* was adapted with scarcely a word changed, the critic James Agee said it was 'one of the world's worst plays', and the screenwriter Robert Buckner that it was 'sheer hokum'. A recent 'whodunnit' ('Not so much a whodunnit as who cares' ran the headline) with its 'tired sequence of jokes', was seen off with 'If you expect to find a night at the theatre an utter bore than you will not be disappointed with this comedy-thriller.'

The life of a play after its initial production is often dictated by the response it gets from reviewers. Good notices will not only mean bigger houses but the possibility of a transfer to the West End.

Although I learned that bad reviews are always couched in stronger language than the good ones – the West End's latest musical to close was panned as 'a grim night … of babble, balderdash and baloney' – as far as theatre audiences are concerned they seem to matter little. A standing ovation or a high score on the clapometer can by no means be extorted from an audience, neither can an attentive silence or an involuntary gasp.

According to one of Britain's leading playwrights – who has found himself increasingly staying at home with a video rather than risking yet another disappointing evening – eight out of ten theatre productions are tedious. So infrequently are audiences engaged by what they see that it is rare for them to emerge from a theatre discussing the play rather than the mileage on their car or whether to go for a Chinese. 'Good theatre ought to both challenge and reaffirm your view of the world. Like life, it ought to have feelings of pain and anguish and fun – and be a little bit illuminating.'*

* John Godber

The Play's the Thing

Home Truths continued to play to very good houses in which the play was extremely well received; remarks such as 'I could kick myself for not coming earlier in the week so that I could have seen it twice' and 'how rarely we get such a good evening in the theatre, something to make you think' were heard in the bar; as as far as a well-satisfied management was concerned, word of mouth had got round and none of them had had such a well-attended play for a long time; although many reviews had been favourable – 'it holds the interest from the first moment till the last' (*Newark Advertiser*), 'the play is thought provoking, clever and original' (Peterborough *Evening Telegraph*) – and the audiences appreciative, the comments which followed the Estelle débâcle coupled with the large cast and expensive nature of the play, put the kibosh on *Home Truths* as far as West End producers were concerned.

All, however, was not entirely lost. While *Home Truths* was rehearsing at Kennington, I was introduced to Michael White (*Beauty and the Beast*) the 'godfather' of theatre impresarios with *Oh! Calcutta*, *Sleuth* and *The Rocky Horror Show*, amongst other successes, to his credit. Always on the lookout for new work, he took an interest in the progress of *Home Truths*, which he promised to see, and asked me to send him the script of my next play *The Gift of Life* which I had by that time finished.

The Gift of Life, a play waiting to happen, came about because I was asked by Professor Julia Polak of the Royal Post Graduate Medical School of the Hammersmith Hospital, to help raise funds for the Julia Polak Lung Transplant Fund. Julia herself, an attractive middle-aged woman, was found to be suffering from primary pulmonary hypertension, a life-threatening condition which paradoxically she was herself researching, and had undergone a heart-lung transplant at the hands of her boss, Professor Magdi Yacoub. Having made a successful recovery she was anxious to raise funds for further research into the illness for which there was a shortage of donor organs.

Novels for the most part being unprofitable, I had suggested a stage play about heart-lung transplants as being, *if* it were successful, the best way to raise money. The only reaction I had had so far was from the actress Anna Massey who was over the moon about *The Gift of Life* and found it 'the most compelling script' she had ever read. Unfortunately she no longer appeared on stage and wanted me to rewrite it for her for TV which at this stage I was not prepared to do.

Having travelled to Guildford to see *Home Truths*, an evening he declared in no way wasted – coming from him this was praise indeed – Michael White said that in its present form, with its large cast, the play was too financially risky for London in which in a single week some 21 new plays were opening. He was, however, interested in *The Gift of Life*, provided he could get the right casting which to my surprise was either the flavour of the month Emma Thompson, or the equally hot number from *The English Patient*, Kristin Scott-Thomas. If anyone could entice these ladies on to the stage it was Michael White. Even if he did not it was gratifying to get endorsement from such a highly respected source for my work for the stage.

Home Truths finished its run at the Theatre Royal Norwich on 5 July 1997. The house was good and the cast, having got over all the teething troubles, superb. Over drinks in the dress-circle bar, encircled by autograph hunters, we said goodbye to each other hugging and kissing the members of what had become, over the course of almost four months, 'family'.

The sadness of parting from my new friends was followed by

the final striking of the set which was trucked to its resting place in Clapham where it would remain in store until, hopefully, it could be used again, and the ignominious tearing down of the last posters.

All I was left with was a few programmes, a few playbills and photographs and some heart-warming fan letters from members of the public. If the reviews were not all as good as I had hoped, at least *Home Truths* was not jeered by the gallery as was Noël Coward's *Sirocco* in 1927, nor was I chased up Charing Cross Road like John Osborne after the opening of *The World of Paul Slickey* in 1959. If the play was not as comprehensible as it should have been during its first run neither was *The Cherry Orchard* nor *The Seagull* (a catastrophic first night sent Chekhov home to bed with a blanket over his head) which was famously misunderstood, while both Pinter's *The Birthday Party* ('an insane, pointless play...') and Becket's *Waiting for Godot* were given the thumbs down by the critics and after the audience's utter incomprehension of his first play, Arthur Miller vowed never to write for the theatre again. What mattered was that as well as being a novelist with 18 published titles under my belt, I had now had a play produced and could legitimately call myself a playwright.

CHAPTER TWENTY-FOUR

The Running out of Time

━━━▷◆◁━━━

Cato learned Greek at eighty; Sophocles
Wrote his grand Oedipus, and Simonides
Bore off the prize of verse from his compeers,
When each had numbered more than four score years...
Chaucer, at Woodstock with the nightingales,
At sixty wrote the Canterbury Tales;
Goethe at Weimar, toiling to the last,
Completed Faust when eighty years were past.

Longfellow

Monteverdi composed his most influential works in his mid 70s and Monet started painting his water lilies at the age of 76. Why does the writer keep on writing? Because – like Picasso, who felt wholly alive only when he was painting – he finds that beside it every other activity palls into insignificance. Unlike the tightrope walker, the writer *never* completes what he sets out to do and in his heart of hearts regards every new book as

356

only a draft – or the draft of a draft – for what he really intends to write.

This is as it should be. The reason that we are unable to give up writing is because no matter how hard we try 'to move the stars to pity' the most we manage to do is '...beat out tunes for bears to dance to' and it is always the next book which is going to be 'the one'.

Although writing novels never gets any easier, it is, together with composing, the most rewarding of all the liberal arts. One does not have to wait for Van Gogh before one can visualise a vase of sunflowers or a chair, but one cannot hear the *Emperor Concerto* or read *Anna Karenin* until Beethoven has cast his spell or Tolstoy conjured up his characters and given them life.

'The novel is not merely an art, even less a profession. It is above all a passion which takes complete hold over you, and enslaves you. It is also a need, perhaps to escape from oneself, to live, at least for a time, by one's own will in a world of one's own choice. Who can say whether it is not also and above all a way of ridding oneself of one's phantoms by giving them life and throwing them into the world. That is undoubtedly the reason why one does not choose one's characters, be they sad or gay, worried, nervous or utterly serene. The novel is more than all this. For him who writes it is also a deliverance.'*

Is writing however a worthwhile job? Is it like being on permanent holiday or is it a real occupation like banking or making ball-bearings? The writer develops early the knack of distancing himself from disaster. When I see the homeless

* Georges Simenon

sleeping on park benches not 100 yards away from where I live, or apathetic and gutted youngsters begging or touting the *Big Issue* outside the supermarkets, when I listen to news bulletins about famine, or consider the plight of the elderly, the disabled and the disadvantaged, I am consumed with guilt about how I spend my days. In cultivating my garden I have fulfilled no social purpose, delivered no moral message. I write for the sake of the pleasure it gives me. How can I justify the fact that not only have I done nothing for the 'huddled masses' of the world into which I was born what seems a very long time ago now, but that I have exploited that world – and shall continue to exploit it – as material for fiction? Napoleon's claim, that he would rather have written *Werther* than won his battles, and Mallarmé's proposition that the aim of the universe is the creation of *le Livre*, reinforce my own conviction that happiness lies in the act of creation.

'I write for the sake of the pleasure it gives me and for the difficulty. I like composing riddles and finding elegant solutions'.*

There is no other justification. Have I succeeded? Does it matter? Suppose no one bothered to play tennis because they couldn't make Wimbledon? The row of novels bearing my name on my bookshelf is no measure of success, which is surely a question of how one feels about oneself. The wish to earn money, the wish to be famous, the wish to be great, is unimportant. Authors are not indifferent to money, but if earning huge sums of it is a principal objective, writing is hardly the profession to be advised.

'I am dying and the whore, Bovary will live for ever.'† The

* Vladimir Nabokov
† Gustav Flaubert

358

ambition of the writer, if he is honest, is not only to work, but to produce work that is good enough to remain. Whilst the author hopes that his books will survive him, he must, at the same time, arrange things in such a way as to convince posterity that he never lived.

'...my life may have been a shamble of error and non-recognition, but if my book has truth and beauty enough it will endure. There are those as yet unborn who shall read it, as I read the classic on my table.'*

The writer knows only too well that she should be a good human being first, and a wordsmith second. What she is worth is not what she has achieved – no artist ever fulfils his/ her creative aspirations – but what she is. She has, none the less, to be single-minded often at the expense of those around her. She not only writes when she is writing, but when she is thinking, when she is reading, when she is experiencing. She needs time to reflect and to work things out, and everything is significant to her purpose. Perpetually storing and making over her impressions, the true artist is unable to give her un-divided attention to anything other than the rigorous demands of her work.

'...the advantages and dangers of the author's calling are offset by an advantage so great as to make all its difficulties, disappointments, and maybe hardships, unimportant. It gives him spiritual freedom. To him life is a tragedy and by his gift of creation he enjoys the catharsis, the purging of pity and terror, which Aristotle tells us is the object of art. For his sins and his follies, the unhappiness that befalls him, his unrequited love, his physical defect, illness, privation, his hope abandoned, his

* Homer

griefs, humiliations, everything is transformed by his power into material, and by writing it he can overcome it. Everything is grist to his mill, from the glimpse of a face in the street to a war that convulses the civilized world, from the scent of a rose to the death of a friend. Nothing befalls him that he cannot transmute into a stanza, a song, or a story, and having done this be rid of it. The artist is the only free man.'*

Plus ça change, plus c'est la même chose. Every writer has to fight against the multitude of books published, and it has never been difficult to find excuses – crisis time in the industry, national disaster, decline in literacy, middle-class materialism, unemployment, the weather – for the fact that one's novels are not reviewed or do not do well.

'The publishers and booksellers between them are destroying the sale of books other than bestsellers.' No, not last week's *Bookseller* but Leonard Woolf writing in 1935!

More than 60 years later the dissolution of the Net Book Agreement continues to arouse passions at all levels in the publishing industry. Its demise gave rise to outcries – similar to those of Dickens and Carlyle who publicly opposed its overthrow in 1852 (it was reinstated in 1900) – as well as credence to the views of such as Gore Vidal who believes that the novel is no longer the *lingua franca*, no longer part of people's lives:

'After some 300 years the novel in English has lost the general reader (or rather the general reader has lost the novel) and I propose that he will not again recover his old enthusiasm.'

The Net Book Agreement, supported by The Society of Authors but widely attacked in the 1980s and early 1990s by

* Somerset Maugham

politicians and press as a barrier to free trade, was an agreement between publishers that if they chose to sell books at 'net' prices, they would ensure that (with certain exceptions) book-sellers would not then sell those books at less than the recommended 'net' price.

The Reed Group (which included Heinemann, Methuen, Secker & Warburg etc.) were the first unilaterally to walk away from the agreement in 1993. In December 1994, Hodder Headline followed suit by heavily discounting certain titles to the tune of 80 per cent higher sales than those of previous works by the same authors.

The issues which raged around this debate were complex and opinions volatile. Not the least of these was that the abolition of the NBA (or retail price maintenance) would drive cut-price bestsellers on to the supermarket shelves where, in theory at any rate, their sales potential would be as large as that for Persil or Carling Black Label. In the face of this 'pile 'em high, sell 'em cheap' approach for *a limited range* of titles, hundreds of small bookshops, which existed on stringent financial margins, would be forced into receivership.

Authors saw the collapse of the NBA as the death knell of British literary tradition. It would not only lead to a bestseller culture, in which there would be more restrictive practices by publishers in the selection of authors and titles (more eggs being placed in fewer baskets), but the royalties which they had previously been paid on the full price of their books would have to be adjusted and new and more complex contracts negotiated. While some writers (Dannie Abse) thought that authors, other than the most commercially successful, were 'screwed enough already', a few objected to their books being regarded simply as merchandise; and others, such as Doris Lessing and Lady

Antonia Fraser, believed that the abolition of the NBA would 'favour the commercial and the second rate'. They feared that consumer choice would suffer, and that one of the greatest pleasures 'of browsing in a small bookshop' – where there was wide availability of books including those which catered for minority and specialist interests – would cease to exist.

As far as the barricades of the big bookshops were concerned, it was Terry Maher, chairman of Pentos (which owned the Dillon's chain) who spearheaded the revolution by price-cutting certain titles in his shops; he was later restrained by an injunction, brought by the Publishers Association (which administered the NBA), from discounting books covered by the agreement. Maher's argument was that since 40–50 per cent of all customers who enter a bookstore leave with a book they had not initially intended to buy, there was no reason why booksellers should not have the freedom enjoyed by every other retailer to compete for the attention of the public by offering attractive discounts. Selective price promotions would generally encourage more book buying in general (not to mention the fact that it would help increase the Pentos share of the market).

The final collapse of the Net Book Agreement in 1995 brought with it not only a radical change in the large bookshops, which had been languishing since the 1980s, but sadly, and paradoxically, the demise of Terry Maher as a major bookseller as Pentos went to the wall. The emerging pattern of bookchains had long been familiar on the other side of the Atlantic, where bestselling novels could be bought at major discounts in open all day and night giant and brightly lit emporia which not only actively encouraged browsing but incorporated comfortable seating and coffee bars to that end.

The Running out of Time

The huge success of these lifestyle shops, such as Barnes & Noble on New York's upper West Side, has been attributed by cynics to the 'sofa' areas which have become the first port of call for anyone on the lookout for a (bookish) partner.

By dint of the quality of its management and staff, restrained growth, canny marketing (10-day money back guarantee or exchange on books) and judicious purchase of sites for its 24 London stores, the London-based chain Books Etc. – started in the early 1980s by the South African Joseph family with one shop in Charing Cross Road (Foyle's is opposite) – has now been acquired by the biggest American book retailer, Borders, who have just opened *Borders Books and Music* in London's Oxford Street and plan to open superstores across the country with serious discounting as its chief weapon, in what will be an all-out competitive price war.

'Printing a book, sending it to a bookshop which may be thousands of miles away, having it returned and then pulping it is a grotesque waste of time and money. Internet sales could again make trade publishing reasonably possible.'* *Amazon.com*, the leading Internet bookseller (4.2 million titles against 140,000 in a superstore), has acquired a staggering billion-dollar market capitalisation on the US stock exchange although currently making horrendous losses.

Where does all this mean to the author? Will these changes increase the market for bestsellers only, or for books as a whole? Will 35 per cent of all books be returned to publishers (as happened last year in the USA) leading to the cancellations of hundreds of authors' contracts? Will there be room, given the vast acres of shelving in the superstores or on the Net,

* William Rees-Mogg

for the local friendly bookseller who is willing to champion you?

Undoubtedly the scrapping of the NBA will spearhead a price war which will reduce profitability, an outcome seen by the farsighted who opposed it. Certainly it will put greater pressure on publishers to cut down on the risk factor – ignoring the fact that today's new authors might be tomorrow's best-sellers – and invest once again in the familiar litany of sure-fire authors.

Britain has long prided itself on its indigenous writers who reflect the heartbeat of the nation. To supplement their incomes, however, these journeyman authors relied heavily on sales to libraries which serviced not only the high street but – through mobile units – outlets in hospitals, community centres, schools, prisons, geriatric and disability homes, academic and industrial institutions.

The deteriorating state of British libraries, previously used by one-third of the population to the tune of 560 million books a year, reflects countrywide cuts and closures (together with withdrawal of services and sell-offs) of a popular and much appreciated local authority service which once offered unrestricted access for all to an intellectual Aladdin's cave.

Reference and academic books are falling into disrepair and not being replaced (despite increased demand), and where half a dozen copies of a new novel might once have been purchased (to alleviate the waiting lists), a single copy – if any – is now all that can be afforded. Many libraries have been forced to close during hours when they were once open, and staff have been made redundant. Those librarians who remain face increased workloads which have little to do with literature, and spend much of their time at computer terminals. The Library Campaign (set up in 1984 and supported by authors) raises the issues of publicly funded libraries with prospective parliamentary candidates, stages publicity stunts, organises National Libraries week and lobbies MPs about the vital importance of free access to information.

Because many readers who once borrowed from libraries are now obliged to buy their books, the book market has increased in value. While the level of discounting (sparked by the collapse of the NBA) in general has proved less catastrophic than was feared, the concentration on bestsellers (often discounted by as much as 50 per cent) with which the conglomerates now play safe, means that the big writing fish have grown bigger, while many smaller fish have been left to flounder in the sea of commercialism. Some cynics have contended that there are far too many books around anyway, and that just as we pay farmers not to grow things, one way of stemming the tide of words would be to pay some writers not to write. Publishers have been accused of hyping minor books by a small circle of overrated authors to compete with similar promotions by their rivals, while ignoring the literary talents of others who in many cases are superior writers. These cult authors, whose names are often household words, may be seen reading, talking, answering questions and signing copies of their books both in local book-shops and the megastores, as well as at literary festivals where their appearance and personality often takes precedence over their books. With Hollywood interest boosting hype, the gap between writers will grow, with ever larger rewards for the successful few while the rest must make do with minuscule (if any) advances. Authors, as it is, earn considerably less than they would for a commensurate level of expertise in other occupations. A recent survey of the 6,500 members of the Society of

THE WRITING GAME

Authors revealed that 41 per cent received advances against royalties of less than £5,000; 13 per cent between £5,000 and £10,000; 11 per cent between £10,000 and £25,000; and 6 per cent more than £25,000 – for books that would take at least a year to write.

Today's bestsellers are genre novels: the blockbusting thriller, entailing extensive research, considerable writing ability, and the stamina to keep going for well over 500 pages, or sagas (sometimes not very well written) which open the doors to a world of power and money of which the reader can only dream. Many versatile writers have been invited to produce 'formula' or 'bonkbuster' novels complete with explicit sex:

'With these words she climbed on to the bed and lowered herself gradually down on me, quivering her supple torso and going up and down with voluptuous movements; she gave me my fill of intercourse as if I were in a swing, until we were both worn out in mind and body and lay collapsed together, breathing our hearts out in our embraces...'*

That this amorous encounter between a servant girl and the hero of the *Metamorphoses* or *Golden Ass* (familiar to generations of schoolboys), was written by a Platonic philosopher in the *second century* AD demonstrates that sexual explicitness in literature is nothing new.

Problems about sexual outspokenness arise not so much from moral or censorious considerations, but from the fact that we seem to have lost the ability to create the paradox of reality relied upon by nineteenth-century novelists. It is through these paradoxes that, although their begetters are long since dead, icons such as Anna Karenina and Isabel Archer survive. Any

* Lucius Apuleius

366

attempt by the writer to convey sensations which cannot be put into words (like those common to sex and music), must by definition be self-defeating. No novelist was more aware of this than Flaubert:

'I have a fornication coming up that worries me considerably, and which I mustn't shirk, although I want to make it chaste – that is, literary without gross details or lascivious images: *the carnality must be in the emotion.*'

One of the most erotic sequences in all literature is that of Emma Bovary hurtling round Paris with her lover in a closed cab. By allowing the reader to indulge his own fantasies, and with the sexuality evoked through the erratic progress of the vehicle over the cobbled streets, Flaubert managed to convey what Stendhal referred to as *amour-physique*, without a single reference to the human anatomy.

Although to write about love and to exclude sex is counter-productive, the present code of frankness in which no holds are barred and blasphemies spatter the pages, is deemed by some to be responsible for the general malaise of, and absence of *gravitas* in, the novel:

The collapse of taboos, both in the cinema and in the novel, has led to a frenetic search for new works of unparalleled violence and depravity, but a writer who knows his craft can say all he wishes to say 'without affronting the good manners or infringing the conventions of his time. One knows full well that language itself is a convention.'*

Do you think much about growing older? Is it something that worries you? Gulliver, on his journey to the flying island of Laputa, makes the acquaintance of the Struldbrugs who, through

* Jorge Luis Borges

THE WRITING GAME

some accident, never die. Gulliver finds them dispirited, bored, and consumed with envy at the deaths of the old. Whenever they see a funeral they lament that others are gone to a harbour of rest to which they themselves can never hope to arrive.

With the passing of the years I give more thought to the business of growing old. 'If you assume you're going to live to be seventy, seven decades, and think of each decade as a day of the week, starting with Sunday, then I'm on Friday afternoon now.'*

'Like to runners (we) hand the lamp of life One to Another.'† As do all writers, I cling to the irrational hope that although I am in the departure lounge of life my flight will not called until I've finished whatever it is I'm working on and have seen it published.

For Isaiah Berlin, neither art nor life has a purpose. 'The purpose of art is to be art ... The purpose of life is life ...' 'What is the meaning of life?' Olga Knipp asked in a letter to Chekhov, to which he replied: 'It is like asking what a carrot is. A carrot is a carrot and nothing more is known.'

I do not share this cynical view and am convinced, as human beings must be if they are to make any sense at all out of their existence, that something more is known even though its nature remains a mystery. In my ambivalence as a writer, I have not managed to hold many deeply held beliefs, although I envy the passionate commitment of those who do. I share Buber's sense of religiosity rather than conforming to the strait-jacket of religious practices, am apolitical, and find the jargon of politics incomprehensible. If the novelist needs to express his opinion

* Simenon
† Lucretius

concerning the state of the world, he should communicate rather than state it. It is not necessary to adopt a position. The writer is a changeable, volatile creature and the aspects of his own personality will become manifest through his characters.

'*Il faut être un homme vivant et un artiste posthume!*' 'The intellect of man is forced to choose/Perfection of the life or of the work.'*

There are only two things that last, your work and your family. They are what you have to show for how you have lived. Whether the meals I have put on the table, the children I have nurtured, or the millions of words I have written, will turn out to be of more lasting value I can only guess.

'Our common fate is age, sickness, death, oblivion. Our common hope, tenuous but persistent, is for some version of survival.'†

It would be nice if one were able to have one's cake and eat it; while I acknowledge the vital significance of the human aspect of life, I do not underestimate the importance of producing books. My aim as a novelist, a single voice speaking, has been not to write literature but to write life. To believe that the sole purpose of the novel is to entertain the reader is both to deny the author's unique ability to define the world, and to reduce it to its lowest common denominator. There is no need to find a story:

'Simply men in their context of life, in their own atmosphere. Then the little push of the finger that sets them going ... from here on I simply have to let them live. They make up the story and I cannot intervene, since my characters, if they are true,

* W. B. Yeats
† Harold Bloom

have their own logic which cannot be altered by the author's logic.'*

To have made a few people laugh, a few people cry, is the best one can hope for. The happiness inspired by Homer cannot be measured, neither can the tears that Horace transformed into smiles. There is no sell-by date on human emotion.

We have to accept that literature no longer has the appeal that it had when people were brought up to read books, when thriving libraries were stocked with books (rather than magazines, music and CD-Roms) and when there was little competition from other kinds of entertainment. We are not a nation of bibliophiles, and the man on the Clapham omnibus would much rather watch football than go to the lengths of buying, let alone reading, a book. Yet the novel is the most satisfactory distraction from boredom at the least expenditure of time and money. A good book – even at today's prices – is still cheaper than dinner in a restaurant and lingers longer on the palate; it is more portable than a TV; more accessible than a theatre seat; is capable of being read in solitude and can be enjoyed many times over.

The novelist may appear to live as others, going through the motions, but it is not possible for him to do so. He cannot look on a child without fast-forwarding it into middle age, cannot contemplate a wrinkled face without rewinding it back to the innocence of the cradle. He is never happy without at the same time feeling sad, never so miserable that he cannot find something to laugh at in a situation.

The writer is not one man but many, and because he is many he is able to create many. There comes a point however when he

* Georges Simenon

must ask himself if what he has written has any value except to himself. His job is observing the world – seeing it as a subject of wonder rather than didactics – but his inclination is to have nothing to do with the day-to-day running of it. He is aware of the fact that the whole of life is not long enough to learn to write well, and it is with the greatest reluctance, and all the time wishing that he were at his desk, that he goes through the motions of supporting causes, taking workshops and serving on committees.

'We do not write because we want to; we write because we must. There may be other things in the world that more pressingly want doing: we must liberate our soul of the burden of creation. We must go on though Rome burns. Others may despise us because we do not lend a hand with a bucket of water; we cannot help it; we do not know how to handle a bucket. Besides, the conflagration thrills us and charges our mind with phrases.'*

It seems a long time ago now that I sat down to write the first words of No White Coat. Any writer has to fight against the volume of books published and the continued polarisation between the international conglomerate and the smaller, more gentlemanly houses who still appear to be in touch – no matter how tenuously – with the man in the street. It is not only by merit, but luck, that the modern writer succeeds. In learning to say 'yes' to life in all its aspects, I have come to realise that, for the novelist in particular, nothing one sees or feels is ever wasted. The most tedious lecture reluctantly attended will yield a nugget of wisdom, the most unpromising of social activities ignite an idea, furnish a new friend or provide a worthwhile contact; everything can be transformed into art.

* Somerset Maugham

THE WRITING GAME

I have also become adept at saying 'no'. Half way through a book is not the moment to dissipate one's energies by reviewing other people's novels, by undertaking more commitments than are strictly necessary, or by staying out late. I have learned to keep time-wasters at bay, and to take my mental phone off the hook.

As we approach the millennium we seem to become more and more obsessed with the pursuit of 'culture'. As if we didn't have enough to worry about, we fret about being unfamiliar with Lorca or unable to tell a Rembrandt from a Damien Hurst, at not having seats for the current Tom Stoppard, heard the new Madonna album, read the 'Booker', seen the latest Oscar winner, marvelled at the most recent pile of bricks or potted shark at the Tate, at having lost out on tickets for Glyndebourne, missed the Proms and who did you say was Howard Hodgkin?

And what of the much vaunted Internet? With easy access to the worldwide Web, will novels – as we know them – still have a place in the life of the novelist? While the dirge over the future of fiction is ongoing, books seem unlikely to be replaced by personal computers any more than they were made redundant by the advent of radio, the cinema or television. The old is not always obsolete and books – one of the greatest and most ingenious of inventions – are still the cornerstone of many movies and inform much of the media. Contrary to received opinion, the written word merges easily with the white noise of technology which lacks both the personality of the author and his rhetorical powers.

Les Perpendiculaires, a trendy group of young French intellectuals, despise the new technology fearing it will replace human intellect and prevent us from reading books or even communicating with each other. These well-meaning Luddites, see themselves as literary guerrillas and, with as little hope as

The Running out of Time

King Canute, imagine they can stem the technological tide of which, no matter how diligently we surf, we are still very much in the shallows. Like the quill, the fountain pen, the typewriter, the word processor and every other human invention which is here to stay, IT (which is useful provided you've read a good many books first) can be a tool or a weapon and, of all people, the writer can be trusted, once he has managed to tame it, to put it to good use.

'People in general do not willingly read, if they can have anything else to amuse them.'*

We live in a world in which the result of a football match or the peccadilloes of public figures take headline precedence over human disasters; in which everything around us goes 'beep' or 'toot'; in which the demands of the cinema and TV (which feeds off books) and cyberspace leave us little time for irony or illusion, for concentrating on something greater than ourselves or which demands application; in which, in the USA, sales of adult books have dropped for the second year running (even unsold copies of the Bible are being returned); in which publisher HarperCollins Inc lost $7 million in its last financial quarter and cancelled a hundred works (some by award-winning authors) not only scheduled for publication but with fully paid-up advances and approved jacket designs, which one agent compared with a bride being told on her wedding day: 'Look, I'll pay your costs but I'm not going to marry you.'

Despite all this doom and gloom, you have only to remark the faithful in a village bookstore or the *aficionados* among the second-hand stacks in Hay-on-Wye, to spend an afternoon in Blackwell's or Books Etc., to experience the buzz of Borders, to

* Dr Johnson

ride on public transport or take a walk in the park to see that books – poetry, philosophy, *belles-lettres* and Penguin classics as well as blockbusters – are not only being bought but read.

As the world shrinks and our congested minds struggle to keep up with instant culture (fast-food for the brain), there is less time left to remember literary masterpieces or to distinguish between the real and the unreal, and it seems increasingly advantageous for the novelist to lose himself, if only for a few hours each day, in a universe of his own creating. As far as the rest of the day is concerned, there is no happiness outside the ordinary, and I don't understand writers who feel they should not have to do any of the everyday things. The simple actions of filling the car with petrol, standing in line at the cash-point, spending an evening with friends or enjoying an evening stroll, restores one's equilibrium, brings one back to the real world which, after all, is the very stuff of creation.

We must always have our bags packed and be ready to leave. If I were called tomorrow to hang up my tennis shoes or climb into my wooden pyjamas, I would echo Wittgenstein: 'Tell them I've had a wonderful life' or perhaps console myself with the immortal words of Emma Bovary: 'There's not much in dying... I shall go to sleep and it will all be over.'

Convinced, like Socrates, that 'the unexamined life is not worth living' I have in the foregoing chapters attempted to give one writer's view on some of the many aspects of what is after all but a game, amusement, diversion, entertainment, pastime or recreation. If, however, I were asked by an aspiring author to divulge in a sentence the secret of novel writing, the answer would be: 'Get black on white.'* The rest is commentary.

* Guy de Maupassant

Afterword

Golden Boy, inspired by the recession of 1987–8, and *Vintage*, a novel set amongst the vineyards and châteaux of Bordeaux, are my two most recent novels and *Southern Comfort* (written many years ago!) published in a new collection by Serpent's Tail, my most recent short story. Charles Dance turned down the part of *Golden Boy* for TV, as did Pierce Brosnan (who had agreed to play the part) in the USA, after he landed the role of the new James Bond. Ian (*House of Cards*) Richardson still wants the eponymous role in *An Eligible Man* and producer Christine Benson of Blue Heaven is trying to sell the six-parter to the network. Janet Suzman has attached her name to *Rose of Jericho*, Anna Massey is waiting to get her teeth into *The Gift of Life*. *Paris Summer* is still circumventing the film studios, a French film producer has expressed interest in *Vintage*. Linda Seifert, aided and abetted by Peter Cregeen of Stoll Moss Theatres, is looking for a West End producer for *Home Truths*. I am currently writing my third stage play *Happy Birthday Rosenberg* as well as completing my nineteenth novel. My daughters, now serious career women, are always in crisis. My ninth grandchild has just been born while the eldest, now up at Cambridge, is not only broke but has troubles with her love life... So what's new? 'Ours is not to complete the task; neither should we desist from embarking on it.'*

RF, September 1998

* Rabbi Tarphon

Epilogue

'When I am dead, I hope it may be said: His sins were scarlet, but his books were read.'

Hilaire Belloc

Say this when you mourn for me:
There was a man – and look, he is no more.
He died before his time.
The music of his life suddenly stopped.
A pity! There was another song in him
Now it is lost
Forever.

Chaim Nachman Bialik

Bibliography

Ackroyd, Peter *Dickens* London: Minerva, 1991

Bloom, Harold *The Western Canon* New York: Harcourt Brace & Company, 1994

Burgess, Anthony Homage to *QWERT YUIOP* London: Century Hutchinson Ltd, 1986

Burgess, Anthony *You've Had Your Time* London: Penguin Books, 1991

Campion, David *Becoming a Playwright* London: Robert Hale Ltd, 1992

Christian, R. F. (Ed) *Tolstoy's Diaries* London: Flamingo, 1994

Connolly, Cyril *Enemies of Promise* London: André Deutsch, 1973

Elliott, David *A Trade of Charms* London: Bellew, 1992

Flaubert, Gustave *Madame Bovary* London: Penguin Classics, 1950

Gide, André *Journals 1889–1949* London: Penguin Books, 1967

Glendinning, Victoria *Trollope* London: Hutchinson, 1992

Golding, William *A Moving Target* London: Faber and Faber Ltd, 1982

Goldman, William *Adventures in the Screentrade* London: Futura, 1985

Gooch, Steve *Writing a Play* London: A & C Black, 1995

Gray, Simon *Fat Chance* London: Faber and Faber Ltd, 1995

Bibliography

Hamilton, Ian *Writers in Hollywood* London: William Heinemann Ltd, 1990

Hodges, Jack *The Maker of the Omnibus* London: Sinclair Stevenson, 1992

Humphries, Sydney (Ed) *Bacon's Essays* London: Adam & Charles Black, 1962

Janouch, Gustav *Conversations with Kafka* London: Quartet Books Ltd, 1985

Jong, Erica *Fear of Fifty* London: Vintage, 1995

Koestler, Arthur *The Act of Creation* London: Hutchinson & Co., 1964

Leavis, Q. D. *Fiction and the Reading Public* London: Chatto and Windus, 1965

Leavis, F. R. *The Common Pursuit* London: The Hogarth Press, 1984

Leon Edel and Lyall H. Powers (Eds) *The Complete Notebooks of Henry James* New York: Oxford University Press Inc., 1987

Levin, Bernard *Enthusiasms* London: Jonathan Cape Ltd, 1983

Lewis, Jeremy *Cyril Connolly A Life* London: Pimlico, 1998

Llosa, Mario Vargas *The Perpetual Orgy* London: Faber and Faber Ltd, 1987

Lodge, David *The Art of Fiction* London: Penguin, 1992

Mamet, David *A Whore's Profession* London: Faber and Faber Ltd, 1994

Mamet, David *True and False* London: Faber and Faber Ltd, 1998

Maugham, W. Somerset *The Summing Up* London: Penguin Books, 1963

Murray, John G. *A Gentleman Publisher's Commonplace Book* London: John Murray (Publishers) Ltd, 1996

Nabokov, Vladimir *Lectures on Literature* London: Pan Books Ltd, 1983

Pritchett, V. S. *The Living Novel* London: Chatto and Windus Ltd, 1966

Roth, Philip *Reading Myself and Others* London: Penguin Books, 1985

Seger, Linda *Creating Unforgettable Characters* New York: Henry Holt and Co., 1990

Seger, Linda *Making a Good Script Great* Hollywood: Samuel French 1987

Singer, Isaac Bashevis *Love and Exile* London: Penguin, 1986

THE WRITING GAME

Steegmuller, Francis (Ed) *The Letters of Gustave Flaubert* London: Faber and Faber Ltd, 1981

Steiner, George *On Difficulty* Oxford: Oxford University Press Ltd, 1972

Storr, Anthony *Churchill's Black Dog* London: Fontana, 1990

Storr, Anthony *Solitude* London: Flamingo, 1989

Storr, Anthony *The Dynamics of Creation* London: Pelican 1976

Styron, William *Darkness Visible* London: Jonathan Cape, 1991

Tolstoy, Leo *Anna Karenin* London: Penguin Classics, 1954

Trechmann, E. J. (Tr) *The Essays of Montaigne* London: Oxford University Press Ltd, 1927

Updike, John *Odd Jobs* London: André Deutsch, 1992

Vidal, Gore *Palimpsest A Memoir* London: Abacus, 1996

Woolf, Virginia *Women & Writing* London: The Women's Press, 1979

Woolf, Virginia *A Room of One's Own* London: Hogarth Press, 1929